Domestic Animals and Stability in Pre-State Farming Societies

Carol Raish

BAR International Series 579

1992

Published in 2019 by
BAR Publishing, Oxford

BAR International Series 579

Domestic Animals and Stability in Pre-State Farming Societies

ISBN 9780860547341 paperback
ISBN 9781407348780 e-book

DOI https://doi.org/10.30861/9780860547341

A catalogue record for this book is available from the British Library

This book is available at www.barpublishing.com

BAR Publishing is the trading name of British Archaeological Reports (Oxford) Ltd.
British Archaeological Reports was first incorporated in 1974 to publish the BAR
Series, International and British. In 1992 Hadrian Books Ltd became part of the BAR
group. This volume was originally published by Tempvs Reparatvm in conjunction
with British Archaeological Reports (Oxford) Ltd / Hadrian Books Ltd, the Series
principal publisher, in 1992. This present volume is published by BAR Publishing,
2019.

BAR
PUBLISHING

BAR titles are available from:

BAR Publishing
122 Banbury Rd, Oxford, OX2 7BP, UK
EMAIL   info@barpublishing.com
PHONE   +44 (0)1865 310431
FAX   +44 (0)1865 316916
www.barpublishing.com

For my mother, Julia Ann Gotcher, and my daughter, Susan Raish

ABSTRACT

This volume reports the results of a study in pattern recognition and the use of general, cross-cultural information to develop an explanation for that pattern. As such, it stresses the importance of a generalist as opposed to a particularist orientation for archaeological research. Its contributions are both methodological and informational.

This study examines sixteen archaeological sequences from both the Old and New Worlds. They are from the following areas: southern Britain and Europe, the Near East, Egypt, China, India and Pakistan, the Andes, Mesoamerica, and North America. The research identifies a pattern of significantly shorter sequence duration for the pre-state farming period in the New World than in the Old World and Peru. This pattern, which has never been examined before, is of considerable value for research on the development of complex societies in both the Old and New Worlds.

This volume examines one possible cause for this difference in duration in terms of the contributions of medium to large domesticated animals, such as cattle, sheep, goats, pigs, and llamas, to economic stability. These animals were present in the Old World and Peru but absent in the reminder of the pre-contact New World. Information from ethnography, soil science, and nutrition is used to determine the contributions of the animals to human subsistence and cultural stability. Economic problems that might arise in subsistence-level farming economies owing to the absence of domesticated animals are also examined. The argument is made that subsistence-level farming economies with domesticated animals are more stable, measured in terms of duration, than those without these animals. This study follows the tenets of cultural ecology in its assumption that problems or perturbations in the economic/subsistence component of a system can lead to instability in the system as a whole and thus to changes in the level of organizational complexity. It is suggested that systems with a less stable economic component may undergo more rapid development of organizational complexity. The shorter pre-state farming periods in the New World may result from such economic instability.

Thus, this suggested difference in stability has strong implications for research concerning the rise of complex societies in the New World and also for research concerning the pattern of frequent geographical abandonments found in the New World. Local factors have previously been used to explain these occurrences. The importance of this research lies in its recognition of a global pattern of differential stability and in its use of cross-cultural and nonarchaeological information to build a potential general explanation of that pattern.

TABLE OF CONTENTS

CONTENTS

ILLUSTRATIONS

TABLES

ACKNOWLEDGMENTS

This volume and the research reported herein are a direct consequence of work I undertook as a doctoral candidate at the University of New Mexico. I therefore wish to thank the members of my dissertation committee, Linda Cordell, Lewis Binford, Robert Santley, and Andrea Vierra, for the considerable time and effort they contributed to my research and education.

My committee chair, Linda Cordell, was consistently ready to help whenever ideas, suggestions, information, and editing skills were needed. Her enthusiasm and encouragement were crucial to the success of this research. Her promptness in dealing with "long-distance" drafts and queries ensured its completion.

Lewis Binford provided the initial idea to examine the economic role of domesticated animals, as well as a sense of the importance and excitement of large-scale pattern-recognition studies and cross-cultural research. His enthusiastic support of the topic was constant.

Robert Santley gave generously of his time and talent. His suggestions for additions to the manuscript improved it substantially. Discussions with him concerning potential economic difficulties in societies without domesticated animals and concerning the role of state-level organization as a possible buffer of these economic difficulties were also very helpful.

June-el Piper did a superb job of editing and producing both the original dissertation and this volume. Her knowledge, dependability, and willingness to teach were much appreciated. I am also grateful to Ron Stauber for the fine work he did on the figures, one of which he revised and improved considerably. He and Sam Tubiolo drafted the figures in their final form.

This book was produced in Times Roman and Helvetica typeface with Wordstar 6.0 on a Qume PSJet printer.

Carol Raish

INTRODUCTION

This study examines two aspects of archaeological research. It is concerned with the definition and explanation of an archaeological problem and with a method for investigating that problem. The method of investigation emphasizes pattern recognition with the use of cross-cultural ethnographic information to frame a potential explanation of the defined pattern. The research methods used in this study are discussed in the second section of this chapter.

RESEARCH PROBLEM

The research problem under consideration is an apparent difference in duration of the pre-state farming period noted in archaeological sequences from the Old and New Worlds. The sequences used in this study are discussed in detail in Chapters 2 and 3. This research identifies a pattern of shorter sequence duration of this pre-state agricultural period in the New World when compared to the Old World and Peru. This pattern of differential duration has never been examined or explained. It is of considerable interest because such a difference between the two world areas suggests the possibility of a general cause or causes operating above and beyond differences in soil, precipitation, general climate, and crop complexes. As such, it has implications for understanding Old and New World patterns of development at a much broader scale than has been attempted previously. The proposed pattern of differential duration of the pre-state farming period is also important for research concerning the rise of social complexity and state development.

When pre-state village farming societies are examined on a global scale, two major patterns are noted in the Old World and the pre-contact New World (Hayes et al. 1981; MacNeish et al. 1980; Redman 1978; Sanders et al. 1979): the presence/absence of domesticated animals (Peru is included with the Old World in this case) and the presence of different crop complexes. These patterns offer an opportunity to seek a possible general cause for the observed difference in duration of the pre-state farming adaptation. There are also differences in precipitation and quality and availability of land. At the scale used in this study, however, these latter differences "even out" because variations in precipitation regimes and land types occur in both areas, leaving the presence/absence of domesticated animals and the distinct crop complexes as the major differences. The different agricultural crops are

briefly examined in this study. This volume, however, concentrates on examination of the presence or absence of medium to large domesticated animals (such as cattle, sheep, goats, pigs, and llamas) as an important conditioning factor in the difference in duration of the pre-state farming period.

This research uses ethnographic information to explore the contributions of medium to large domesticated animals to economic stability. Information from nutrition and soil science is also presented. It is suggested that subsistence-level farming economies with domesticated animals are more stable, measured in terms of duration, than those without animals. For purposes of this research, stability is defined as persistence through time without major modifications or changes (discussed by Hardesty 1977:46). According to this definition, a stable economy is one that persists through time without major modifications in means of production, organization of production, and resources produced and consumed. A wide range of resources and strategies that diversify the acquisition of energy can aid in reducing subsistence risk and economic perturbations that may lead to instability (Hardesty 1977: 43-45; Santley 1984). This study suggests that medium to large domesticated animals serve as one such alternative strategy (Flannery 1969). Further, this study assumes that problems in the subsistence/economic component of the system can lead to instability in the system as a whole. As Schelberg (1984:6) discusses for Chaco Canyon and Halstead and O'Shea (1982) discuss for the Aegean, attempts to reduce risk and maintain stability can lead to growing organizational and technological complexity. Thus, systems with a less stable subsistence component may indeed undergo rapid development of organizational complexity. The shorter pre-state farming periods and more rapid onset of state development in the New World may result from such economic instability. This study suggests that a cause of this greater instability is the lack of an important alternative subsistence resource present in the Old World and Peru but absent in the remainder of the pre-contact New World.

This research, then, is based partly on the tenets of cultural ecology (Steward 1955:30-42) in its emphasis on the primacy of subsistence activities and economic arrangements as they relate to environment in structuring other aspects of culture. The assumption that problems in the economic/subsistence component of the system can lead to instability in the system as a whole, and thus to changes in the level of organizational complexity, is drawn directly from cultural ecology. This study departs from cultural ecology in the research methods that are used. The approach of this work is generalistic as opposed to the more particularistic approach of cultural ecology.

Of course, other factors might contribute to the observed difference in duration of the pre-state farming period in the two world areas. Nonetheless, singling out the presence of medium to large domesticated animals for in-depth study as a potential cause of this difference provides valuable insight into the problems of growing social complexity in general and the economic role of domesticated animals in particular. It does not exclude the possibility that other factors may also be present.

RESEARCH METHODS

As stated earlier, this research has two primary foci: the definition and examination of an archaeological problem and the development of a research method to investigate that problem. This section presents a discussion of the research methods used in this study.

The research methods used here follow Binford (1983a: 192, 1983b) in framing a research strategy useful for the investigation of a problem of general interest. The methodological side of this study is designed to demonstrate the value and importance of a generalist as opposed to a particularist research orientation. Too often, archaeological research problems and explanations are confined to local or at best regional areas. Consequently, many local explanations for archaeological manifestations stress unique occurrences and special conditions. Climatic deteriorations or changes, which are often applied too widely and freely (Cordell 1984:304-325), are favorites in this line of explanation. Unique causal factors do occur, of course. Volcanic eruptions in the Basin of Mexico that destroyed the farmlands surrounding Cuicuilco are genuine examples of unique occurrences that may have that caused considerable culture change (Sanders et al. 1979; also see Chapter 3). In general, however, area-specific explanations are relied upon much too heavily in the literature. Such particularistic explanations do not aid in an understanding of general cultural processes. Archaeological information, however, has great potential to contribute to the understanding of general processes. This study makes use of that potential by defining a problem of general interest and developing a research strategy to examine that problem on a worldwide scale. A global frame of reference is not common in archaeological studies but is necessary if general cultural processes are to be examined (Anderson and Oakes 1980:12-40; Gilman 1983; Hard 1986).

An outline of the steps used in this research is given below. To begin with, an appropriate archaeological problem must be defined in the archaeological record. This allows definition of a problem of archaeological

relevance: one that can be seen and examined in archaeological terms. The many interesting ethnoarchaeological and contemporary urban behavioral studies in the literature today (e.g., Rathje 1979:1-37) may or may not be relevant to archaeological problems. If the material correlates of a behavior cannot be observed in the archaeological record, there is not much archaeological purpose to recording them in detail in modern society. Another related problem concerns the relevance of present examples to past behaviors. Care must be taken to assure that contemporary analogs have been properly warranted before they are used to help to develop explanations for the behavior of past systems. This critique is not intended to negate the value of ethnoarchaeological and urban behavioral studies but simply to reinforce the view that the problem of interest should first be identified in the archaeological record (Binford 1983a, 1983b). Building a body of information on present-day behaviors and their material correlates that may prove archaeologically useful is not an efficient research strategy unless this body of research has been warranted and is tied to a problem of archaeological interest.

Once a problem of interest has been observed, further archaeological research can then determine if the identified problem is a general pattern that seems to occur in other archaeological cases. The importance of examining a local problem in terms of its possible occurrence in other areas stems from the fact that this research can lead to explanations of general cultural relevance as opposed to narrow, unique case reconstructions. The possibility of a general cause in operation should always be explored before unique or local causes are accepted, owing to their limited explanatory power (Binford 1983a, 1983b). To reiterate, the pattern identified and examined in this study is that of the longer duration of the pre-state farming period in the Old World and Peru when compared to the remainder of the New World.

After an archaeological research problem has been identified and the presence of a general pattern has been determined, an explanation must be developed for the observed pattern. The archaeological record is a present-day phenomenon in which patterns can be observed. Simple recognition of an archaeological pattern does not explain what produced that pattern (Binford 1983a, 1983b). An explanation must be developed using information independent of the archaeological problem. This study emphasizes the use of ethnographic and ethnohistoric information, with ancillary material drawn from sources on nutrition and soil science, to build an explanation for the observed difference in duration of the pre-state farming period. As discussed previously, the potential explanation examined in this research focuses on the contributions of medium to large domesticated animals to the economic stability of subsistence-level farming societies.

Ethnographic sources are especially valuable because they offer dynamic, present-day information to help to interpret the static remains that constitute the archaeological record. The only place from which to obtain direct information on the actual operation of subsistence-level farming societies, outside experimental studies, is the body of ethnographic and ethnohistoric information that describes those societies. This type of information can only be inferred from archaeological remains.

The role of ethnographic data in this research is not to "flesh out" the archaeological record in a descriptive sense, which occurs when one or two ethnographic cases are described and then used to explain archaeological information. This study examines a substantial number of ethnographic cases that are controlled for level of agricultural intensity and animal husbandry to determine the degree to which a common pattern is in evidence. The economic contributions of domesticated animals to pre-state village farmers are thus examined under a wide range of geographical conditions. From this examination, four general uses are defined and studied in detail: *(a)* use of animal meat and by-products as a food source; *(b)* use of dung as fertilizer; *(c)* use of animals as a means of amassing wealth, as a back-up resource in lean times, and as a form of live storage; and *(d)* use of animal traction for transport and plowing. The importance of these categories in the economic life of the subsistence farming societies that were studied indicates the value of domesticated animals to these groups. Their value increases as other subsidiary resources, such as hunted game, decline with growing human populations and growing intensity of agriculture (Harris 1977; Murdock 1967). This study argues for the importance of domesticated animals as means of resource diversification and risk reduction. Domesticated animals also increase soil fertility through manuring and widen options for trade and interaction when they are used for transportation.

Warranting of the argument for the importance of domesticated animals to the economic stability of pre-state farming societies, as measured by duration, is accomplished by a listing of the ethnographic groups showing each of the uses. As such, it is an argument of enumeration, which is indeed weaker than the highly desirable causal argument. It is strengthened, however, by the use of a substantial number of controlled ethnographic cases, along with ancillary information concerning the decline of wild game with agricultural intensification, the importance of animal protein to nutrition, and the importance of animal manure to soil fertility. This combined body of information makes a strong case for the contribution of domesticated animals to economic stability even though the argument is one of enumeration. This type of controlled and strengthened enumerative argument, though not as powerful as a causal argument, has considerable explanatory power in its own right. It can also be used as a starting point to develop a causal argument.

VOLUME OVERVIEW

The final portion of this introduction briefly reviews the organization of this volume and the contents of each of the chapters. Chapters 2 and 3 present the archaeological data used to define the pattern of greater duration of the pre-state farming adaptation in groups that possess domesticated animals. Chapter 2 begins with a discussion of the conditions used to define pre-state village farming groups for purposes of this study. Criteria for group definition for both archaeological and ethnographic groups are given, since both of these types of groupings are examined in this study.

The remainder of Chapter 2 is devoted to a review of basic information on the selected archaeological sequences representing pre-state societies with domesticated animals. They are discussed in order of the duration of the pre-state farming period (beginning with the longest sequence): Carpathian Basin, south-central Bulgaria, Thessaly, Konya Plain, southern Britain, northern Mesopotamia, Ayacucho Basin, northern China, Indus River of Pakistan, Upper Egypt, and southern Mesopotamia. Each sequence review contains the same set of basic information on sequence duration, the use of domestic animals and their secondary products, the farming system, and settlement pattern and social organization. Chapter 3 presents the same set of information for the archaeological sequences that do not include medium to large domesticated animals (also listed in order by duration of pre-state farming period): Tehuacan Valley, Valley of Oaxaca, Basin of Mexico, Cahokia, and Chaco Canyon.

Chapter 4 discusses the identified pattern of differential duration of the pre-state farming period between the group without domesticated animals and the group with domesticated animals. Two statistical tests run on the data from both of the groupings indicate that the difference in duration between the groupings is statistically significant. Specific variations in length among the sequences within the same general grouping are also examined. Factors that might contribute to these variations in sequence length by speeding the process of growing social complexity are reviewed. These factors include population growth, land constriction, necessity of some form of water control, and intra- and inter-regional trade and exchange. The roles of irrigation and land constriction in hastening the growth of complex social organization are emphasized in this examination. They seem to have had a strong impact on several of the sequences, including those of Upper Egypt and southern Mesopotamia.

The final portions of Chapter 4 focus on an examination of the differences and similarities between the Ayacucho Basin sequence and the three Mesoamerican sequences with respect to duration, farming system, crops, population growth, land constriction, irrigation, and trade. This comparison is particularly instructive because all of these sequences are in the New World, yet only the Andean area has domesticated animals and a relatively long pre-state farming period.

Chapter 5 presents a discussion of the ethnographic information used in this research. The selection criteria for the 15 ethnographic groups chosen for detailed study are examined first. The selected groups are subsistence-level, mixed farmers as opposed to casual horticulturalists, pastoralists, or groups whose primary reliance is on cash cropping. These conditions help to ensure that the ethnographic cases are as comparable to the archaeological cases as possible. The following groups are used in this research: Balinese, Bambara, Coorg, Ifugao, Irish (Rural), Kikuyu, Kurds, Mapuche, Miao, Rif, Serbs, Shluh, Tallensi, and Zuni.

The four previously mentioned uses of domesticated animals were chosen based on information from these societies: *(a)* use of animal meat and by-products as a food source; *(b)* use of dung as fertilizer; *(c)* use of animals as a means of amassing wealth, as a back-up resource in lean times, and as a form of live storage; and *(d)* use of animal traction for transport and plowing. Each of these uses is explored in detail in the second section of Chapter 5. The importance of the economic contribution of each use is also assessed.

Chapter 6 presents descriptive models of the economic operation of societies with and without domesticated animals. The data for these models are drawn from both archaeological and ethnographic sources. The economic roles of agricultural crops and farming techniques, land-use patterns, hunted resources, domesticated animals, and trade and interaction are examined. A discussion of the ways in which domesticated animals are integrated into the village farming economy is also included. A comparison of the economic strategies of the two types of systems is presented along with a discussion of the situations in which economic problems might arise in the absence of domesticated animals. These comparisons focus on the importance of animals as means of increasing productivity through their use as sources of food, fertilizer, and traction. The ways in which growing societal complexity, especially the state level of integration, might ameliorate economic difficulties in the absence of animals in these situations are examined. The role of the state in agricultural intensification and in wars of conquest for land and tribute, which could include both agricultural produce and wild game, is examined. State-organized relocations of personnel and state control of trading networks are also discussed. These functions suggest the ways in which states can increase productivity and widen spheres of interaction to buffer areas of potential economic risk.

Chapter 7 concludes this study. The chapter begins with a brief review and summary of the major points of this research. The second section of the chapter examines the theoretical and methodological contributions of this type of study to archaeological research in general. It emphasizes the point that pattern-recognition studies at a global scale enable research to move beyond historical explanation to the examination of general cultural processes. This type of explanation is central to the purpose of anthropological research, which focuses not only on describing cultural and behavioral patterns but also on explaining them in the broadest possible terms. Thus, the underlying purpose of this study is to examine one possible cause of growth in social complexity. The cause examined here is economic instability. The study then focuses on the examination of one possible cause of that economic instability in the form of the absence of domesticated animals as an added subsistence resource for village farming economies.

The third and final portion of the concluding chapter reviews some of the implications generated by information derived from the present work. These include a brief discussion of the changing roles of hunted game and domesticated animals in early village farming societies. This section also includes an examination of the growing role of edible, secondary animal products. Another topic deals with the changing importance through time of the different animal domesticates and what factors seem to be conditioning these alterations. Another implication is illumination of the way in which state-level sociopolitical organization can serve as a means of buffering economic risk by increasing productivity.

The third section of Chapter 7 also presents a detailed exploration of a topic of considerable interest, centering on the New World systems and focusing on possible reasons for the different developmental trajectories seen in Mesoamerica and in several of the North American areas. The specific developmental difference concerns the growing social complexity and state development that occurred in Mexico, as compared to the growing social complexity followed by decline or abandonment seen in some North American areas. The Southwest and the Middle Mississippian area of the Midwest are examined in particular, and both areal and site abandonments are discussed.

ARCHAEOLOGICAL SEQUENCES
WITH DOMESTICATED ANIMALS

DEFINITIONS

This chapter describes the pattern of interest and discusses the archaeological cases with domesticated animals, in which one side of the pattern of interest can be observed. Chapter 3 presents information on the archaeological cases without domesticated animals, which constitute the other side of the pattern of interest. In any archaeological study the areas of interest must be delimited, be they chronological, spatial, or artifactual. Because this study examines patterning in the duration of pre-state agricultural societies, these societies must be defined in terms relevant to this research. Since the interest lies in the duration of a particular economic and sociopolitical organization, its beginning and ending points must be defined. The basic question concerns how long the farming lifeway persisted in an area before the appearance of the state as the form of sociopolitical integration. Because many sequences from widely varying geographic areas and research traditions are examined, no single criterion can be used to determine beginning or ending points of the time period of interest.

The starting point of the time period of interest is the beginning of the farming lifeway in an area. Determination of this beginning point is discussed first. Since this study uses both ethnographic and archaeological information, the beginning point of the farming lifeway must be determined in both ethnographic and archaeological terms.

The phrase *farming lifeway* as used here is not synonymous with the first appearance of domesticated crops. Rather, it is a period within which agricultural crops became important components of subsistence, contributing in the neighborhood of at least one-third of the subsistence base. The ethnographic descriptions of village or subsistence-level farming that are used here are drawn from several sources and are tailored to fit the needs of this study. In economic terms, these groups can best be described as having a domestic mode of production (Sahlins 1972:41-99, 101-148). The majority of production and consumption is at the household level or within the village. There is little circulation of goods beyond the household and village. In most respects, these communities can be classed as economically independent with respect to basic subsistence needs.

The type of agriculture and land use practiced by these groups can be either shifting/extensive farming, as described by Hardesty (1977:96-97) and Boserup (1965: 16), or advanced/intensive farming (Boserup 1965:16). In reality, groups often seem to practice a combination of the two types of strategies, as can be seen in infield-outfield systems. Often, certain fields are cultivated intensively each year while others are cultivated on a shifting basis, with considerable fallow time between periods of cultivation. These types of cropping systems can be difficult to distinguish archaeologically. The important point for this study is not necessarily how the fields are cultivated, but how important domestic crops are in the overall subsistence base.

The sociopolitical organization of these communities fits most easily into the lower end of the nonegalitarian societies, such as that of Fried's (1960) ranked society category. In Service's terms (1962) they would be described as tribes or at the very low end of the chiefdom scale (Redman 1978:204), in contrast to the band organization characteristic of hunters and gatherers. At the beginning of the time period under examination there may be some limited access to valued status positions. Access may be dependent on birth order or birth into a particular family.

If economic redistribution is present in these groups, it primarily occurs within the village itself. Other mechanisms of village and intervillage integration, such as sodalities and warrior and religious societies, may also be present. Intercommunity exchange of goods, services, and members occurs, but one community is generally not dependent on another for basic subsistence resources on a regular trading or redistributive basis. The above characterizations are taken from Fried (1960), Redman (1978: 179, 201-213), Sahlins (1972:101-148, 277-301), and Service (1962).

The regional settlement pattern demonstrated by these sequences is one of communities that usually have much fewer than 1000 persons but are larger than the 30- to 100-person groups suggested for the band level of integration. These communities are of relatively similar size and are located with respect to both wild resources and suitable farmland. No large centers are present, and communities do not generally locate themselves with respect to other communities (Redman 1978:201-213). Shifting of villages may occur if long-fallow agriculture is practiced (Boserup 1965:16). In other cases, these groups may practice some form of seasonal transhumance. The village-farming settlement pattern is best observed archaeologically or ethnohistorically. The current prevalence of state-level societies virtually ensures the presence of at least a regional capital, which disrupts the above-described pattern in the ethnographic cases.

The village farming lifeway, just described ethnographically, begins the period of interest. Recognition of these groups in the archaeological record presents the problem of determination of preservable material correlates of ethnographically described behavior. Redman (1978:178-213, 214-243) discusses archaeological indicators suitable for use in the present research. The intent of this research is to be conservative in selection of appropriate indicators of both the beginning and ending points of the period under study. Consequently, only the most commonly observed, best documented indicators are used.

According to Flannery (1972b:23-53) and Redman (1978: 178-213, 214-243), the beginning of the village farming lifeway is generally inferred by the presence of villages of from 100 to 200 people, with houses constructed of masonry, adobe, jacal, or some combination of these materials. The structures are often, but not always, rectilinear. In some areas, pithouse villages also occur. The two basic criteria used in this study are the presence of villages in combination with the presence of the remains of domesticated crops. Ideally, the domesticated crop remains should be indicative of their use as an important food resource (at least one-third of the subsistence base, for purposes of this study) and not as a back-up resource. Unfortunately, preservation problems and the difficulties inherent in determining dietary percentages of food remains make exact determination of percentage of contribution very difficult. However, every effort has been made to determine that domestic food crops are an important resource to the group before it is considered to be at the village farming level. In this study the opinions of the primary investigators in each area concerning the appearance of the farming lifeway are normally accepted.

Growing economic, social, and political complexity can be discerned throughout the agricultural time periods before the appearance of the state as the means of sociopolitical integration. These changes are seen in the archaeological record. In combination with an agricultural subsistence base, one sees the development of public architecture and differential dwelling size and elaboration. Evidence of craft specialization and intercommunity economic cooperation also appears during these time periods. In addition, the regional settlement pattern may feature communities that are unequal in size and appear to be located with respect to other communities as well as to needed natural resources (Redman 1978:178-213, 214-243).

The end of the time period of interest comes with the definition of a state level of society by the primary

researchers of that area. The beginning of local state development can be either pristine or secondary. Conquest of a region by a neighboring state-level society or abandonment of an area also constitutes an end to the period of interest.

The presence of a state-level society in an area is used as an endpoint for the period of interest for several reasons. The interest of this study lies in examining the duration of the village farming lifeway prior to the onset of measurable social, political, and economic complexity. After considerable research, it was decided that the appearance of the state in an area is the most reliable, best documented, and most standardized measure of that complexity. Forms of complexity do appear earlier, but they can be extremely difficult to measure (Feinman and Neitzel 1984). The state is considerably easier to define and determine archaeologically than either the beginnings of social complexity or complex chiefdoms, which tend to vary with every different investigator who attempts to examine them (Feinman and Neitzel 1984). Since a wide range of sequences from varying geographic areas is used in this research, a somewhat standard measure becomes very important.

Any typological classification that seeks to define societal levels exhibits the problems inherent in all categorizations (Feinman and Neitzel 1984; Lightfoot 1985). This is as true for definition of village farming level groups as it is for definition of state-level societies. Typological categories do indeed inhibit the study of sociopolitical change through time by forcing groups into predefined pigeonholes (Lightfoot 1985). These categories are static and descriptive, but they do allow comparisons of the subject matter under consideration. For this reason, and because the better-defined, descriptive categories are needed as sequence beginning and ending points and not as springboards for further sociopolitical research, typological categories are appropriate for use in this study.

Various researchers (Flannery 1972a; Flannery and Marcus 1983; Redman 1978; Wright and Johnson 1975) have discussed what constitutes a state-level society in both ethnographic and archaeological terms. There is a good deal of convergence among investigators on this topic. Flannery and Marcus's discussion of the beginnings of the state in Oaxaca is used here as an example of both archaeological and ethnographic definitions of the state (1983:79-83). They examine the Valley of Oaxaca in terms of the appearance of four characteristics. They consider a highly centralized government with a professional ruling class to be one indicator of a state-level society. An archaeological expression of this type of government is the true palace, a monumental structure consisting of both habitation areas and audience halls (Flannery and Marcus 1983:80). Another indicator is the presence of public buildings, including religious buildings and full-time specialists to maintain a state religion. The archaeological correlate they use is the appearance of the traditional two-room Zapotec temple, which appears almost simultaneously with the true palace (Flannery and

Marcus 1983:82). Their third characteristic is the presence of a four-tiered administrative hierarchy, observed in the archaeological record as a site-size hierarchy consisting of primary, secondary, and tertiary centers and small sites with no evidence of public architecture (Flannery and Marcus 1983:82). Flannery and Marcus are careful to note, however, that there is ambiguity concerning the relationship between an administrative hierarchy and a site-size hierarchy, and a direct relationship cannot be assumed (Flannery and Marcus 1983:82). The last category they consider concerns the time period when the valley groups began to wage war, exact tribute, and levy taxes. These activities are discerned archaeologically in the form of "town conquest slabs" and evidence of Monte Alban (the primary center) occupation in adjacent areas (Flannery and Marcus 1983:82-83).

The majority of investigators cited in this research follow a similar format to develop a case for the presence of a state-level society in an area. On the whole, their arguments are sound and are accepted for use in this research. Exceptions are discussed on a case-by-case basis.

Within the defined framework of pre-state agricultural societies, the groups of interest are further limited geographically and with respect to the major subsistence resources. The archaeological groups of interest are located in temperate zone, inland areas rather than tropical or coastal areas. The main agricultural crops are grain as opposed to root crops. The geographic restriction is more relaxed for the ethnographic cases since many of the present-day subsistence farmers are located in tropical areas. The added subsistence information on the ethnographic cases allows better control of exactly how much reliance is placed on coastal resources and root crops. Thus, tropical groups that are heavily reliant on coastal resources and root crops can be identified fairly easily and have been excluded from this study. When domestic animals are present, they are medium to large animals, such as cattle, llamas, sheep, goats, and pigs. The economic effects of such domesticates as dogs, chickens, or guinea pigs are not examined. These restrictions aid in the control of critical variables over the many groups that are being examined. Each of these restrictions is briefly reviewed below.

The needs and interests of this study dictate the use of groups that emphasize grain crops and either possess or do not possess medium to large domestic animals. Interest lies in determining how the presence or absence of this type of animal affects the economy of the group, especially with respect to stability. Grain crops are selected because they are the type of crop emphasized by the majority of the temperate zone groups and the majority of the complex societies. Inclusion of groups that place an emphasis on root crops might introduce unknown variation, which could not be monitored. Thus, the decision has been made to hold constant the use of grains as the major crop. The same line of reasoning holds for the exclusion of groups that emphasize a different sort of domesticate, such as chickens, with

minimal or no use of medium to large animals. This kind of use produces additional variability that could disrupt the results of the study.

Coastal groups are excluded from this study if they show a heavy reliance on fish or shellfish. Since one of the major economic contributions of domestic animals is as a source of protein, the importance of their contribution is clouded or altered if another major source of protein is readily obtainable. Fish and shellfish constitute one such source for coastal groups. Thus, the contribution of domestic animals to these groups cannot be accurately assessed.

This study, then, examines the duration of the pre-state, village farming lifeway as shown in archaeological sequences from a wide range of geographic areas. Ethnographic information is also used. The period of interest begins with the definition of the village farming lifeway in an area and extends until the appearance of the state. Temperate zone, noncoastal groups with primary agricultural reliance on grain crops are emphasized.

SELECTION OF ARCHAEOLOGICAL SEQUENCES

The pattern of differential duration of the village farming lifeway was identified using sixteen archaeological sequences from eight general areas (Figure 1): southern Britain and Europe, the Near East, Egypt, China, India and Pakistan, the Andes, Mesoamerica, and North America. Table 1 lists the specific sequences used in this study. These groups were selected because they give wide areal coverage and also because sufficient information on them is available. The sequences vary in geographic extent, number of sites, and amount of information in general, owing to the varying amount, intensity, and quality of research that has occurred in the different areas. A brief review of information on each sequence with domesticated animals is presented here.

Each review follows the same format and includes the same types of information whenever possible. The first section on each sequence presents the beginning date, ending date, and total duration in years of the pre-state farming lifeway. Establishment of agriculture in an area is also discussed. Time periods, phases, and cultures into which this larger time span is divided are listed next. The second major section discusses the domestic animals present and their changes through time. The use of secondary animal products is also discussed in this section. The farming system and any changes or intensifications that it may have undergone are the subjects of the third section of the review. The final section describes changes through time in the settlement pattern and social organization of the geographic area under consideration.

The dates used in this study follow those given by the researchers in the several areas under examination. Some

Figure 1. Locations of the archaeological sequences

Table 1.   Archaeological Sequences Listed by Group and by Order of Appearance in Text (numbers refer to location in Figure 1)

Sequences with Domestic Animals	Sequences without Domestic Animals
Southern Britain (5)	Mexico (Valley of Oaxaca) (14)
Central Europe (Carpathian Basin, Great Hungarian Plain) (1)	Mexico (Basin of Mexico) (13)
Southeastern Europe (South-central Bulgaria) (2)	Mexico (Tehuacan Valley) (12)
Greece (Thessaly) (3)	North America (Chaco Canyon) (16)
Anatolia (Konya Plain) (4)	North America (Cahokia) (15)
Northern Mesopotamia (Hassunan, Halafian, Samarran) (6)	
Southern Mesopotamia (Sumer) (11)	
Upper Egypt (10)	
Pakistan (Indus River system) (9)	
Northern China (Chung Yuan or Central Plain) (8)	
Peru (Ayacucho Basin) (7)	

studies use bristlecone pine–calibrated radiocarbon dates; others do not. This review follows Champion et al. (1984), Sherratt (1981), and others in using "B.C." for calibrated radiocarbon dates and "b.c." for uncalibrated radiocarbon dates. (In some cases, the original reports may refer to dates as "B.C." even when they have not been calibrated.)

Use of both calibrated and uncalibrated dates in this study is not a problem, as long as both the sequence beginning and ending points are calculated in the same way. Beginning and ending points are not compared across sequences, only durations are compared. Calibration tends to lengthen the sequences somewhat (Klein et al. 1982), but this does not constitute a problem for the current research. The mix of Old World calibrated and uncalibrated figures tends to balance out. Some sequences may be a bit longer whereas others are a bit shorter. With respect to the dates from the five New World non-animal cases, two are uncalibrated, two are calibrated, and one does not require calibration because it is based primarily on tree-rings. Again, the figures tend to balance each other out.

The individual sequence reviews for the archaeological cases with domesticated animals are presented in the remaining portion of this chapter. Reviews of the sequences without domesticated animals are presented in the following chapter.

SOUTHERN BRITAIN

Sequence Duration and Phases or Cultures Represented

Farming in southern Britain began with the appearance of wheat, barley, sheep, and goats. None of these foods is native to the British Isles; Smith (1974:281) reports that they were presumably brought in by colonists, whereas others (Barker 1985:203; Dennell 1983) argue that adoption of introduced cereals and stock into the local forager economy is more likely. In any event, the farming lifeway began around 4300 B.C. (ca. 3500 b.c.). The period of interest to this study ends with state formation in the century or so before the Roman invasion of Britain in the first century before the birth of Christ (Barker 1985:218; Champion et al. 1984:297-325; Renfrew 1982: 1-8). Thus, approximately 4000 to 3500 years of pre-state agricultural societies are represented in southern Britain before the first appearance of the state. (The maximum duration of pre-state level farming groups is listed in Table 2.) This time span encompasses the Early Neolithic (ca. 3500-2500 b.c.), the Late Neolithic and Early Bronze Age (ca. 2500-1500 b.c.), the Late Bronze Age (ca. 1500-500 b.c.), and the pre-Roman Iron Age (ca. 500 b.c. to the Roman Conquest; Barker 1985:xviii, 197, 203, 211, 218).

For the British sequence, as well as for all the other sequences examined in this study, definition of the state and the factors that led to state formation are by no means unanimously agreed upon. It is not the purpose of this review, however, to examine the various factors considered by local researchers to have led to state formation in each of the areas under study. Instead, the time of the first appearance of the state, as agreed upon by the majority of workers in an area, is the one used here.

Domestic Animals and Secondary Animal Products

Major crops and domesticated animals in pre-state southern Britain included wheat, barley, sheep, goats, cattle, and pigs. Emmer and six-row barley were the

Table 2.   Durations of the Pre-State Farming Period
            from Sixteen Archaeological Sequences

Sequence	Years
Central Europe	6200
Southeastern Europe	6200
Greece	5000
Anatolia	4600
Southern Britain	4000
Northern Mesopotamia	3660
Peru	3650
Northern China	3150
Pakistan	3000
Upper Egypt	2400
Southern Mesopotamia	1900
Mexico (Tehuacan Valley)	1750
Mexico (Basin of Mexico)	1400
Mexico (Valley of Oaxaca)	1400
North America (Cahokia)	1073
North America (Chaco Canyon)	800

main cereals, along with einkorn, flax, bread wheat, and spelt (Barker 1985:198; Helbaek 1952). Of the domestic animals, cattle and pigs are native to Britain. From their first appearance, domestic plants and animals seem to be by far the major means of subsistence (Rowley-Conwy 1981:85-96).

The faunal data show this emphasis, although Neolithic sites with fauna are scarce. They are mainly causewayed camps, which are considered primarily ceremonial as opposed to domestic. For this reason, the data must be viewed with some caution, but even so, the preponderance of domestic animals over hunted game can be seen in several Neolithic samples. The Neolithic fauna from Hambledon consists of cattle (55%), pig (25%), and sheep and goat (15%), with red and roe deer and dog comprising the remainder (5%; Legge 1981:172). The Stepleton fauna is very similar, as is the pre-enclosure fauna from Windmill Hill (Legge 1981:172). The Bronze Age fauna from Grimes Graves, which was used as a domestic site during this time period, is similar in species composition to the earlier faunas. The main difference is that pigs are more common in the earlier assemblages whereas sheep and goats are more strongly represented at Grimes Graves. The Grimes Graves fauna consists of cattle (52.5%), sheep and goat (31.9%), pig (5.7%), red deer (4.1%), horse (3.3%), and roe deer (2.5%; Legge 1981: 170). All of these assemblages illustrate the preponderance of domestic animals over hunted game from the Neolithic on. Sheep increase in importance along with cattle in the later times, presumably owing to the drier and more open environment (Barker 1985:205) and also to the increased importance of secondary animal products

(Champion et al. 1984:156-160). During Iron Age times, sheep outpace cattle in importance in some areas (Barker 1985:218).

Secondary animal products, such as milk, milk products, and wool, are an extremely important aspect of the maintenance of domestic animals within mixed farming systems. Certain general information concerning secondary animal product use and the evidence for its presence are presented now. This evidence applies to all of the following sequences as well as to the British sequence.

The use of secondary animal products can be inferred from several lines of evidence. The age/sex structure of archaeological faunas is one of the indicators used by many investigators. For example, a high juvenile kill-off rate for males, with more females surviving into adulthood, is taken to indicate dairying (Legge 1981:172; Sherratt 1981:283-285). A high survival rate of both male and female adult sheep can indicate both dairying and wool production (Sherratt 1981:283-285). In contrast, when animals are raised purely for meat, it is more economical to slaughter them while they are relatively young; thus, fewer survive into adulthood (Sherratt 1981: 283). Other lines of evidence for the use of secondary products include the presence of special vessels associated with milking, pictorial representations of milking and of wool sheep, and ethnographic practices (Sherratt 1981: 275-283). The earliest definite secondary product use in Britain seems to date to the Late Neolithic and Early Bronze Age (Barker 1985:206; Sherratt 1981:275-283, 294).

Legge (1981:169-181) argues for an earlier beginning for the use of secondary products, with a dairying economy from the Early Neolithic on. This earlier beginning is rejected by both Clutton-Brock (1981:218-220) and Sherratt (1981:276-283) in general discussions of secondary product use in mixed farming economies. These discussions center on the time required to develop both the humans' readiness to use and the animals' ability to provide milk. For example, animals that are not specifically bred for milking do not let down their milk readily to the herdsman. They also do not produce large surplus quantities of milk. Pictorial representations show the small udders on early cows and the use of an insufflator to stimulate the milk ejection response. In addition, most human adults are not equipped to digest milk owing to lactose intolerance. The tolerance present in northern European and Euroamerican populations today is the result of a relatively recent evolutionary episode, and adult milk drinking is a late and restricted feature of human diet (Kretchmer 1972; Simoons 1969, cited in Sherratt 1981:280). The Late Neolithic and Bronze Age is suggested as the most clearly defined beginning point for the spread of the milking complex. This judgment is based on the above information, on the appearance of specialized vessels associated with milking, and on pictorial representations that appear during the Bronze Age (Sherratt 1981:279-282, 294).

Farming System

From the earliest Neolithic on, agriculture in well-watered, temperate southern Britain consisted of mixed farming, with domestic stock playing an important role (Barker 1985:203). Early interpretations held that the first farming was slash-and-burn cultivation in heavily forested areas, but this interpretation has been reassessed (Barker 1985:197-198; Barker and Webley 1978; Rowley-Conwy 1981:85-96). The question of the primacy of slash-and-burn versus permanent-field farming systems is not central to the issues examined in this study. The debate is mentioned here as background information, since this controversy also appears in the literature on several of the other areas. It is currently suggested that a natural mix of vegetation types was present at the time of Early Neolithic farming rather than blanket forest, with open country and light woodland on the higher ground and closed forest and wet pasture in the river valleys (Barker 1985:198; Barker and Webley 1978). In this type of environment swidden farming would not be necessary (Barker 1985:198; Barker and Webley 1978; Rowley-Conwy 1981:85-96). Instead, Barker (1985:198) suggests that the distribution of Early Neolithic monuments and subsistence data indicates a model of more or less sedentary mixed farming, with each community using a transect of land from river floodplain to upland plateau. The most attractive low-technology farming soils would be the light, freely drained soils carrying open woodland (Barker 1985:198; Barker and Webley 1978).

During the later time periods, mixed farming remained the primary means of subsistence and grew in intensity. The following brief description of farming in the Late Neolithic, Early and Late Bronze Age, and Iron Age is taken primarily from Barker (1985:203-223). During the Late Neolithic and Early Bronze Age (ca. 2500-1500 b.c.), the range of farmed soil types increased, with heavier lands coming into use. Ard furrows have been found under several barrows from this time period, but it is possible that the ox-traction ard was in use during the earlier farming periods as well (Barker 1985:202; Rowley-Conwy 1981:94). By the end of the Early Bronze Age (ca. 1500 b.c.), the beginnings of planned field systems indicate the formalization of land tenure, suggested to be a response to growing populations and increasing pressure on the agricultural system.

The Late Bronze Age (ca. 1500-500 b.c.) shows continued development of bounded field systems and ard cultivation. There is evidence of rotational cropping and manuring of fields. The evidence for crop rotation consists of macrobotanical and pollen information. The evidence for manuring consists of spreads of household rubbish in former field areas (Barker 1985). Loom weights and spindle whorls are common, indicating the growing role of wool as a secondary animal product. The pre-Roman Iron Age (ca. 500 b.c. to the Roman conquest) shows continued development of these trends toward intensification of the mixed farming economy. There is

additional evidence of rotational cropping and spring and fall planting, with cattle and sheep used to manure the arable land. As previously stated, growing population is seen as the spur for the agricultural intensification.

Settlement Pattern and Social Organization

Agricultural intensification is paralleled by changes in settlement type and growing social and political complexity. This information is summarized by Sherratt (1981:294) and is also a major topic of discussion by Renfrew (1973:539-558). Sherratt describes the Early Neolithic communities as basically egalitarian, undifferentiated villages and hamlets. During the Late Neolithic and Early Bronze Age, funerary monuments and regional centers were added to the lattice of villages and hamlets. Sherratt views the social system of this time as that of a big-man system, whereas Renfrew argues for chiefdoms beginning in the Late Neolithic. The Late Bronze Age and pre-Roman Iron Age saw the development of regional chiefdoms and later the state as the form of sociopolitical integration. Barker (1985:218) and Champion et al. (1984:297-325) discuss the acceleration in cultural complexity in southern Britain in the last century before the arrival of the Romans, as shown by the presence of massive nucleated settlements called *oppida*. These settlements were seats of tribal governments and centers of both regional and long-distance trade. During this time, there were centralized production and marketing of certain items, such as wheel-made pottery, as well as standardized units of measure for trade. State-level societies were probably present, with the oppida serving most of the functions of the Roman towns that replaced them (Collis 1971:97-104; Cunliffe 1974; Haselgrove 1976:25-49, cited in Barker 1985:218; Champion et al. 1984:297-325). These figures for the appearance of state-level society in southern Britain yield a total of roughly 4000 years of pre-state farming societies.

CENTRAL EUROPE

(CARPATHIAN BASIN – GREAT HUNGARIAN PLAIN)

Sequence Duration and Phases or Cultures Represented

The farming lifeway on the Great Hungarian Plain dates from ca. 5300 b.c. (in the neighborhood of 6300 B.C. if calibrated dates are used; Champion et al. 1984:117) with the appearance of settlements of the Koros culture (Barker 1985:90, 95-97). Wheat, barley, millet, and flax are present in these sites along with sheep and goat (Kosse 1979:128; Sherratt 1982:16). According to the traditional interpretation, the farming lifeway was introduced into central and southeastern Europe by colonists from Greece and the eastern Mediterranean (Milisauskas 1978:44-46; Sherratt 1982:16). More recently, it has been suggested that farming in central and southeastern Europe was the result of adoption of introduced species by indigenous populations — perhaps in combination with local domestication of some species, possibly einkorn and sheep (Barker 1985:97-98). A realistic interpretation from Champion et al. (1984:100-101), one that is accepted in this study, suggests that the introduction of farming probably resulted from a combination of colonization in some areas and adoption of introduced domesticates by local groups in others. Some local domestication may also have occurred. The period of pre-state farming groups came to a close in the first century before Christ with the appearance of state and quasi-state societies in the regions surrounding the Roman world (Barker 1985:110; Champion et al. 1984:298-321). Thus, pre-state farming groups endured from a minimum of 5200 years to a maximum of 6200 years in the central European area of the Great Hungarian Plain (Table 2).

Sequences and phases from this long time span are somewhat confusing because terminology and time ranges vary from author to author (Barker 1985:84-111; Champion et al. 1984; Milisauskas 1978; Sherratt 1982: 13-26; Whittle 1985). For the purposes of this study, a generalized summary will be presented using the sequences described by Milisauskas (1978). The upper end of this sequence range is presented with both uncalibrated and calibrated dates. The Early Neolithic began with the appearance of the first farming societies and was followed by the Middle Neolithic in 3900-2600 b.c. (4540-3180 B.C.) and the Late Neolithic in 2600-1900 b.c. (3180-2180 B.C.). The Early Bronze Age, 1900-1450 b.c. (2180-1680 B.C.); Middle Bronze Age, 1450-1250 b.c. (1680-1480 B.C.); and Late Bronze Age, 1250-750 b.c. (1480-840 B.C.), follow. The period of interest ends during the pre-Roman Iron Age, from 750 b.c. (840 B.C.) to A.D. 1. This time span encompasses the following named cultures and phases: Koros, Linearbandkeramik (LBK), Tisza, Tiszapolgar, Bodrogkeresztur, Baden, Unetice, Tumulus, Urnfield, Hallstatt, and La Tene.

Domestic Animals and Secondary Animal Products

Major agricultural crops evident in the Carpathian Basin sites include wheat, barley, millet, and flax (Kosse 1979: 128). Sheep and goats, the domestic animals present in the earliest farming sites, are the most common species in the assemblages. Both fish and wild game were extremely important components of the subsistence base during the Early Neolithic, however, with hunted game (exclusive of fish) making up 20-30% of the faunal samples (Bokonyi 1964 and 1974, cited in Barker 1985: 96-97). Thus, the economy of the Koros communities consisted of mixed farming, hunting, fishing, and foraging.

During the middle and later Neolithic, which encompasses the Tisza and Tiszapolgar/Bodrogkeresztur cultures, domesticated cattle, which are native to the area,

predominated heavily over sheep and goats. This finding caused Sherratt to suggest that cattle breeding and trading were major activities during the Tisza period (1982:17-20). The percentages of game decreased and of both domesticated plants and animals (including pigs) increased, suggesting that systematic mixed farming was firmly established (Barker 1985:100). During Late Neolithic Baden times, sheep again increased in importance over cattle, probably owing to a growing emphasis on the use of secondary animal products (Sherratt 1982: 19). During this time, the animal component of the economy in general increased in importance as agriculture expanded to less productive areas where larger herds could be grazed during necessary fallow periods (Champion et al. 1984:162). This trend continued through the Middle Bronze Age when degradation of marginal soils and climatic deterioration forced farming settlements back onto the more productive arable land (Champion et al. 1984:205-209). Domestic animals, however, maintained their important role throughout the remainder of the Bronze Age and Iron Age.

Although Barker presents evidence of the use of milk, wool, and cattle for traction prior to the Late Neolithic, their systematic and widespread use seems to date to the Late Neolithic Baden culture in central Europe (Barker 1985:106; Champion et al. 1984:156-160; Sherratt 1981). The secondary product categories apparent at this time period include the plow and cart, with associated animal traction; wool from sheep; and milk from domestic animals. Horse bones are common for the first time in Baden burials. Two Baden burials contain paired oxen or cattle, and several models of four-wheeled carts have been found in burials and settlements in Hungary (Bokonyi 1974, *inter alios*, cited in Barker 1985:106). Manure is also mentioned as a consequence of large numbers of domestic animals grazing fallow fields and was used to maintain the fertility of permanent fields (Champion et al. 1984:156-160).

Farming System

The central European farming system during the Early Neolithic Koros and LBK cultures was originally considered to have been shifting or slash-and-burn cultivation (Bogucki 1983; Harris 1972a:245-262). Recently, a different type of farming system has been suggested for the area. Kosse (1979:128) suggests that cultivation centered on the seasonally inundated river levees planted in wheat, barley, millet, and flax. Cultivation was on a small scale, and the fertility of the levees was renewed by seasonal inundation (Barker 1985:97; Kosse 1979:128). Milisauskas considers Early Neolithic farming in the area to have involved the shifting or rotation of fields but not the frequent movement of villages because ample land surrounded the LBK villages (1978:76-80). The emphasis on cultivation of river levees, with renewed fertility through inundation, would require little shifting anyway. Bogucki (1983) summarizes the arguments against shifting, slash-and-burn type cultivation by emphasizing the natural fertility of these floodplain areas and of the post-glacial European loess in general. This information contradicts Harris's (1972a:245-262) view of shifting, slash-and-burn agriculture in the Early European Neolithic and argues for small-scale farming on relatively permanent fields.

In the Middle and Late Neolithic, cultivation spread to less productive areas in the Alfold and Carpathian foothills and northwest to the Pannonian plain (Barker 1985:99-100). In the Koros heartland subsistence intensification has been noted. Caches of harvested crops have been found, including emmer and six-row barley in particular, but also einkorn, bread wheat, millet, and legumes (Barker 1985:100). During the Late Neolithic there is also solid evidence for use of the plow or ard and the cart, as well as the full range of secondary animal products and manure, as mentioned previously.

The trend toward agricultural expansion continued through the Middle Bronze Age, with a wide range of cereals and legumes being cultivated. The presence of rye and spelt at the end of this time could indicate cooler and wetter conditions at the beginning of the Late Bronze Age (Barker 1985:109). Also during this time, degradation of marginal soils forced farming settlements back onto the more productive arable land. Bounded field systems are known from some areas of Europe during this time, probably as a response to the contraction of available arable land (Champion et al. 1984:205-209). Only hints of these phenomena are known in west-central Europe, however, probably owing to lack of discovery as opposed to genuine absence (Champion et al. 1984:206). Unfortunately, subsistence data from the Bronze Age and later periods from the Carpathian Basin lags considerably behind information from Britain and western Europe, because studies in the former region have been focused on prestige goods and culture histories (Barker 1985:109-110; Champion et al. 1984:205-206, 304). Thus, the more detailed descriptions of later farming techniques that are available for Britain, for example, are not available for the Carpathian Basin. Similar types of bounded fields, rotational cropping, and manuring were probably in use, however. In the closing stages of pre-Roman times, metal dominated agricultural technology. Iron plow shares enabled the cultivation of heavier soils that had previously been reserved for animal husbandry, producing the pattern of farming that survived to the recent period (Barker 1985:110).

Settlement Pattern and Social Organization

The long time span under discussion also saw considerable changes in settlement and social organization. The early Koros and LBK sites were dispersed along tributaries of the major rivers and were egalitarian villages and hamlets (Bogucki 1983; Sherratt 1981:294, 1982:17). During the Middle Neolithic, changes occurred in settlement organization with aggregation into fewer settlements

and the first appearance of true tells. Sites were larger, but Sherratt views them as continuing to be basically egalitarian in nature (1982:17-23), with aggregation the result of defense or production needs. No fortifications are present on these sites, however. During the later Middle Neolithic, sites were once again dispersed, and differences in grave goods indicate that a big-man type of system may have been in operation (Sherratt 1982:18-23). During the Late Neolithic, settlements were often fortified (Barker 1985:106), and there is evidence of the beginning of a site hierarchy in the form of small hamlets and larger nucleated settlements. This pattern reverted to one of smaller, dispersed settlements during the long Late Neolithic time span, however (Champion et al. 1984:162). Social organization remained at the level of big-man organization (Sherratt 1981:294). Bronze Age communities were also often fortified or located on defensible promontories. Hillfort villages were common in the upland margins of the basin (Barker 1985:108). Champion et al. (1984:214) refer to these hillfort sites as fulfilling "central place" functions and discuss Early Bronze Age central Europe in terms of the appearance of chiefdoms. Sherratt (1981:294) also refers to chiefdoms having developed during the Early Bronze Age and continuing until the appearance of the state in the century or so before Christ. This latter development is signaled by massive increases in settlement densities shown by the appearance of major nucleated settlements (*oppida*; Barker 1985:110; Collis 1982:73-78) and by other developments in production and distribution previously discussed for Britain. The appearance of the state during this time period in central Europe indicates the end of roughly 6200 years of the pre-state farming lifeway.

SOUTHEASTERN EUROPE

(SOUTH-CENTRAL BULGARIA)

Sequence Duration and Phases or Cultures Represented

Farming in southeastern Europe, as represented by the sequence and sites from south-central Bulgaria, probably began before ca. 5500 b.c. (ca. 6500 B.C. if calibrated dates are used; Champion et al. 1984:117). Archaeological information from this geographic area comes from excavations at various large tell sites, such as Karanovo, Azmak, Kazanluk, and Chevdar. The farming lifeway began in the Karanovo I time period with the presence of einkorn, emmer, barley, flax, and pulses. Domestic animals included sheep, goats, pigs, and to a lesser extent, cattle (e.g., Dennell 1978; J. Renfrew 1969, 1973). Not all species of plants and animals are present on every site, but they are all present on sites within the area. As discussed previously for the Carpathian Basin, the appearance of farming in southeastern Europe is best explained in terms of a combination of colonization, adoption of introduced domesticates by local groups, and possible local domestication of some species (Champion et al. 1984:100-101; Whittle 1985:54-55). The long period of pre-state farming societies ends in the Bulgarian portion of southeastern Europe with the appearance of the short-lived, low-level state of the Thracian Seuthes at the end of the fourth century B.C. (Barker 1985:110-111; Champion et al. 1984:316). The duration of the pre-state farming period in this region, then, is 5200-6200 years (Table 2).

This time span includes the following sequences described by Barker (1985:90-111) and Champion et al. (1984). The Early Neolithic began with the appearance of the first farming villages at ca. 5500 b.c. and ended at roughly 4500 b.c. The Middle Neolithic ran from ca. 4500 to 4000 b.c., and the Late Neolithic continued from 4000 to 3000 b.c. The following phase, referred to as the Initial Bronze Age in southeastern Europe, lasted from ca. 3000 to 2000 b.c. It was followed by the Early, Middle, and Late Bronze Ages. The earlier Bronze Age (composed of the Early and Middle Bronze Ages) ended at approximately 1100 b.c. The local Iron Age is generally considered to have lasted from 750-700 b.c. to A.D. 1. This period covers the following cultures and phases: Karanovo I-VII, Ezero, Final Ezero, Urnfield, and Thracian. The time period of concern to this research ends at the end of the fourth century B.C. with the appearance of the Thracian state.

Domestic Animals and Secondary Animal Products

Major domesticated crops and animals in the south-central Bulgarian sites consist of einkorn, emmer, barley, flax, pulses, sheep, goats, pigs, and cattle (e.g., Dennell 1978; J. Renfrew 1969, 1973). These domesticates are present in Early Neolithic sites along with small numbers of red deer, roe deer, small mammals, birds, and fish (Barker 1985:92; Dennell 1978). Domestic animals, however, represent the main faunal component, with sheep and goats predominating over cattle.

Dennell (1978) suggests that fodder was grown for the animals and that the sheep and goats were taken to the hills in the summer while the cattle and pigs stayed at the settlements. Dennell's argument is based on evidence from the sites of Chevdar and Kazanluk. The same type of farming system, involving a mobile pastoral component, was probably also present in the primary zone of tell settlement, the Nova Zagora region (Barker 1985:92-93), where Karanovo, Azmak, and Ezero are located. During later Neolithic times, the same system of mixed farming with a mobile pastoral component continued. Sheep remained the most important domestic animal. During the Initial Bronze Age, further intensification in sheep pastoralism is noted at sites like Ezero and suggested as a response to the lack of additional arable land that could be brought into cultivation (Dennell 1978). (This intensification is discussed in more detail below.) As mentioned for the Carpathian Basin sequence, subsistence information from the later time periods has suffered from the emphasis by researchers on prestige goods and culture histories. Thus, less is known concerning subsistence during these time periods. Domestic animals, especially sheep and cattle, retained their important role in subsistence throughout the remaining time periods, however (Barker 1985:110).

Barker (1985:92-94) suggests that the age structure of faunal remains from domestic animals at the Bulgarian tells indicates the use of secondary products from the earliest Neolithic. Manure is also mentioned for this time period, but the evidence for its use is not stated. Thus, manure use during this time period is not a certainty. The possibility of cattle traction and the scratch ard is mentioned for the Middle Neolithic in the Balkans (Barker 1985:100). Some evidence for the use of secondary products is also known from the Late Neolithic (Barker 1985:101; Champion et al. 1984:139). Solid evidence for the widespread use of secondary products and cattle traction comes with the Initial Bronze Age in southeastern Europe (the Ezero phase in south-central Bulgaria), which is roughly comparable to the Late Neolithic in areas farther north. These uses are similar to those described for the Carpathian Basin (Champion et al. 1984:156-160; Sherratt 1981).

Farming System

The Bulgarian farming system from the time of the first Neolithic settlements was a stable, mixed farming system with permanent fields and a mobile pastoral component. Rotational cropping and some manuring are suggested for this time period (Dennell 1978). This system remained unchanged until Initial Bronze Age times when the component of sheep pastoralism intensified. This intensification is suggested as a response to the lack of additional arable land around the major settlements (Dennell 1978). Climatic changes may have been a factor in decreasing the amount of arable land available and producing a more open landscape better suited to sheep and goat pastoralism (Barker 1985:105). This increase in the pastoral component may also have resulted in further degradation of the arable land around the major tell sites owing to erosion from overgrazing of the uplands. This erosion may have caused the washing of massive sheets of clay down onto the arable land (Dennell and Webley 1975, cited in Barker 1985:105). Most of the tell sites were abandoned during the Initial Bronze Age, presumably for the reasons discussed above.

During the later time periods of the Bronze and Iron Ages, subsistence information is scant. It appears that intensive mixed farming systems with rotational cropping and manuring continued, though settlements were now more dispersed. The pastoral component also retained its importance. Unfortunately, no information exists concerning the presence or absence of bounded field systems. As in central Europe, metal came to dominate agricultural technology towards the end of this period, which enabled the cultivation of heavier soils (Barker 1985:110).

Settlement Pattern and Social Organization

South-central Bulgaria saw changes in both settlement pattern and social organization during the period spanning the Early Neolithic through the Iron Age. Fairly large, permanent settlements (possibly up to 400-500 people at the larger communities) began in the Early Neolithic and continued into the Initial Bronze Age (Barker 1985:94). These large tell sites were located at the junction of the hills and the plain, affording access to both farming and grazing lands (Dennell and Webley 1975, cited in Barker 1985:92). The sites grew in size and complexity through time, but the basic settlement pattern did not alter until their abandonment during the Initial Bronze Age.

Social organization at the tell sites is not clearly known. Differential distribution of such items as fine pottery, figurines, and clay altars suggests some status distinctions (Barker 1985:91). These distinctions are not high level, however, and are not inconsistent with a basically egalitarian village structure. During the later Neolithic and Initial Bronze Age, a big-man system of organization may have developed as discussed by Sherratt (1981:294).

During the later Bronze and Iron Ages in nearby areas, settlement dispersed to smaller communities, some of which were located on hilltops and were fortified. This dispersal is seen as a continuation of the trend begun during the Initial Bronze Age with the abandonment of many of the tell sites of the region. The smaller, dispersed sites are seen as facilitating the growing importance of pastoralism in the economy (e.g., Barker 1985: 105-111). Social organization during these later periods continued to increase in complexity with the development of complex chiefdoms during the later Bronze Age (Sherratt 1981:294) and the appearance of the short-lived Thracian state at the end of the fourth century B.C. (Barker 1985:110-111; Champion et al. 1984:316). Thus, the south-central Bulgarian sequence represents 6200 years of agricultural societies before the development of the state.

GREECE

(THESSALY)

Sequence Duration and Phases or Cultures Represented

There are many archaeological sequences from Greece. The sequence from Thessaly was chosen for this study because it provides some of the most complete information for the earlier Neolithic sites. Unfortunately, the area is less informative for the Bronze Age. Thus, developments in some of the other areas, such as Crete, will be mentioned during discussions of the Bronze Age.

The village farming lifeway began in Thessaly in northern Greece at approximately 7000 B.C. with the appearance of farming villages that later developed into large tell sites (Halstead 1981; Renfrew 1972:64). Such sites as Argissa, Souphli, Sesklo, and Achilleion show the presence of barley, millet, einkorn, and emmer as well as sheep, goats, cattle, and pigs (Barker 1985:64; Renfrew 1972:64). It has been suggested that the first farmers in Greece were emigrants from Anatolia (Renfrew 1972:64). A more current view is that indigenous groups domesticated some local species (einkorn, barley, and sheep) in the early Holocene and later adopted other introduced species (emmer and bread wheat, which appear at some sites; Barker 1985:71). For the purposes of this study, the time period of interest ends with the beginning of the small, minor Minoan state on Crete at approximately 2000 B.C. (Champion et al. 1984:230; Milisauskas 1978: 246-252; Renfrew 1972:363-370). This cut-off date is used to prevent the extension of the Thessalian sequence past the time when state development is present in the area. Using this cut-off date yields a total of approximately 5000 years of pre-state farming villages in Thessaly (Table 2). The time span on Crete is approximately the same, since the site of Knossos also has an early beginning date that is comparable to those of the sites in Thessaly (Renfrew 1972:64).

As categorized by Halstead (1981:335), this time span begins with the Early Neolithic (ca. 7000-6000 B.C.) and continues through the Middle Neolithic (ca. 6000-5000 B.C.), Late Neolithic (ca. 5000-4000 B.C.), Final Neolithic (ca. 4000-3000 B.C.), and Early Bronze Age (ca. 3000-2000 B.C.). The following cultures and phases are represented: Proto/Pre-Sesklo, Sesklo, Dhimini, Larisa/ Rakhmani, and Early Thessalian I-III (Champion et al. 1984:117; Renfrew 1972:116-117).

Domestic Animals and Secondary Animal Products

Early Neolithic sites show evidence of subsistence based on cereals and pulses. Remains of sheep, goats, pigs, cattle, and wild game are also present. Sheep and goats predominate by a considerable margin, and domestic animals in general predominate over wild game (Barker 1985:63-64; Renfrew 1972:64-65, 270-274). The flocks probably remained near the villages for most of the year during this time period (Halstead 1981:319). During the later Neolithic (Middle and Late Neolithic), cattle and pigs dominated sheep and goats in terms of the numbers of domestic animals being maintained. The actual percentage of pigs in the fauna, however, remained fairly stable through time. Goats were more numerous than sheep during this period (e.g., Bokonyi 1973b, cited in Barker 1985:65). Halstead (1981:324) describes this change in the following way. The predominance of sheep in the Early Neolithic can be taken to indicate that most of the grazing was on stubble and fallow fields. Fields were relatively permanent, with very little cleared land abandoned and left to revert to browse for goats and cattle. During the long periods of the later Neolithic, more vegetation was gradually disturbed, creating the lower browse favorable for goats and cattle at the expense of mature woodland. Halstead (1981:324) feels that this situation did not result from a change to a bush fallow system but from gradual depredation of the area surrounding the major sites by humans for firewood and by animals for fodder. During the Final Neolithic and Early Bronze Age, sheep again predominated, indicating an increase in the amount of open areas, probably cleared for permanent fields. There are also suggestions that transhumance was being practiced during this time period, with flocks grazing lowland fallow fields in winter and upland pastures in summer (Halstead 1981: 328).

Secondary product use in Thessaly is discussed by Halstead (1981:319, 322-331). Animal and human manure, as well as household refuse, was probably in use from the earliest farming times on. Other secondary products came into use much later. The heavy death rates of immature animals found in Neolithic faunas indicate that these herds were exploited primarily for their meat. Not until the Early Bronze Age is there good evidence for the use of milk, wool, and cattle traction, with both the ard and cart in use. In actual time range, this evidence corresponds with the beginning of secondary product use in other areas of Europe.

Farming System

Farming in Thessaly more than likely involved autumn sowing of crops and a summer harvest, since winters are wet and warm whereas summers are periods of heat and drought (Barker 1985:55-57, 63-64). As discussed for southeastern Europe, agriculture in northern Greece from the time of the first Neolithic villages was a stable, mixed farming system with permanently cultivated fields, manuring, and probable crop rotation of some form (Halstead 1981:317-320). Fallowing was probably rare or short-term, with cultivated fields located in wooded areas on the diluvial soils at the junction of the alluvial plains and the mountainous hinterland (Barker 1985:63-64; Halstead 1981:320). By the end of the Neolithic, barley, millet, oats, einkorn, emmer, bread wheat, and pulses were being grown (Barker 1985:64; Renfrew 1972:274-276). Stock was maintained near the communities, though there is evidence in the later Neolithic of cattle pastoralism in the wetlands of western Thessaly (Halstead 1981:325-326). This type of mixed farming continued throughout the Neolithic.

During the Early Bronze Age, the cultivated areas around the growing farming communities were expanded. Use of the plow and cart, as well as other animal secondary products, also occurred during this time period. The plow and cart undoubtedly made the use of these more distant fields profitable. Sheep grew in numbers and importance during this time period, probably because of the growing importance of secondary products. Greater expanses of fields around the communities also provided more winter fallow land for larger flocks to graze. Summer movement of the flocks to the uplands during this time may have occurred because the stubble fields provided insufficient summer fodder for the larger flocks. Growing community size is seen as an initial stimulus for the above-described changes (Halstead 1981:327-331).

Settlement Pattern and Social Organization

Permanent farming settlements, which grew in size through time, remained a feature of the Thessalian landscape throughout the time period of interest. During the Final Neolithic, external ditches appear around such sites as Dhimini and Sesklo. Stone retaining walls also appear around the acropolis areas at these two sites, as do large megaron buildings. These features suggest defensive considerations along with possible social differentiation (Whittle 1985:148-150). The precise nature of the social organization at these sites is not known, however. Egalitarian communities during the earliest Neolithic are presumed to have given way to more complex forms of social organization as communities grew larger in the Final Neolithic and Early Bronze Age.

These large nucleated settlements remained during the Early Bronze Age. Some settlement relocation occurred in Thessaly during the third millennium, perhaps because of the growing importance of pastoralism and the use of animal traction (Halstead 1981:330). In general, however, life in Thessaly remained much the same as it had been during the Late Neolithic (Renfrew 1972:117). In fact, social organization in the north probably altered little until the developments of the eighth through the sixth centuries B.C. in the south that produced the Greek city-states and regionwide interactions (Champion et al. 1984: 240-264). Using this as an ending time for village farming in the north would produce a very long span of roughly 6200 years. For purposes of this study, however, the development of the first minor state on Crete will be considered the cut-off point, yielding a time span of approximately 5000 years.

ANATOLIA

(KONYA PLAIN)

Sequence Duration and Phases or Cultures Represented

Farming villages appear on the Konya Plain at ca. 6500 b.c. (Mellaart 1967a:52-53, 1972:282). (All dates used in the following discussion of the Konya Plain are uncalibrated and use the "b.c." designation, though "B.C." may have been used in the original reports.) The large site of Catal Huyuk is the main site during the early time period and shows evidence of the presence of both domesticated plants and animals from the beginning of its occupation (Mellaart 1967a, 1967b). The level from ca. 6250 b.c. contains evidence of cattle, sheep, and goats. Domesticated plants include emmer, einkorn, bread wheat, two-row barley, six-row naked barley, peas, and bitter vetch (Mellaart 1967b:8). Other sites on the Konya Plain include Can Hasan, Reis Tumegi, and Keyren, which are all permanent settlements that were occupied for a considerable length of time (French 1966:113-124; Mellaart 1972:279-280). These farming villages are considered to have developed locally out of earlier sedentary villages whose inhabitants used wild resources and perhaps some domesticates (Redman 1978:153-165, 182). The time period of interest ends at ca. 1900 b.c., the beginning of the Middle Bronze Age in the area, with the appearance of small city-states (Lewy 1965:11; Mellaart 1967b:43-44). Thus, approximately 4600 years of pre-state agricultural societies are known for the Konya Plain before the appearance of a more complex form of social organization (Table 2).

Included within this time span are the following periods: Early Neolithic (up to 5750 b.c.), Late Neolithic (ca. 5750-5600 b.c.), Early Chalcolithic — essentially a continuation of the Late Neolithic (ca. 5600-5000 b.c.), Middle/Late Chalcolithic (ca. 5000-3500 b.c.), Early Bronze Age I (ca. 3500-2800 b.c.), Early Bronze Age II (ca. 2800-2300 b.c.), and Early Bronze Age III (ca. 2300-1900 b.c.; Mellaart 1965, 1967b, 1972:279-280). In general, prehistoric developments in Anatolia are discussed in terms of the above-listed time periods in the various geographic areas, such as the Konya Plain, without reference to specific phases or cultures.

Domestic Animals and Secondary Animal Products

Subsistence based on grain crops and domesticated animals is apparent from the time of the Early Neolithic. Domestic animals include sheep, goats, and cattle, with cattle predominating (Mellaart 1967b:8; Perkins 1969, cited in Redman 1978:183; Redman 1978:183). In fact, cattle bones outnumber the bones of all other animals, both wild and domestic, in the faunal remains from the main mound of Catal Huyuk (Cohen 1970:122-123; Mellaart 1966). Hunted game was also very important and included wild cattle, wild sheep, onager, half-ass, and red, roe, and fallow deer (Mellaart 1967b:8; Perkins 1969, cited in Redman 1978:183; Redman 1978:183). Transhumance is suggested for the Anatolian Neolithic by Mellaart (1972:281), with a portion of the population from the settled communities taking the animals to the uplands for summer grazing. The animals would then be returned after the harvest to graze on the stubble fields. During the later Neolithic and Chalcolithic in the area, sheep rose in importance at some sites, as is the case during the much later Roman period (Cohen 1970:123; French 1972:233-237). Pigs also appeared as a domesticate during this long time span (Mellaart 1972:282). All of these domesticated animals — sheep, goats, cattle, and pigs — retained their importance throughout the following time periods (French 1972:233-237).

Mellaart (1967a:224-225) suggests that animal secondary products, such as milk and wool, were in use from the time of the Early Neolithic. Sherratt's (1981:261-305) discussion of the advent of secondary product use, which has been summarized earlier in this sequence review, indicates that this date is probably too early. Evidence for use of the cart in eastern Turkey comes from ca. 2800-2700 b.c., with evidence for use of the plow at a somewhat similar time, although the form of plow that was used in Anatolia is not known (Sherratt 1981:263-267). Milking appears during the Early Bronze Age in Anatolia, as does wool use (Sherratt 1981:280-285). This information for Anatolia in general gives a picture of what was probably occurring in the Konya Plain in particular.

Farming System

Farming on the Konya Plain seems to have begun with settled communities and relatively permanent fields. The agricultural system was mixed farming, with domestic plants and animals being of considerable importance. Hunted game and wild plants were also important during the earlier periods. By 6250 b.c. at Catal Huyuk, emmer, einkorn, two-row barley, lentils, bitter vetch, and peas were being grown as well as bread wheat and six-row naked barley (Helbaek 1964, 1970:1, cited in Redman 1978:183). The latter two crops probably required some form of simple irrigation on the arid Konya Plain (Mellaart 1972:282; Redman 1978:183). As mentioned above, Mellaart (1972:281) suggests limited transhumance, with stock being taken to summer pasturage in the uplands, and a spring and a fall planting. Both of these suggestions are based on current practice, however, and may not have been the case in the Neolithic.

There is less information concerning regional farming practices for the later time periods owing to the nature of research in the area. At the end of the Early Bronze Age II period, ca. 2300 b.c., an apparent depopulation of the Konya Plain and other areas of Anatolia occurred, which lasted through the Early Bronze Age III period. The reasons for this depopulation are not entirely clear, but the lack of sites suggests the rise of pastoralism in the area (Mellaart 1965:46-50). This suggestion is discussed further in the section on settlement pattern. By the Middle Bronze Age, beginning at ca. 1900 b.c., intensive mixed farming with irrigation seems once again to have been the dominant form of subsistence (Mellaart 1967b: 28).

Settlement Pattern and Social Organization

From the beginning of the Neolithic, permanent farming settlements, which altered in size and number through the millennia, were present on the Konya Plain. During the Neolithic and Chalcolithic, small egalitarian communities were the rule (French 1972:232-233). Neolithic Catal

Huyuk, a very large site for the time period, is an exception. This community may also have been more complexly organized, but the evidence is not sufficient to make this determination (Redman 1978:182-187, 206).

During the Early Bronze Age periods in general, sites grew in size and number on the Konya Plain. More than 100 large Early Bronze Age I and II mounds are known in the area (Mellaart 1965:5-6), indicating the existence of prosperous communities. During the Early Bronze Age I and II, social organization was presumably beyond the egalitarian village level but had probably not yet attained a state level of organization (French 1972:233-236). During the Early Bronze Age III period, there was an apparent depopulation of the area, which Mellaart considers to be the result of invasion and of use of the area by pastoralists (Mellaart 1965:46-50). A detailed discussion of this presumed depopulation is beyond the scope of this study. Two large sites were still present in the area, however, and could simply represent extreme aggregation during this time period (French 1972:234). Definite fortifications appear for the first time on the plain during this period, which indicates that defense was indeed a consideration in community planning (French 1972:234). Whether or not the area was invaded and truly depopulated is simply not known.

By the beginning of the Middle Bronze Age at ca. 1900 b.c., a four-level site hierarchy was present in the Konya Plain. Approximately 25 large mounds of city size, one of which is Karahuyuk-Konya, were scattered over the area, and the regional settlement is discussed in terms of kingdoms and small city-states (Lewy 1965:11; Mellaart 1967b:43). Thus, the time period of interest ends with the beginning of the Middle Bronze Age, yielding a total of 4600 years of pre-state agriculture on the Konya Plain.

NORTHERN MESOPOTAMIA

Sequence Duration and Phases or Cultures Represented

The region referred to as northern Mesopotamia is quite large and includes the region referred to as Assyria in later times. The majority of sites discussed in this study are located in Iraq, north of Baghdad and between the Tigris, Euphrates, and Diyala rivers. Some sites also occur in northeastern Syria, southeastern Turkey, and western Iran (Redman 1978:20, 181). Village farming began in this area at about 6000 b.c. with the Umm Dabaghiyah culture (Kirkbride 1972, 1973a, 1973b, 1974, 1975; Mellaart 1975:135-141). (As discussed for the Konya Plain sequence, all the dates used in the following review are uncalibrated and use the "b.c." designation). Cultivated emmer, einkorn, barley, sheep, goats, cattle, and pigs are present on these sites (Bokonyi 1973a; Helbaek 1972), which represent movement down to lower elevations by farming groups from the Zagros Mountains and their foothills (Redman 1978:188). The pre-state farming adaptation ends in northern Mesopotamia with

the conquests of Sargon, King of Agade, in the north. The period, then, ends with the beginning of Sargon's rule in 2340 b.c. and covers a time span of 3660 years (Table 2; Bottero 1967:107, 129-130; Redman 1978:309-314).

The following, somewhat overlapping cultures and phases are commonly mentioned in discussions of northern Mesopotamia: Umm Dabaghiyah (ca. 6000-5500 b.c.); Hassunan, Samarran, and Halafian (ca. 5500-4800 b.c.); 'Ubaid 1-4 (ca. 5500/5300-3600 b.c.); Early and Late Uruk (3600-3100 b.c.); Jemdet Nasr (ca. 3100-2900); and Early Dynastic (ca. 2900 to 2340 b.c.; Edzard 1967:52-90; Falkenstein 1967:1-51; Mellaart 1975:135-179; Redman 1978:189-201, 245-251). The Uruk period represents the beginning of city-state development in the south, but in the northern portion of the area under discussion only towns were present during the Uruk (Redman 1978:293), and cities do not occur until later.

Domestic Animals and Secondary Animal Products

A mixed farming economy consisting of grain crops and domesticated animals was present in northern Mesopotamia from the time of the first village occupations. Sheep, goats, cattle, and pigs were present, with sheep and goats predominating. At the early site of Umm Dabaghiyah, hunted game was considerably more important than domestic animals, with onagers (68%) and gazelles (16%) constituting the majority of the bones found (Bokonyi 1973a). In the later Hassunan, Samarran, and Halafian cultures domestic animals attained positions of greater importance. They consisted of sheep, goats, cattle, and pigs, with sheep and goats still predominating (Mellaart 1975:147, 152, 155, 160-161; Oates 1973; Redman 1978:196, 201). During the following 'Ubaid period in northern Mesopotamia, the animals that were being herded remained essentially the same (Redman 1978:257). In the Uruk, Jemdet Nasr, and Early Dynastic periods in the north, sheep and goats still predominated, with the ratio of sheep to goats increasing significantly through time (Oates 1973; Redman 1978:269). The growing importance of sheep can be viewed in terms of the growing importance of secondary products and the continued clearance and use of fields, producing a more open landscape. This type of landscape would de-emphasize the secondary browse preferred by goats in favor of the type of grazing preferred by sheep.

Secondary animal product use in northern Mesopotamia is discussed by both Redman (1978:268-270) and Sherratt (1981) and appears to have begun at about the same time for all the different uses. Since secondary product use itself seems to have developed first in Mesopotamia, it appears earlier in both northern and southern Mesopotamia than in any other area studied here. Uruk period pictograms and cylinder seals give definite evidence of use of the plow (ard), cart, milk, and wool (Redman 1978: 254; Sherratt 1981:263, 266, 271, 275, 279). Sherratt (1981:271) feels that the plow and cart were developed somewhere in northern Mesopotamia during Uruk times and spread from there. Thus, the period from 3600 to 3100 b.c. can be used as a solid date for the beginning of secondary animal product use and animal traction in northern Mesopotamia. The sources do not mention the use of manure, though it undoubtedly was used.

Farming System

The first farming in northern Mesopotamia represents movement by farming communities from higher mountain and foothill locations down to upland, piedmont locations. The new locations are areas in which rainfall agriculture is possible but not always completely reliable, but irrigation was not practiced at these sites (Oates 1972: 300-301; Redman 1978:188). The first communities, such as those of the Umm Dabaghiyah culture and the early Hassunan culture levels, may not have been completely sedentary (Kirkbride 1972, 1973a, 1973b, 1974, 1975; Lloyd and Safar 1945). The community, or portions of the community, may have moved with the herds to the better-watered uplands during years of inadequate rainfall (Redman 1978:194). Emmer, einkorn wheat, and barley are present on these early sites (Helbaek 1972:35-48).

Later Hassunan, Samarran, and Halafian sites represent settled agricultural communities, though some transhumance may have been practiced by the more northerly communities (Redman 1978:190-194). Major sites of the three cultures are Tell Hassuna, Tell es-Sawwan, Choga Mami, and Tell Arpachiyah. In very general terms, Hassunan sites appear first in the northern portion of the area under study and represent farming groups practicing rainfall agriculture. Halafian sites, which appear in this area later, also represent rainfall agriculturalists. Samarran sites overlap in time with both Hassunan and Halafian sites. The majority of Samarran sites occur farther to the south on the edge of the Mesopotamian alluvium. Irrigation agriculture of various forms was practiced at these sites (Mellaart 1975:141-170; Redman 1978:189-201).

Agricultural crops present on Hassunan sites include dry-farmed emmer, einkorn, bread wheat, and two-row hulled barley (Mellaart 1975:147). Halafian sites show the same range of crops (Redman 1978:201). Samarran sites contain emmer, bread wheat, six-row naked barley, two-row hulled barley, and linseed. The bread wheat, six-row naked barley, and linseed could not have been grown in the climate characteristic of Samarran sites without irrigation. The smallness of the grains suggests that irrigation was fairly simple and consisted of seasonal flooding of the fields as opposed to regular canalization (Helbaek 1964b, 1972b, cited in Redman 1978:195-196).

Farming at 'Ubaid period sites in the north was primarily rainfall farming with a continuation of the same range of crops that was grown during earlier times (Redman 1978: 251). During the later Uruk, Jemdet Nasr, and Early Dynastic periods in northern Mesopotamia, communities grew in size and developed into towns in some areas (Redman 1978:293), but the farming system remained essentially the same as during earlier periods. Arboreculture, the cultivation of figs, was added during the Jemdet Nasr period, but elaborate forms of irrigation agriculture were not necessary and were not practiced.

Settlement Pattern and Social Organization

The earliest farming villages of the Umm Dabaghiyah and Hassunan cultures were small, with perhaps a minimum of 50-100 or 200 people (Oates 1972:301; Redman 1978: 209). The population of the site of Umm Dabaghiyah itself may have been even smaller and primarily oriented toward hunting (Kirkbride 1972, 1973a, 1973b, 1974, 1975). In general, however, these communities represent small, agricultural villages with a probable transhumant component. The sites seem to represent egalitarian, tribal communities (Redman 1978:205).

The later Halafian and Samarran sites also represent agricultural villages and small towns. Halafian sites are quite variable in size; Samarran sites are also variable in size but are generally larger than the previous communities (Redman 1978:194-199). Choga Mami, for example, may have had a population of more than 1000 (Oates 1973). Samarran sites also show defensive considerations, such as ditches and walls, towers guarding entrances, and bent-axis approaches to entrances (Redman 1978:196).

Halafian sites are very widely distributed in the rainfall-agriculture belt of the north in an area that includes the earlier Hassunan region but also stretches beyond it. Samarran sites are located along rivers in areas where seasonal flooding provided waters for crops or where irrigation channels were possible (Oates 1972:302-303). Another favored location was at the base of a mountain range, where damming and canalization of runoff was adequate for agriculture (Redman 1978:210). The level of social complexity suggested for both Samarran and Halafian communities is the chiefdom (Redman 1978: 206).

During the later time periods from the 'Ubaid through the Early Dynastic in northern Mesopotamia, communities grew in size and number. Large towns developed but did not reach the organizational level of city-states owing to their small size and lack of emphasis on central institutions and specialized activities (Redman 1978:293). A state level of organization was not reached in the north until the appearance of Sargon of Agade at ca. 2340 b.c., resulting in a period of 3660 years of pre-state farming.

SOUTHERN MESOPOTAMIA

(SUMER)

Sequence Duration and Phases or Cultures Represented

Southern Mesopotamia, also referred to as the Mesopotamian Plain, includes roughly the land from Baghdad south to the Persian Gulf in the area of the Tigris and Euphrates rivers (Redman 1978:247). Farming in southern Mesopotamia commenced with colonization of the alluvium by sedentary agriculturalists, probably from the north, at ca. 5500-5300 b.c. (Mellaart 1975:170; Redman 1978:245-251). The sequence began with the 'Ubaid 1 period occupation, which is found on virgin soil at several of the large tell sites (Redman 1978:247). Considerable alluviation has occurred on the Mesopotamian Plain, and it is quite likely that earlier settlements may lie buried beneath these deposits in some areas. Sites in nearby regions, such as Khuzistan, indicate the presence of earlier occupations in the vicinity. The Deh Luran Plain of Khuzistan shows occupation from 8200 B.C. (Hole 1977). However, the earliest currently known settlement in southern Mesopotamia occurs with 'Ubaid 1, so this period is used as the sequence starting point.

Despite the potential problem presented by alluviation and despite the brevity of sequence duration, the southern Mesopotamian sequence is included in this research for two reasons. First, southern Mesopotamia is used because it is a critical region for discussion of the development of states, cities, and civilization. Second, the sequence is used precisely because it is so short. This sequence, and the one from Upper Egypt, serve to keep this study "honest." The pattern of differential duration was not defined using only the longest Old World sequences — two of the shortest were also used.

The domesticated plants and animals apparent in northern Mesopotamia were also present from the first in the south and include emmer, bread wheat, barley, flax, sheep, goats, pigs, and cattle (Redman 1978:269). City-states appear in the region during the Uruk period at approximately 3600 b.c., bringing the early farming period to a close (Redman 1978:260, 286; Wright and Johnson 1975). The duration of the period is 1900 years (Table 2), which makes this the shortest sequence in which domesticated animals are present. Possible reasons for this brevity, aside from the burial of early sites owing to alluviation, are discussed in greater detail at the end of the present review and in the overall discussion of the domestic animal sequences. The pre-state periods of interest to this study are the 'Ubaid 1-4 periods (ca. 5500/5300-3600 b.c.; Edzard 1967:52-90; Falkenstein 1967:1-51; Mellaart 1975:170-179; Redman 1978:245-278).

Domestic Animals and Secondary Animal Products

From the first appearance of farming villages in southern Mesopotamia, domesticated plants and animals have been the mainstays of subsistence. Fishing, too, is of importance to these communities, but it is overshadowed by domesticated crops and animals. The full range of domesticated animals is present from 'Ubaid times on, but pigs declined sharply in importance during the later time periods (Harris 1977). Cattle outnumbered sheep and goats throughout the entire time span of interest. Sheep were second in importance, partly owing to their secondary products, especially wool (Redman 1978:269). The primacy of cattle seems to have resulted from several factors. They adapted readily to the hot plain; they produced important secondary products, such as milk and milk products; and they could be used for plowing and as beasts of burden (Redman 1978:269). A seminomadic segment of the economy, which moved with its herds during lean agricultural years, is suggested for all time periods (Adams 1972:744; Lees and Bates 1974; Redman 1978:268).

The information concerning secondary animal product use, including milk and wool, and animals used for pulling both plows (ards) and carts, is essentially the same for southern Mesopotamia as that discussed for northern Mesopotamia. The use of plows, carts, milk, and wool can definitely be dated to the Uruk period, ca. 3600-3100 b.c., on the basis of representations found on pictograms and cylinder seals, but it probably began earlier (Redman 1978:254; Sherratt 1981:263, 266, 271, 275, 279). As is the case for northern Mesopotamia, the use of manure is not mentioned in the sources.

Farming System

The earliest farming communities of the 'Ubaid period are found in the lowest levels of such sites as Tell Al 'Ubaid and Eridu. Later, state-level Uruk period occupations are known from excavations at Uruk (Warka) and Eridu, among others. The shorter Jemdet Nasr period is known primarily from Uruk and several other sites (Redman 1978:247-260). From the first, agriculture in southern Mesopotamia relied on irrigation (Redman 1978:247), which grew more complex through time as the population grew and more land was brought into cultivation. Communities were permanent, though a portion of the community may have moved with the herds seasonally or during lean agricultural years. Extensive farming was practiced on lands without access to irrigation waters, and these lands were allowed to lie fallow in alternate years (Redman 1978:268). Introduction of the plow and wheeled transport, probably during Uruk times or earlier, aided agriculture on and communication over the hard alluvial clays of lowland Mesopotamia (Redman

1978:268). The crops grown throughout the time span of interest consisted of emmer, bread wheat, two-row hulled barley, six-row naked barley, and flax. During the later Early Dynastic period, salt-tolerant barley overtook wheat as the main grain crop produced, as salinization progressively became a more severe problem (Redman 1978: 269). During the periods under study, however, wheat remained the dominant grain crop.

Settlement Pattern and Social Organization

Early 'Ubaid occupations were sparsely scattered agricultural villages of modest size, evenly dispersed along what are presumed to have been the watercourses of the time (Adams and Nissen 1972:9-11; Redman 1978:262). By the end of the long 'Ubaid period, a few of the settlements had grown into large population aggregates, and 'Ubaid culture had stretched throughout Mesopotamia and beyond (Redman 1978:262). At its maximum, Eridu, the best-known site from this time period, probably had 2000 to 4000 people (Redman 1978:245). Communities such as this indicate that already by the 'Ubaid period there was a marked degree of social differentiation and complexity (Adams and Nissen 1972:11).

During the Uruk and Jemdet Nasr periods, communities grew in size and complexity. Materials from these periods are also widespread throughout Mesopotamia. They are best known from the site of Uruk (Warka) and its surrounding area and from the work of Adams and Nissen (1972). Wright and Johnson (1975) define the appearance of the state during Uruk times.

During these periods, the growing population tended to settle in small clusters of communities instead of in the more scattered communities of 'Ubaid times. The number of rural communities reached its peak during Late Uruk and Jemdet Nasr times and began to decline somewhat during the Jemdet Nasr period. This decline in rural population escalated during the Early Dynastic as the large urban centers, such as Uruk, drew in local rural populations, producing an extreme form of aggregation. Also from Jemdet Nasr times on, the settlement emphasis moved from the small stream channels that were useful for short-range irrigation of small areas to the main stream channels that could be canalized to irrigate large areas of permanent fields to support the growing population. During these time periods, the community of Uruk attained urban status and may have had a population of 10,000.

As mentioned at the beginning of the section on southern Mesopotamia, this sequence exhibits the shortest pre-state farming period in which domesticated animals were present. Several possible reasons will be briefly mentioned here. Many of the factors considered to have led to changes in social organization, or growing social complexity, came together in southern Mesopotamia (Flannery and Marcus 1983; Redman 1978:215-243). This

combination of factors may have hastened the development of organizational complexity and state-level society in the south. The following forces contributing to complexity were present in southern Mesopotamia (Redman 1978:247-251, 253-266).

Southern Mesopotamia was an area of population growth from both internal expansion and external migration into the area. In combination with this growing population, the area of best agricultural land, on which irrigation was possible, was limited. Full-time farming communities are not possible on the Mesopotamian alluvium without irrigation, which requires some degree of organization even in its simpler forms. Groups moving into the area had to be aware of this technology to set up successful farming communities. In addition to these factors, southern Mesopotamia lacks several critical resources — wood, stone, and metals, for example, which were items of trade from early times on. Thus, the combination of population growth, limited access to good land, the necessity of irrigation, and trade may have hastened the appearance of organizational complexity in southern Mesopotamia.

UPPER EGYPT

Sequence Duration and Phases or Cultures Represented

Farming communities appeared in the upper portion of the Nile Valley at ca. 5500 B.C. This approximation is based on several thermoluminescence dates, which have large standard deviations, from the site of Hemamieh (Caton-Thompson and Whittle 1975; Whittle 1975, cited in Hassan 1985:106). Thus, they do not permit a firm temporal placement of the earliest village farming in Upper Egypt (Hassan 1985:106-107). They are a best estimate, however, and are useful for this study. Somewhere within the range of 5500 to 5000 B.C. is probably a safe estimate for the beginning of the village farming lifeway in Upper Egypt. As is the case throughout, the maximum duration is listed in Table 2.

Farming arrived late in the Nile Valley relative to other areas, but it made its first appearance as fully established agricultural villages. Domesticated crops and animals included emmer, barley, flax, cattle, sheep, and goats, with hunting and fishing also forming an important component of the subsistence base (Arkell and Ucko 1965: 150-151). Since the farming lifeway appeared fully developed and rather late in Egypt, it has been suggested that the concept and technology of agriculture came to Egypt from southwest Asia (discussed in Redman 1978: 281). A more recent view is that farming technology and crops may have spread into the Nile Valley from the western desert areas, where earlier farming villages have been found and where conditions were wetter than they are at present (Hoffman 1979:218-221). The pre-state farming adaptation in Upper Egypt ranks as one of the shortest domestic animal sequences. It ends at 3100 B.C.

with the unification of Egypt and formation of the early pharaonic state (Hassan 1985:110-113; Redman 1978: 284). Possible causes for this duration of 2400 years are discussed at the end of this review and in the general discussion of domestic animal sequences.

The following culture and phase terms are used for Upper Egypt: Early Predynastic (Badarian, ca. 5500-4000 B.C.), Middle Predynastic (Nagada I, ca. 4000-3650 B.C.), Late Predynastic (Nagada II, ca. 3650-3300 B.C.), and Terminal Predynastic (Nagada III, ca. 3300-3150/3100 B.C.; Arkell and Ucko 1965:145-166; Hassan 1985:95-116; Hoffman 1979:16, 140-147). All of the dates used in this discussion have been checked against Hassan's compendium of radiocarbon dates; terminology also follows Hassan (1985:95-116).

Domestic Animals and Secondary Animal Products

At the first farming communities in Upper Egypt domesticated plants and animals, as well as hunted game and fish, were of importance. During the Early Predynastic (Badarian) period, cattle, sheep, and goats were present (Arkell and Ucko 1965:150-151). By the beginning of the Middle Predynastic (Nagada I) in Upper Egypt, evidence from such sites as Tasa, Badari, Nagada, and Abydos indicates that dogs, sheep, goats, cattle, geese, and pigs were fully domesticated (Lamberg-Karlovsky and Sabloff 1979:126). During the subsequent Late Predynastic (Nagada II) and Terminal Predynastic (Nagada III) periods, the domestic animal component of the economy remained much the same; hunting declined in importance but was still present. Fishing always played an important role in the subsistence economy (Hoffman 1979:151-153). A pastoral component, consisting of the herding of cattle, sheep, and goats by a portion of the farming community, is suggested throughout the Predynastic (Lamberg-Karlovsky and Sabloff 1979:132). The sources do not indicate if one or another of the domesticated animals predominated at any particular point in time.

The use of secondary animal products and animal traction in Egypt is unfortunately not well reported, and the majority of uses appear somewhat late compared to their appearance in other areas. This delay may be more apparent than real, because knowledge of these practices relies on pictorial evidence alone. The types of faunal studies needed to document secondary product use in earlier times have not been conducted on Egyptian materials in the great majority of cases.

The use of pack animals is an exception: pack donkeys are reported perhaps as early as Nagada II times (ca. 3650-3300 B.C.), which fits well with their appearance during the fourth millennium in other areas (Sherratt 1981:272, 1983:96). Information on wheeled transport is scant, however. Evidence for the use of the plow, dairy products, and wool all appear during the period ca. 2500-

2000 B.C., which is late in comparison to other areas. According to Sherratt (1981:266-267), the first solid evidence of the plow in Egypt is during the mid-third millennium in a Third Dynasty context, later than the time period of interest to this study. Dairying is suggested by Hoffman (1979:152) during Nagada III times (ca. 3300-3100 B.C.), but specific evidence for the practice is not presented. Sherratt discusses a representation of a cow being milked in the tomb of Ti in the Old Kingdom (ca. 2500 B.C.; Klebs 1915:63, cited in Sherratt 1981:280). Milking is also shown on some central Saharan rock drawings, but their date is unknown (Simoons 1971, *inter alios*, cited in Sherratt 1981:280). Milking undoubtedly occurred earlier than ca. 2500 B.C., but this is the first solid evidence for the practice thus far discovered. Wool genuinely seems to have appeared very late in Egypt owing to the hot climate. Wool sheep were not introduced into Egypt until the Middle Kingdom at ca. 2000 B.C.

As is the case for Mesopotamia, manure is not mentioned in the sources. Manure was probably not critical in Egypt for the majority of agricultural lands because of the annual flooding of the Nile.

Farming System

The earliest farming settlements in Upper Egypt were permanent communities with farming lands whose fertility was renewed by the seasonal inundations of the Nile. Wadis a few miles out into the desert were also farmed under the wetter conditions of the Neolithic Subpluvial. These latter sites may have been seasonally occupied (Hoffman 1979:145-164). Wheat, barley, and flax were cultivated throughout the Predynastic period (Arkell and Ucko 1965:150-151; Hoffman 1979:145-154). Crops were sown in either late October or November after the Nile floods, which occur from late June through late September. Harvest took place in late March or early April (Hoffman 1979:163). Agriculture became more developed through time with increasing use of substantial irrigation works (Redman 1978:285-286) to support a growing population.

Settlement Pattern and Social Organization

The Upper Nile Valley is narrow, with rock escarpments close to the river enclosing a narrow cultivable plain (Redman 1978:282). From their first appearance, settled communities were located parallel to the river on elevated hillocks in the alluvial bottomlands, on raised portions of the low desert, or along the channels of the larger wadis a few miles out into the desert (Hoffman 1979:148). Early Upper Egyptian Predynastic villages were generally small and spread out, with freestanding houses of wattle and daub surrounded by outbuildings in a barnyard type of community pattern (Hoffman 1979:146-147). Early Predynastic villages, such as Hemamieh, seem to have been egalitarian communities. Middle Predynastic communities, though slightly more numerous and somewhat larger and richer, were located in the same areas and were still small with freestanding wattle-and-daub houses (Arkell and Ucko 1965:151-153; Hoffman 1979:143-154). Their social organization may have been slightly more complex than that of the earlier communities.

During Late Predynastic and Terminal Predynastic times, rectangular, pueblo-style, mud brick dwellings appear on some sites, as do town walls (Arkell and Ucko 1965:153; Hoffman 1979:147-149). During much of the Predynastic in the south, especially in these later periods, the settlement pattern consisted of two large towns, with the majority of people living in the small villages that have been previously discussed. Only two important population centers, Nagada and Hierakonopolis, were present (Kemp 1977:198; Lamberg-Karlovsky and Sabloff 1979: 132). These centers fit the description of temple-towns (Redman 1978:202) and were probably organized as complex chiefdoms.

During the century before formation of the pharaonic state, this distribution changed as described by Kemp (1977:198) and Lamberg-Karlovsky and Sabloff (1979: 132-133). Their description of the settlement distribution is presented here. Many of the small settlements that surrounded Hierakonopolis and Nagada were abandoned as these two towns grew. Their growth was both internal and external as they drew in the population of the small, abandoned villages. Rivalry existed between the two towns. Nagada may have been the first capital of Upper Egypt but was soon replaced by Hierakonopolis, which continued to become larger. In about 3100 B.C., as the result of warfare and conquest, Upper and Lower Egypt were unified under the first pharaoh, who came from the south. This date is considered to be the date of the founding of the Egyptian national state, which limits the time period of interest to 2400 years.

The Upper Egyptian sequence has one of the shortest durations of any of the domestic animal sequences. It is similar to the Sumerian one, in that the same factors promoting rapid state development in southern Mesopotamia were also operating in the Nile Valley. Growing population, constriction of prime agricultural land, advancement in irrigation technology, and an active trading system seem to have hastened the appearance of the state in Egypt, as they did farther to the east in Mesopotamia.

PAKISTAN

(INDUS RIVER SYSTEM)

Sequence Duration and Phases or Cultures Represented

Settled, mixed farming first appeared in the western margins of the Indus River system at ca. 5500 b.c. at the site of Mehrgarh, which is located at the transition of the

uplands of Baluchistan and the plains of the Indus River (Allchin and Allchin 1982:103). This site is emphasized in the following review, since it provides evidence of some of the earliest farming occupations in the area and has been subjected to modern analytic techniques. The early village occupation at Mehrgarh shows evidence of domesticated two-row hulled barley, six-row barley, einkorn, emmer, and bread wheat. Fully domesticated cattle, sheep, and goats are present in this level and outnumber by a considerable margin the larger, wild forms of these species, which are also present (Jarrige and Meadow 1980:122-124). In earlier, undated levels, the larger, wild forms outnumber the domesticated ones (Meadow 1979:153-166). Meadow feels that the considerable size diminution through time shown in the faunal remains from the site precludes sexual dimorphism alone and indicates the growing importance of domesticated animals over wild ones. He believes that goats were introduced into the area in their domesticated form, whereas cattle and sheep may have been domesticated at Mehrgarh and other sites in the area (Meadow 1979:161-166). These conclusions are also based on size diminution, or the lack of it, evident through time in the faunal remains. The period of pre-state farming comes to an end in the Indus River system with the appearance of the state-level society of the Mature Harappan or Mature Indus period at roughly 2500 b.c. (Allchin and Allchin 1982:126, 166-169). Thus, the pre-state farming adaptation lasted for roughly 3000 years (Table 2).

For the portion of eastern Pakistan containing the Indus River system, the following culture and phase terms are used: Neolithic (5500?-3500 b.c.), Chalcolithic (ca. 3500-2900 b.c.), and Early Indus or pre-Harappan (ca. 2900-2500 b.c.). The sequences of interest end at 2500 b.c. with the advent of the Mature Indus or Mature Harappan (Allchin and Allchin 1982:126, 162-166).

Domestic Animals and Secondary Animal Products

By the beginning of the time period of interest at ca. 5500 b.c., both domesticated plants and animals were in the majority on Neolithic sites at the western border of the Indus system. Domesticated cattle, sheep, and goats were herded in roughly the same proportion throughout the time period of interest. From 5500 b.c., cattle increased in importance over sheep and goats, with goats remaining slightly more important than sheep. Cattle remained the primary domestic animal throughout the Neolithic, Chalcolithic, and Early Indus (Meadow 1979:153). By ca. 5000 b.c., wild game had declined tremendously in importance and scarcely appears in the faunal remains of later periods (Jarrige and Meadow 1980:124). Based on ethnographic practice, transhumance between the plains and the uplands is suggested, with summer pasturage located in the cool, moist uplands (Meadow 1979:146).

In order to examine possible secondary product use, Meadow (1979:166) carried out survivorship studies on

Neolithic faunal remains from Mehrgarh levels dated to ca. 5000 b.c. The kill-off pattern for sheep and goats during this time period was consistent with that of a meat herd, whereas the pattern for cattle was not. Male cattle were allowed to survive longer into adulthood than would be consistent with their exclusive use as a meat source. Meadow suggests that cattle might have been used as pack or traction animals during this time period. Unfortunately, the assemblages from the later time periods are not as amenable to survivorship studies as the earlier ones.

After Meadow's very early date for traction animals, the next dated appearances of traction animals are during the Early and Mature Indus periods. Cart models are found in early- to mid-third millennium contexts, and evidence of the use of the plow in the form of plow marks occurs in later third millennium contexts (Mughal 1974:112; Sherratt 1981:266-267). Milk and wool were undoubtedly also in use by the Harappan period and probably earlier. Suggested dates for the first appearance of these uses were not found, however.

Farming System

The earliest Neolithic farming communities in the Indus system, such as Mehrgarh, were permanent villages located at the western edge of the plains near the transition to the uplands. A full range of crops, including two-row barley, six-row barley, einkorn, emmer, and bread wheat, was grown at these sites (Jarrige and Meadow 1980:122-124). Winter planting is suggested for the area, with some form of fairly simple water control being necessary. From observation of traditional farming systems in the area, it is suggested that early cultivators practiced a form of shifting cultivation in which irrigated fields were abandoned as they became too saline. They were reclaimed after they were allowed to lie fallow for a number of years. Moisture and soil fertility were replenished by trapping fresh silt from floodwater behind field walls and diversion dams (Meadow 1979:146).

During the later Chalcolithic period, the basic farming regime remained the same but production was intensified. Two species of barley, five forms of wheat, and oats were grown. These crops were also grown throughout the remaining Harappan times (Jarrige 1979:110).

Also during the Chalcolithic period the first occupations of the Indus floodplain itself are evident at ca. 3500 b.c. As yet undiscovered earlier occupations may be buried under the ruins of later cities or under the alluvium (Wenke 1980:509). These earliest communities practiced much the same type of agriculture and grew the same crops as their more westerly counterparts. The Indus plain has so little rainfall during the average year that irrigation from the river is necessary and was practiced from the time of the first occupation of the area (Wenke 1980:507).

During the Early Indus period, the farming system of fairly simple irrigation used to produce the same crops as during earlier periods continued on the Indus floodplain and its western margin. It was not until the later, Mature Indus period that complex irrigation works and flood-control features appeared, much as in southern Mesopotamia and Egypt (Wenke 1980:522).

Settlement Pattern and Social Organization

The Neolithic communities of the Indus system were relatively small, scattered, permanent agricultural communities consisting of structures of unbaked mud brick (Jarrige and Meadow 1980:122). Social organization at these sites was apparently relatively simple (Allchin and Allchin 1982:103). During the later Neolithic, similarities in ceramics indicate wide contacts among sites of the western Indus/Baluchistan area, such as Mundigak and Kili Ghul Muhammad; these contacts were maintained during later time periods as well (Allchin and Allchin 1982:107-108).

By the Chalcolithic and Early Indus periods, many more communities appeared throughout the Indus plain. Such sites as Gumla, Sarai Khola, Kot Diji, Jalilpur, and Amri are known from this time period (Allchin and Allchin 1982:109-111). Some communities of considerable size developed, often surrounded by town walls, indicating that at least some defensive considerations were necessary. For example, remains from this time period at Mehrgarh encompass almost fifty hectares. Though the entire area was not necessarily occupied simultaneously, the size of the site does indicate a considerable population (Jarrige 1979:107, 110). Also during this time, very widespread pottery styles indicate regional contacts (Allchin and Allchin 1982:162-165).

The level of social complexity at these sites is not completely known. Size, interregional connections, defensive works, structures interpreted as granaries, and possible specialized craft-production areas (Allchin and Allchin 1982:100-169) argue against egalitarian, village-level integration, however. By sometime around 2500 b.c., cities and the state-level society of the Mature Indus period appeared in the area, limiting the time period of interest to a duration of 3000 years (Allchin and Allchin 1982:169).

NORTHERN CHINA

(CHUNG YUAN OR CENTRAL PLAIN)

Sequence Duration and Phases or Cultures Represented

The earliest farming groups in northern China appear at approximately 5000 B.C. with settlements of the Yang-shao culture in the Chung Yuan or Central Plain of China (Barnard 1975, 1979, 1980; Chang 1977:84, 119-143). These groups cultivated millet, vegetables, and hemp (Chang 1977:95; Chang 1983:66; Wenke 1980:530-533). Domesticated animals included pig, cattle, sheep, and goats (Chang 1977:95); silkworms were also raised (Chang 1977:95). Millet agriculture is indigenous to northern China, whereas other grain crops, such as wheat and barley, were introduced during later time periods (Chang 1977:91; Chang 1983:65-70). The period of pre-state farming ends in the Chung Yuan area of northern China with the appearance of the Shang state at approximately 1850 B.C. (Chang 1977:218; Fried 1983:467-493). Thus, pre-state farming lasted for 3150 years (Table 2).

Sequences and phases from the Central Plain are those given by Chang (1977:173), unless otherwise noted. The first farming groups are represented by the Yang-shao culture, lasting roughly from 5000 to 3200 B.C. This culture was followed by the Miao-ti-kou II, or Lung-shanoid, culture from ca. 3200 to 2500 B.C. Huber (1983:179) dates the beginning of the Miao-ti-kou II earlier, at 3684 B.C., but provides the same ending point given by Chang. The difference in beginning dates for the Miao-ti-kou II is not critical to this study, and Chang's dates are used throughout. The Lung-shan culture is the final culture of interest to this study. It lasted from ca. 2500 to 1850 B.C. and ended with the formation of the Shang state.

Domestic Animals and Secondary Animal Products

By ca. 5000 B.C., millet agriculture and domesticated animals were major subsistence components in northern China, though hunting and gathering were also still important (Wenke 1980:530-533). The most prevalent domesticated animals at these Yang-shao communities were dogs and pigs; cattle, sheep, and goats were much less common (Chang 1977:95). Since dogs are not a topic of this study, they will not be discussed further.

During the Miao-ti-kou II period, or the Chung Yuan Lungshanoid, pigs retained their primary position among the domesticated animals, but cattle and sheep began to rise in importance (Chang 1977:152, 157). By the time of the fully developed Lung-shan culture, domestic faunal remains included those of pig, cattle, water buffalo, and sheep. Pig remains were still the most numerous, however (Chang 1977:174-178). Hunting and fishing retained their importance during both Lungshanoid and Lung-shan times (Chang 1977:169, 174-178).

The use of animal secondary products and animal traction did not attain the early importance in northern China that it did in other world areas. Several factors may have contributed to this delay. Sherratt (1981:289) suggests that lactose intolerance among the Chinese precluded the development of a pastoral sector with a dairying focus and thus limited a ready supply of draft animals. In

addition, the pig has been the prime Chinese domesticated animal from the time of the earliest farming communities (Chang 1977:95). It is well suited to the northern Chinese climate and serves as both a meat source and a village scavenger (Harris 1977:224-229); however, it is not useful for traction or secondary product production. Along the same lines, the silkworm has also been raised in China since the Yang-shao Neolithic (Chang 1977:95). It serves as a source of clothing and tradable manufactured goods, much as wool does in other areas. The animal traction/secondary products complex associated with cattle, sheep, and goats did develop in north China, but later than in other Old World regions.

Wheeled vehicles appeared in China during the Shang period in the second millennium B.C. (Sherratt 1981:266). The plow did not appear until the Eastern Chou period in the first millennium B.C. (ca. 770 B.C.), and it was relatively rare even then (Chang 1977:355; Sherratt 1981:267). It never replaced the spade and the hoe as cultivating tools and was not common until the Han dynasty (202 B.C.-A.D. 220; Chang 1977:356). Wool was apparently in use on the western periphery of the Chung Yuan during Lung-shan times but is not mentioned for the Central Plain area itself (Chang 1977:199), where silkworm raising had a long tradition. The milking complex was not important prehistorically in northern China owing to lactose intolerance among Chinese populations, even though such products as cheese and yogurt can be consumed by lactose-intolerant populations (Sherratt 1981:289). Fertilizer is mentioned as a possibility during Lung-shan and Shang times but is not discussed in detail (Chang 1976:30, 1977:289).

Farming System

The early Yang-shao farming communities of the Chung-Yuan area practiced shifting cultivation of millets, vegetables, and hemp (Chang 1977:95, 97-100; Chang 1983:66; Wenke 1980:530-533). Pig herds were maintained within the villages, where they scavenged, were fed on substandard crops, or rooted in the forested areas associated with slash-and-burn cultivation (Harris 1977:224-229). Hunted and gathered resources were of considerable importance to the Yang-shao economy, as well as to all other Chinese groups of interest to this study. Their role declined in importance during the later times, however (Chang 1977:95-96).

During the Lungshanoid period, shifting cultivation gave way to permanent, settled farming communities (Chang 1977:152-153). Millet remained the primary cultivated crop in the Central Plain. In addition, there is scant evidence for the presence of rice during this time period from the site of Yang-shao-ts'un. The introduction of rice is considered to indicate influence from the southern part of China, where rice cultivation was probably first mastered (Chang 1977:169). From this period on, cattle and sheep gained in importance, though pigs maintained their primary role throughout the periods of interest. It is not known whether some form of transhumance was practiced with the cattle and sheep.

The Lung-shan period continues the tradition of settled, advanced farmers practicing millet agriculture with the addition of rice and possibly wheat and barley (Chang 1983:77). Definite evidence for the latter two crops does not appear until Shang times, however, when they occur on inscriptions on bone oracles (Chang 1983:77). Chang (1976:30) suggests that irrigation, the use of fertilizer, the fallowing of fields, and the improvement of cultivating tools and techniques may all have occurred during the Lung-shan, but there is no definite evidence.

By the time of the state-level Shang society, agriculture was based on millet, rice, wheat, and vegetables. Fertilizers and a prototype of the plow may have been in use, and irrigation was practiced, but there is little evidence of large irrigation systems anywhere in the Shang domain (Chang 1977:289; Wenke 1980:540).

Settlement Pattern and Social Organization

The Chung Yuan or Central Plain of northern China is the area comprising the river basins and alluvial plains of the middle Huang Ho Valley (Chang 1977:119). It is extensively cultivated today but was probably covered by deciduous, broad-leaved forest in pre- and protohistoric times (Li 1983:28). Yang-shao communities of the Chung Yuan represent the shifting settlements of swidden farmers, which were often reoccupied (Chang 1977:97-100). They are small villages of wattle-and-daub pithouses often scattered along the ridges overlooking fertile river valleys (Wenke 1980:531). In the center of some of the villages is a much larger structure interpreted as a big-man's house or as a communal house (Watson 1974:26, cited in Wenke 1980:532). These sites represent primarily independent, egalitarian villages, with ceramic similarities showing some contacts among them (Chang 1977:114).

The later, Lungshanoid settlements are considered to represent relatively permanent communities of settled agriculturalists (Chang 1977:152). Villages are larger than they were during Yang-shao times but still consist of wattle-and-daub pithouses arranged around a central "long house" (Wenke 1980:533). Some degree of craft specialization in pottery manufacture and differences in burial patterns indicate the beginnings of social differentiation within these villages during Lungshanoid times (Chang 1977:172). Very widespread ceramic and artifact styles indicate regional contacts during this period, but villages still appear to be independent and peaceful (Chang 1977:144, 172).

By the Lung-shan, the last period of interest to this study, considerable changes had come about. Communities still consisted of wattle-and-daub pithouses, but they had shifted to the low terraces of river valleys and were larger than the earlier communities (Chang 1977:174; Wenke 1980:533-534). Continued craft specialization and variation in the richness of grave goods indicate social differentiation beyond that attained during the Lungshanoid. Defensive walls around communities and weapons appear frequently in Lung-shan sites and indicate conflict and raiding not present before (Chang 1976). Settlement patterns for this time period are poorly known; however, they do not indicate the type of aggregation and community spacing reflective of one community's dependence on another or on a major population center (Wenke 1980:534). Thus, the Lung-shan settlements do not show the settlement pattern trends associated with complex chiefdoms or state-level societies (e.g., three- or four-level site-size hierarchy and placement of small communities in proximity to much larger ones; Flannery and Marcus 1983). Chang describes the Lung-shan as a "warlike and ranked society preparatory for the formation of civilization and the state" (Chang 1977:144). Perhaps the Lung-shan groups were organized in some form of chiefdom-level society of advanced farming villages as described by Redman (1978:202). By 1850 B.C., however, state-level society was present in the Chung Yuan with the appearance of the Shang state (Chang 1977:218; Fried 1983:467-493), which marks the end of the pre-state farming period after a duration of 3150 years.

PERU

(AYACUCHO BASIN)

Sequence Duration and Phases or Cultures Represented

The farming lifeway began in the Ayacucho Basin of Peru with the Cachi phase at 4000 B.C. (Johnson and MacNeish 1972:4-5; MacNeish et al. 1980:11-12, 1981:17). Cultivated crops included corn, squash, beans, gourds, tara, lucuma, and possibly cotton, pepper, quinoa, and achira as well as potatoes (MacNeish et al. 1980:11). Domesticated guinea pigs and camelids were also present by this time period (Lynch 1982:212, 1983:169, 1984:419; MacNeish et al. 1980:11; Wheeler 1984:196-198; Wing 1978:180). Local domestication within the Peruvian highlands areas is indicated for both animals and the major plant crops (MacNeish et al. 1980:9-10; Wheeler 1984:196-198; Wing 1978:167-196). The years of pre-state farming end with the beginning of the Caja phase at 350 B.C., when local city-states are considered to have formed (MacNeish et al. 1980:13). These dates yield a total of 3650 years for the pre-state village farming adaptation (Table 2).

The following phases pertain to the period of interest in the basin: Cachi (ca. 4000-2200 B.C.), Andamarka-Wichqana (ca. 2200-1100 B.C.), and Kichkapata-Chupas-Rancha (ca. 1100-350 B.C.). The period of interest ends with the formation of small, local states during the Caja-Huarpa-Cruz Pata period beginning at ca. 350 B.C. (MacNeish et al. 1980:11-13).

26

Domestic Animals and
Secondary Animal Products

Around 4000 B.C. domesticated plants and animals became major contributors to subsistence in the Ayacucho Basin, though hunting and gathering retained their important role, as they did throughout the time period of interest (MacNeish et al. 1980:11-12). During the Cachi phase, the domestic animals consisted of guinea pigs and camelids (MacNeish et al. 1980:11; Wing 1978:180). Guinea pigs may have been domesticated, or at least tamed, as much as 1000 years earlier (MacNeish et al. 1980:9-10). They remained an important food source throughout Andean prehistory but are not treated further in this study because of their size. The domesticated camelids consist of both the larger llamas and the smaller alpacas (Wing 1978:180). Faunal data from the phase immediately preceding the Cachi phase from Pikimachay Cave in the Ayacucho Valley indicate the presence of both the larger and smaller forms at this time (Wing 1978:180). Seasonal, high-elevation herding of camelids is suggested for this period (MacNeish et al. 1980: 11-12).

Both the use of alpacas and llamas and high-elevation, seasonal herding continued throughout the remaining time periods of interest (MacNeish et al. 1980:12-13). During the Andamarka-Wichqana phases, the fullest development of the combination of high-elevation herding of camelids and their introduction and use in lower-elevation valley sites occurred, and this level of use continued until the time of the Spanish conquest (Wing 1978:185). During the latest period, the Kichkapata-Chupas-Rancha, the size difference indicating the presence of both alpacas and llamas is quite clear (MacNeish et al. 1980:12) and grows clearer throughout the prehistoric sequence.

The use of secondary products in the Andean area did not include the use of milk or milk products, nor were animals used for plowing. The larger llamas were used as beasts of burden at least by the time of the Kichkapata-Chupas-Rancha period (MacNeish et al. 1980:12) and possibly earlier. The use of wool is suggested by MacNeish et al. (1980:11) for the Cachi phase on the basis of the presence of bone weaving swords and artifacts that may have been used to pluck wool from the camelids. The difference in camelid size that appears in the Kichkapata-Chupas-Rancha period indicates to MacNeish et al. (1980:12) that by this time period the alpaca may have been used primarily for wool, whereas the larger llama was used for meat and transport, as it was during later times. Dung from the camelids was used for both manure and fuel at least by Inca times (ca. 1450 A.D.; Rowe 1946:216) and probably much earlier.

Farming System

The following discussions of both farming system and settlement pattern/social organization are taken from MacNeish et al. (1980:11-13) unless otherwise cited.

During the Cachi phase, the Andean "vertical" economy appeared for the first time. Presumably segments of the same group or of related groups interacted in this economic system. One group participated in a pattern of seasonal transhumance that consisted of high-elevation (Puna) camelid herding and hunting during the dry season and lower-elevation (Low Puna or Humid Woodland) potato cultivation during the wet season. The other group occupied even lower elevations in the valley, where such crops as corn, beans, squash, gourds, and all the others mentioned in the first section of this discussion were grown. Agricultural terraces were present on some of these sites. Camelids were also present and were introduced from the higher elevations. Exchange, kinship, and ritual ties linked these two systems together.

During Andamarka-Wichqana times, the high-elevation herding/potato growing and low-elevation seed agriculture subsistence patterns remained substantially the same. The amount of corn grown increased, however, as did the number of communities with agricultural terracing. Some form of water control was also present, since some of the terraces were apparently watered from large storage tanks.

The agricultural system and the crops grown remained the same during the following Kichkapata-Chupas-Rancha period. The use and complexity of the irrigation system increased, however. Terraces continued to be watered from tanks, but these tanks were now connected by long canals whose sources were dams or springs. By the following period, when small city-states appeared, the water-control system had grown increasingly complex, with the majority of irrigation features radiating out from four large towns, which were possibly the capitals of the local city-states.

Settlement Pattern
and Social Organization

The Ayacucho Basin is located in a major valley in the Central Highlands of Peru. Considerable vertical relief results in several varied ecozones. Ecozones of special interest to this study include the High and Low Puna, which are the native habitats of the camelids, and the Humid Woodland, which is ideal for growing potatoes and quinoa. The lower-elevation zones, such as the xerophytic ecozone, are used for growing the other crops. Irrigation is necessary in parts of the lower valley areas owing to frequent droughts (MacNeish et al. 1981:2-3).

The settlement pattern during Cachi times consisted of seven or eight small hamlets in the lower-elevation zones, with hunting and herding camps in the Puna and Humid Woodland zones. These latter camps often featured corrals. Considerable numbers of lowland trade items in highland camps and vice versa indicate active interaction between the groups. The level of social integration at this time period is that of egalitarian, village-level societies.

During the following Andamarka-Wichqana phase, occupation of the uplands and lowlands continued. The settlement pattern consisted of resource-procurement camps, hamlets, and five ceremonial centers. The hamlets and centers were at the lower elevations. The centers are identified on the basis of the presence of pyramids. Associated with these sites were clusters of hamlets and camps. Circular storage buildings and corrals with camelid bones at the centers suggest to MacNeish et al. (1980:12) that these sites may have been loci of economic redistribution. Some form of a chiefdom type of social organization may have been present during this time period.

During the final phase of interest to this study, the Kichkapata-Chupas-Rancha, the pattern that appeared during Andamarka-Wichqana times continued and intensified. Camps and hamlets clustered around the five ceremonial centers, which had grown and become more elaborate. Two of the sites were surrounded by fortification walls. State-level society was not reached, however, until the following Caja-Huarpa-Cruz Pata period, when four huge towns are considered to have been the capitals of local city-states. This yields a duration for the pre-state farming period of 3650 years.

SUMMARY

These eleven cases form the body of information on archaeological groups with domesticated animals. Information on chronology, domesticated animals, farming system, settlement pattern, and social organization has been reviewed. Chapter 3 presents the same information for the selected archaeological cases without domesticated animals. This combined body of information is used in an examination of the pattern of differential duration between groups with animals and groups without animals in Chapter 4. These archaeological data are then used in combination with ethnographic data in Chapter 6 to outline descriptive economic models of the operation of the animal-using and non-animal-using systems.

ARCHAEOLOGICAL SEQUENCES
WITHOUT DOMESTICATED ANIMALS

This chapter presents information on chronology, domestic animals, farming system, settlement pattern, and social organization for the five New World sequences from Mesoamerica and North America. The final section of this chapter consists of a tabular presentation of the combined data from Chapters 2 and 3.

MEXICO

(VALLEY OF OAXACA)

Sequence Duration and Phases or Cultures Represented

The beginning date of the village farming lifeway in Oaxaca is poorly known and may be anywhere within about a 500-year period. This study follows Whalen (1981) in setting the beginning of the Espiridion complex, and thus the beginning of village farming, in the middle of the disputed period at ca. 1600 b.c. This date is probably fairly realistic since it fits in well with the other beginning dates for village farming in Mesoamerica. By this time, cultivated maize, along with other domesticated plants, was making an important contribution to subsistence (Flannery and Marcus 1983:41-43). Maize is native to the general Mesoamerican area, though it may have been introduced into the Valley of Oaxaca. The pre-state farming adaptation ends in Oaxaca at 200 b.c. with the appearance of state-level organization during Monte Alban II times (Flannery and Marcus 1983:80). These dates result in a pre-state farming period of 1400 years (Table 2).

These dates are uncalibrated, as are all the dates used in this discussion of Oaxaca. The question of calibrated versus uncalibrated dates is not of great significance for the New World examples, since the difference between calibrated and uncalibrated dates narrows as A.D. 1 is approached (Klein et al. 1982). The New World, non-animal sequences all begin much closer to A.D. 1 than their Old World counterparts. Thus, the difference between the two types of dates is only a matter of several hundred years. The durations also balance out somewhat since two of the New World sequences are uncalibrated, two are calibrated, and one is not dated using radiocarbon samples.

Village farming began with the Espiridion complex (ca. 1600-1400 b.c.), which was followed by the Tierras Largas phase (ca. 1400-1150 b.c.). The Early San Jose (ca. 1150-1000 b.c.), Late San Jose (ca. 1000-850 b.c.), and Guadalupe (ca. 850-700 b.c.) phases are related; the Guadalupe phase only occurred in a portion of the Valley of Oaxaca, while the Late San Jose phase continued in the other areas. These phases were followed by the Rosario (ca. 700/650-500 b.c.) and Monte Alban I (ca. 500-200 b.c.) phases. The sequences of interest end at 200 b.c. with the appearance of the Zapotec state at the beginning of Monte Alban II times (Flannery and Marcus 1983:41-80).

Domestic Animals and Secondary Animal Products

The Oaxaca sequence is the first in this discussion for which medium to large domestic animals are not recorded. Domesticated dogs and turkeys were present and did serve as food sources (Flannery 1976:103-117; Flannery and Marcus 1983); because of their size, however, these animals are not under consideration in this study and will not be discussed further.

Farming System

The crops and farming regime in use in Oaxaca during the time periods of interest are not discussed in detail for each phase in the sources examined for this study. Thus, a summary of crops and farming techniques for the entire pre-state period is presented here. By Tierras Largas times maize, accompanied by and perhaps interplanted with teosinte, was grown along with avocados and other domesticates (Flannery and Marcus 1983:44). By San Jose times the full range of crops, including maize crossed with teosinte, chili, squash, avocado, and beans, was grown (Flannery 1976:107-108). According to Ford (1976:267), the maize yield increased after 500 b.c. with removal of teosinte from the fields and stabilization of the genetic pool of corn.

Farming occurred primarily in the humid alluvium of the Pleistocene floodplain of the Atoyac River; dry farming also occurred on the gently sloped piedmont near the base of the mountains (Flannery 1976:106). Agriculture was often possible in the fertile humid soils without irrigation (Ford 1976:261), but some of the lands required it. Although canal irrigation was probably practiced during earlier periods, two canal systems are definitely known from Monte Alban I times. This period also saw the spread of farming communities into the more marginal agricultural lands, such as along both major and minor tributaries of the Atoyac and back into the steeply sloping piedmont. A greater variety of crops was also grown during this period (Flannery and Marcus 1983:96). The intensification in both crops grown and areas farmed probably resulted from population growth in the valley.

Settlement Pattern
and Social Organization

The Valley of Oaxaca is semiarid and semitropical and has been divided into four physiographic zones by researchers in the area: the low alluvium or present river floodplain, the high alluvium or level alluvial plain representing the Pleistocene floodplain of the river, the piedmont or gentle slopes near the base of the mountains, and the mountains. The major agricultural areas are the high alluvium and the piedmont. Generally, the archaeological sites representing the early villages in the valley are located on piedmont spurs or low rises near the river, but some communities are located in the upper piedmont along tributaries of the river (Flannery 1976:105-106). All the following information is taken from Flannery and Marcus (1983), unless otherwise cited.

Small hamlets of wattle-and-daub houses occurred during the Espiridion complex and the Tierras Largas phase. By Tierras Largas times, sites occurred throughout the valley. The majority were tiny hamlets, but San Jose Mogote was a small village at this time. All were egalitarian in social organization.

During San Jose, Guadalupe, and Rosario phase times, ranked society appeared in the Valley of Oaxaca along with wider trading contacts as shown by use of Olmec symbolism, which was especially prevalent during San Jose times (Flannery 1968; Drennan 1976). Ceremonial centers with lime-plastered public buildings were built. San Jose Mogote, by that time a ceremonial center, may have housed 700 people. The site-size hierarchy includes the first-order ceremonial center of San Jose Mogote, several second-order communities that would be classed as villages, and a large number of third-order settlements or hamlets.

At the beginning of the Monte Alban I phase, several sites in the valley, including Tierras Largas, San Jose Mogote, Fabrica San Jose, and Huitzo, suffered considerable population losses. These losses coincide with the founding of Monte Alban and suggest that these villages contributed to its founding. Monte Alban's location on a mountain top indicates that defensive considerations were important. During Monte Alban I, striking growth is evident in the number and size of sites in the valley. During this time period hamlets, large and small villages, secondary centers, and a regional and administrative center in the form of Monte Alban are in evidence. Flannery and Marcus (1983) do not consider a state level of organization to have been present during this time period, however. They see clear indications of the state in the following Monte Alban II period at 200 b.c., with signs of the appearance of a professional ruling class, state religion, four-tiered administrative hierarchy, and wars of conquest. This cut-off point gives a duration to the pre-state sequence of 1400 years.

MEXICO

(BASIN OF MEXICO)

Sequence Duration and
Phases or Cultures Represented

The village farming lifeway began in the Basin of Mexico with the colonization of the southern part of the area by farmers from the south, probably Morelos, at ca. 1500 B.C. (Sanders et al. 1979). Maize, amaranth, beans, squash, and chili peppers were cultivated (Santley and Rose 1979:194). According to Sanders et al. (1979:108, 302-305), the pre-state farming adaptation ended at ca. A.D. 100 with the full development of the Teotihuacan state. Brumfiel (1976:234-249), Earle (1976:196-223), and Santley (personal communication, 1987) all suggest that the state may have formed several hundred years earlier during the period from ca. 300 to 100 B.C. This study follows this latter view and concludes the village farming period at 100 B.C., resulting in a total of 1400 years for the entire sequence (Table 2). The decision to use the 100 B.C. date is discussed in greater detail below.

The following phases are examined for this discussion of the Basin of Mexico: Early Horizon (ca. 1500-1150 B.C.), First Intermediate: Phase One (ca. 1150-650 B.C.), First Intermediate: Phase Two (ca. 650-300 B.C.), and First Intermediate: Phase Three (ca. 300-100 B.C.). The sequence of interest ends with the appearance of the state at 100 B.C. (Brumfiel 1976; Earle 1976; Santley, personal communication 1987). Throughout the remainder of this discussion, the First Intermediate phases are referred to simply as Phase One, Phase Two, and Phase Three.

Domestic Animals and
Secondary Animal Products

As discussed previously for Oaxaca, medium to large domestic animals were not present in the Basin of Mexico before the Spanish conquest. As was also the case for Oaxaca, domesticated dogs and turkeys, which are not under consideration, were present (Sanders et al. 1979; Santley and Rose 1979:193). According to Lamberg-Karlovsky and Sabloff (1979:327), these Mesoamerican domesticates had a minor dietary role at best.

Farming System

Santley and Rose (1979:193-194) present a reconstruction of the dietary importance of the major domesticated plant crops, based primarily on archaeological information from both the basin and the Tehuacan Valley. Maize was always the major domesticated crop, rising in importance from an estimated 30% of the diet in Early Horizon times to 65% by Phase Five/Middle Horizon times. Beans also rose in importance, while the other domesticates remained fairly constant. Gathered plants played a role in subsistence throughout the Basin of Mexico sequence, though they declined considerably in importance during the later times.

The first settled, village farmers colonized the well-watered southern portion of the basin where rainfall agriculture was possible during the Early Horizon (Sanders et al. 1979:95-96). By Phase One times, occupation of the more arid portions of the basin occurred, with settlements extending as far north as the Teotihuacan Valley (Sanders et al. 1979:96). During the span of the First Intermediate period, groups in the drier portions of the basin began to experiment with hydraulic agriculture. This included small-scale drainage and permanent canal irrigation. At Teotihuacan the process of agricultural intensification, coupled with increasingly complex water-control systems, moved faster than in other areas of the basin. Teotihuacan's location in the zone of highest agricultural risk, and its proximity to two permanent springs, made it an extremely favorable location for hydraulic intensification. By Phase Three and Four times, agriculture was highly intensified in the zone surrounding Teotihuacan, with a concomitant maximal expansion and elaboration of the irrigation system (Sanders et al. 1979:94-108).

Settlement Pattern and Social Organization

The following discussion is drawn from Sanders et al. (1979:94-116, 302-397), unless otherwise cited. The Basin of Mexico is an elevated plain located in the heart of the Central Highlands of Mexico (Santley and Rose 1979:192). The combined lakes of Zumpango, Xaltocan, Texcoco, and Chalco-Xochimilco occupy a central portion of the basin. During the time periods of interest, the primary agricultural zones of the basin were the deep soil alluvium, the upland alluvium, and the lower/middle piedmont.

During the Early Horizon, hamlets, small villages, and large villages were present in the southern portion of the basin. During Phase One, the numbers of all types of sites increased, and hamlets appeared in the more arid northern portions of the basin. There was also population growth in the deep soil alluvium and lower/middle piedmont zones. During Phase Two, civic ceremonial centers appeared for the first time in the basin along with the hamlets and small and large villages. The settlement

pattern suggests four or five separate settlement clusters that may have sociopolitical significance. Phase Three shows an approximate doubling of the population from earlier times and the presence of two very large regional centers, Teotihuacan and Cuicuilco. Defensive considerations are also apparent during this period, as indicated by the presence of the Tezoyuca hilltop centers, which are considered to be defensive. Thus, large and small regional centers, large and small villages, and hamlets were present in addition to the defensive loci. Population was now clustered into six major groupings separated by what are interpreted as buffer zones of sparse occupation between hostile polities. As mentioned above, Brumfiel (1976:234-249), Earle (1976:196-223), and Santley (personal communication 1987) are of the opinion that the state was forming during Phase Three. The above description is more than sufficient to consider the Basin of Mexico at the state level of integration by the end of Phase Three. For purposes of this study, then, a state level of organization is considered to have been present by 100 B.C., yielding a total of 1400 years of pre-state farming.

MEXICO

(TEHUACAN VALLEY)

Sequence Duration and Phases or Cultures Represented

The Tehuacan Valley was one of the Mesoamerican loci in which the initial domestication of maize and other plant crops occurred several thousand years before settled village farming was established as a way of life in the valley (MacNeish et al. 1967:10-11). The farming lifeway was definitely present by the beginning of the Ajalpan phase at 1900 B.C. and may have developed earlier (Johnson and MacNeish 1972:5; MacNeish et al. 1967:11-12). The preceding Purron phase is not well known, however, so village farming is considered to have begun with the Ajalpan phase. Crops that were cultivated include maize, squash, gourds, amaranth, beans, chili peppers, avocados, sapotes, and cotton (MacNeish et al. 1967:12). The pre-state, village farming phases end with the appearance of state-level society at 150 B.C. during the Palo Blanco phase (Johnson and MacNeish 1972:5-6; MacNeish et al. 1967:12-13). These figures yield a total of 1750 years for the pre-state farming adaptation (Table 2). The phases of interest to this study are the Ajalpan (ca. 1900-1000 B.C.) and the Santa Maria (ca. 1000-150 B.C.; Johnson and MacNeish 1972:5).

Domestic Animals and Secondary Animal Products

None of the domestic animals under consideration in this study were part of the Tehuacan economy. Dogs and turkeys were present, as in Oaxaca and the Basin of Mexico.

31

Farming System

The following discussions of farming system and settlement pattern/social organization are taken from MacNeish et al. (1967:3-13), unless otherwise cited. During the earlier time periods in the valley, domesticated crops were a part of the dietary mix but apparently made up less than one-third of the diet. The seasonal round was oriented toward hunted and gathered resources rather than settled, village agriculture. By Ajalpan times at approximately 1900 B.C., village agriculture, based on the previously mentioned crops, was well established. Maize was the most important crop, and early hybrid forms of corn were grown. The prime farming lands were the alluvial deposits of the valley and canyon floors (Woodbury and Neely 1972:95). According to MacNeish (1967:306-309), shifting cultivation was not common during the time periods of interest. Crops were planted in barrancas, by the side of springs or the River Salado, in arroyo bottoms or on low arroyo terraces, and on the alluvial floodplains. Though small-scale forms of water control may have been in use, elaborate irrigation systems were not present during this time period.

During the Santa Maria phase, manioc, tomatoes, and a new form of beans were added to the repertoire of cultivated crops. In addition, productive hybrids had been developed from many of the cultivated plants by this time. True irrigation was first used in this period, and the water-control system grew increasingly complex during the long span of the phase. During the later portion of the Santa Maria phase, irrigation was used to produce two, and perhaps three, maize crops per year (Woodbury and Neely 1972:95).

By Palo Blanco times, peanuts, small lima beans, and guavas were being cultivated in addition to the previously known domesticates. Complex and elaborate systems of irrigation were in use and remained so throughout the remainder of the prehistoric sequence in the valley.

Settlement Pattern
and Social Organization

The Tehuacan Valley is a highland desert valley in south-central Mexico (MacNeish 1967:307). During the Ajalpan phase, the people were full-time agriculturalists who lived in villages of small wattle-and-daub houses. These villages contained from 100 to 300 inhabitants. The villages seem to have been egalitarian in social organization. During the following Santa Maria phase, the settlement pattern consisted of villages oriented toward a single larger village, or ceremonial center, with a religious structure. Pottery similarities show that the Tehuacan groups were interacting with groups from Monte Alban, the Valley of Mexico, and the coast of Veracruz. Chiefdoms of some form were probably present during this time period.

By the Palo Blanco and Venta Salada phases, true urban communities and city-states supported by full-time specialists and ruled in the end by dynasties appeared (Johnson and MacNeish 1972:6). For the Palo Blanco period in particular, hamlets, large and small villages, and large hilltop centers were present. Some of the centers covered entire mountain tops and could be classed as cities, though probably sacred ones, in terms of population. These centers contained elaborate stone pyramids, plazas, ball courts, and other structures. This phase begins at ca. 150 B.C. and marks the end of the time period of interest, yielding a total of 1750 years.

NORTH AMERICA

(CHACO CANYON)

Sequence Duration and
Phases or Cultures Represented

Though domesticates were present in the American Southwest from the Archaic period on, in Chaco Canyon the farming lifeway is considered to have begun with Basketmaker III at ca. A.D. 500 (Windes 1987). The major domesticates were brought into the Southwest from Mexico and were adopted by local groups. Major cultivated crops include corn, beans, and squash (Toll 1985:247-277). The Chaco chronology is based primarily on a combination of dendrochronological dates, archaeomagnetic dates, dated pottery types, and radiocarbon dates, with the emphasis on dendrochronology (Hayes et al. 1981). Chaco is the first sequence discussed in this volume in which the farming period ended without state formation. The farming period ended sometime in the neighborhood of A.D. 1300 with the effective abandonment of the canyon by village farming groups (Windes 1987), yielding a total of 800 years of village farming in Chaco Canyon (Table 2).

The phases of interest to this study are taken from Windes (1987): La Plata (essentially Basketmaker III; A.D. 500-ca. 725), White Mound (ca. A.D. 725-900), Early Bonito (ca. A.D. 900-1040/1050), Classic Bonito (ca. A.D. 1040/1050-1100), Late Bonito (ca. A.D. 1100-1140), McElmo (ca. A.D. 1140-1200?), and Mesa Verde (ca. A.D. 1200-1300). These phases cover the span from Basketmaker III through Pueblo I, II, and III.

Domestic Animals and
Secondary Animal Products

None of the domestic animals that are under consideration in this study were present. Dogs and turkeys are known from Chacoan sites, as they are from other New World areas.

Farming System

The village farming adaptation got fully underway in the canyon at approximately A.D. 500 with the cultivation of corn, beans, and squash. Reliance on these major cultigens increased steadily through time (Judge et al. 1981:9-10). Chaco Canyon was always a marginal area for agriculture, especially with respect to precipitation and growing season, and hunted and gathered resources were always an important component of the subsistence system (Clary 1984:265-279; Schelberg 1983).

The early, settled farming in the canyon was probably floodwater or akchin farming without evidence of water-control devices (Judge et al. 1981:9-10). The canyon bottom lands at the mouths of drainages were always the most favored field locations. Fields were also located next to dune deposits, which were probably the best dry-farming locations in the canyon (Truell 1986:319), and on the mesa tops (Hayes et al. 1981:49).

The agricultural intensification that increased with the use of water-control devices probably began in the canyon in the later part of the period between A.D. 950 and 1150 (Lagasse et al. 1984:189, 202), which corresponds to the Classic and Late Bonito phases. Vivian (1970:75) dates the beginning of irrigation in the canyon to A.D. 1000, which corresponds to the Early Bonito phase. Water control in Chaco, always relatively simple, was based on using runoff from along the canyon margins for agricultural fields in the canyon bottom. Runoff water was transported through small ditches to fairly complex masonry headgates, which probably regulated water flow to the fields (Lagasse et al. 1984:187). The Chacoan system of both dry-farmed and irrigated fields survived several droughts but was evidently severely stressed by a major and extended dry period from A.D. 1134 to 1181 (McElmo phase; Schelberg 1983). After this period, regional interaction shifted to the north, population declined, and Chaco was eventually abandoned by village farmers (Schelberg 1983).

Settlement Pattern and Social Organization

The Chaco Plateau is a rolling plain with gentle relief, except for the sharply incised stretch of Chaco Canyon. The canyon bottom is fairly flat and ranges from a quarter- to a half-mile wide (Hayes et al. 1981:1-4). The climate of the Chaco country is that of a cold desert or steppe (Brand et al. 1937, cited in Hayes et al. 1981:4). Chaco has a relatively short frost-free period and is relatively dry; both combine to make Chaco marginal for corn agriculture (Schelberg 1983).

During the La Plata phase, also known as Basketmaker III, the people lived in pithouse villages or scattered pithouse groupings ranging from one to twelve houses. The favored location, as during all time periods, was the

canyon bottom. Use of the mesas was somewhat limited but remained nearly constant throughout the Chacoan occupation. After Pueblo I (roughly equivalent to the White Mound phase), there was a gradual movement from the plains and plateaus to the canyon (Hayes et al. 1981:23-24, 49). Population declined in the canyon during the McElmo and Mesa Verde phases, and the canyon was effectively abandoned after the Mesa Verde phase (ca. A.D. 1300).

During the White Mound phase (Pueblo I), above-ground pueblos, which were constructed primarily of jacal and adobe, appeared. As time passed, more masonry was integrated into pueblo construction. Subsurface structures presumably evolved into kivas and became religious in nature. Individual housing units range from five to fifteen rooms that are often quite close and may have been parts of the same community (Hayes et al. 1981:24-27).

The Early Bonito, Classic Bonito, and Late Bonito phases span the time period of the traditional Pueblo II and early Pueblo III periods and were times of major construction in the canyon (Lekson 1984:56-71). During the Early Bonito phase, the construction of towns began. These pueblos were generally large, multistoried, arc-shaped structures consisting of living and storage rooms. Smaller pueblos were also constructed. During the later portion of this period, some large structures were built quite close together, such as Chetro Ketl and Pueblo Bonito. Lekson (1984) considers these large sites to be local elite residences. The major sphere of interaction was within the canyon itself during the Early Bonito phase.

During Classic Bonito times, construction consisted mainly of additions to already existing structures. Elevated circular rooms, or raised kivas, appeared during this time period. Expansion of the large sites shows either population growth or aggregation at these sites, according to Lekson.

Chacoan construction is considered to peak in the transition period between the Classic and Late Bonito phases (A.D. 1075-1115), with several massive construction episodes consisting of both additions and new constructions. These additions added considerable numbers of storage rooms, which leads Lekson to conclude that the large structures were functioning as both elite residences and large storage facilities during this time period. He also is of the opinion that during both Classic and Late Bonito times Chaco served as the central focus of a regional system operating beyond the limits of the canyon and its environs. It may, in fact, have encompassed the entire San Juan Basin. "By the middle 1100's, Chaco was much closer to being a city than simply a canyon full of independent agricultural towns and villages" (Lekson 1984:71).

The subsequent McElmo and Mesa Verde phases in Chaco Canyon are no longer considered to represent intrusions from the San Juan. Construction in the canyon tapered off during these periods, and certain items, such as ceramics, indicate increasing contact with, but not a migration from, areas to the north (Lekson 1984:66-71).

For many years the social organization of Chaco Canyon was considered to be egalitarian, primarily because known ethnographic Puebloan groups are considered to be egalitarian in social structure. Recent work, however, contradicts this view and suggests a ranked society (chiefdom level), perhaps from Basketmaker III times on, for the canyon (Schelberg 1983). By Classic times there is definite evidence of a ranked society in the form of differential grave goods, a three-level hierarchy of settlement types and sizes, evidence of part-time craft specialization, and monumental construction. These developments probably came to an end around A.D. 1200. The period of interest for this study ends after 800 years with the effective abandonment of the canyon at ca. A.D. 1300.

NORTH AMERICA

(CAHOKIA)

Sequence Duration and Phases or Cultures Represented

The American Bottom is the portion of the Mississippi River floodplain between the cities of Alton and Chester, Illinois. It extends approximately 114 km in a straight line and includes within its span the major site of Cahokia (Bareis and Porter 1984:3). This area was the heartland of Mississippian culture. Village agriculture seems to have begun in the American Bottom area during the Late Woodland Patrick phase at A.D. 600 (Kelly et al. 1984: 104). (Information examined for this study indicates that the dates from Cahokia are not calibrated.) The first cultigens were local domesticates, such as marsh elder, goosefoot, maygrass, and knotweed, which may have been cultivated from approximately the time of Christ, or the Middle Woodland period (Fortier et al. 1984:85; Kelly et al. 1984:125). By A.D. 300, or Late Woodland times, squash and sunflowers were also cultivated (Kelly et al. 1984:125). Squash, an introduced cultigen, may have been cultivated earlier, since it appears in Early and Middle Woodland contexts in other Midwestern areas (Johannessen 1984:201-202). Maize, which was also introduced from the south and southwest, was only sporadically present and was presumably harvested in the green stage for immediate consumption. It did not become a major constituent of the diet until after A.D. 800, or Emergent Mississippian times (Kelly et al. 1984: 125). Nonetheless, other domesticated floral remains and settlement patterns showing larger floodplain communities located near productive agricultural land seem to indicate the beginning of village farming at least by the Late Woodland Patrick phase at A.D. 600 (Kelly et al. 1984:126-127).

The village farming period in the American Bottom also came to an end without state formation, as in Chaco Canyon. This will be discussed further in the section on social organization. The time period of interest officially ends at A.D. 1673 with the beginning of the Euroamerican exploration and occupation of the American Midwest (Esarey 1984:187), resulting in a farming period of 1073 years (Table 2). In reality, it is probably shorter since only scattered population remnants remained in the area after the decline of Cahokia in the mid-fourteenth century (Milner et al. 1984:186).

Phases of interest to this study are from the following periods: Late Woodland (only the later portion, ca. A.D. 600-800), Emergent Mississippian (ca. A.D. 800-1000), Mississippian (ca. A.D. 1000-1400), and Oneota (ca. A.D. 1400-1600/1673). The late portion of the Late Woodland in this area is known as the Patrick phase. The Loyd, Merrel, and Edelhardt phases are known from the northern portion of the area during the Emergent Mississippian; the southern portion of the area is represented by the Dohack, Range, George Reeves, and Lindeman phases during this period. The Lohmann, Stirling, Moorehead, and Sand Prairie phases are the Mississippian phases, and the Vulcan phase represents the Oneota period (Bareis and Porter 1984:12).

Domestic Animals and Secondary Animal Products

No domestic animals that are under consideration in this study were included in the Cahokia economy. Dogs were present, but turkeys are not known to have been domesticated in this area (Kelly and Cross 1984:215-232) unlike in other New World areas.

Farming System

By A.D. 600, domesticated crops formed a significant part of the subsistence base in the American Bottom. Wild plants, especially nuts and acorns, formed a part of the subsistence base throughout the sequence, however (Johannessen 1984:202-205). A temporal trend noted by Johannessen (1984:207, 214) is the decline in nut use and the rise in cultivated, starchy seed use (such as maygrass, goosefoot, and knotweed, as well as maize). Hunted game and fish were always important contributors to subsistence (Kelly and Cross 1984:215-232).

During the later portion of the Late Woodland period as well as during earlier times, slash-and-burn cultivation of garden plots on forested soils is suggested (Kelly et al. 1984:126). Late Woodland cultigens included marsh elder, goosefoot, maygrass, knotweed, squash, gourds, sunflowers, and possibly maize to a very small extent, although the evidence for maize is almost nonexistent from this time period (Johannessen 1984:202-203). By Emergent Mississippian times, maize was an important dietary contributor along with the previously grown domesticates, which retained their importance (Johannessen 1984:203). Slash-and-burn cultivation is also suggested for this period (Kelly et al. 1984:156). Both the crops grown and the farming system itself changed little throughout the remaining Mississippian and Oneota periods (Milner et al. 1984:185-186). Beans are mentioned as a domesticate during the Mississippian period (Smith 1978:483), but they are apparently not commonly found in Mississippian sites. Relatively permanent garden plots may also have been present in floodplain locales where annual or occasional flooding of the river would renew their fertility.

Settlement Pattern and Social Organization

The American Bottom is a wide portion of the relatively flat central Mississippi River Valley floodplain (Bareis and Porter 1984:3). Resource zones within the general area include the uplands adjacent to the floodplain, the zone of colluvial veneers and alluvial fans (located at the foot of the bluffs or uplands), and the floodplain itself (White et al. 1984:15-17). The soil is fertile, with annual flooding of some areas of the floodplain and periodic flooding of the floodplain as a whole, and the climate is continental (Bareis and Porter 1984:3).

During the Late Woodland, a gradual population increase is evident and continues through the Patrick phase. The Patrick phase settlement pattern consisted of larger, permanent communities widely scattered throughout the floodplain as well as smaller, upland settlements. For the first time, sizable communities of many structures were present in the American Bottom. Houses were set in basins with extended ramps oriented to the southeast or southwest, away from prevailing winds. Larger structures located to the side of each community may have served as men's houses (Kelly et al. 1984:126-127). The organizational bases for these communities are not clear. Their size, uniformity of size, and lack of indications of public architecture or craft specialization suggest that they were egalitarian communities (Kelly et al. 1984:127).

Population is also considered to have increased during the Emergent Mississippian, producing evidence of more communities than are known for earlier times (Kelly et al. 1984:156-157). Settlements were located on the floodplain, on the bluff banks, and in the uplands. They consisted of farmsteads, small villages, and larger communities in which mounds were present. These mounds cannot be definitely associated with the Emergent Mississippian, however, since the communities were occupied during the Mississippian as well. Generally, Emergent Mississippian settlements are considered to represent permanent agrarian communities, which may have been occupied for limited periods consistent with the movement associated with shifting cultivation. Some of the larger communities are more densely occupied and may have had longer occupations associated with more permanent fields. Structure plans were somewhat variable but seem to be semisubterranean set within rectangular basins. They were also variable in size, and some may have been used for storage. Some communities, like the Range site, appear to have had a plaza area. Kelly et al. (1984:157) see the communities that were more densely packed and occupied longer as a possible response to decreasing availability of good agricultural land. According to Kelly et al. (1984:157), there is little or no direct evidence for social stratification during the Emergent Mississippian. The foundation for later ranked society was probably laid during this period, however.

Continued population increase is also apparent during the Mississippian. For this time period, Fowler (1978:455-478) has identified four different types of communities located in the floodplain zone: fourth-line communities, which have no mounds; third-line communities, which have one mound; second-line communities, which are larger and have more than one mound within their limits (such as Mitchell and Pulcher); and one first-line community, Cahokia. The Cahokia site, which extended over five square miles at its peak, has evidence of more than 100 mounds of varying sizes and shapes arranged around what were probably plazas. Platform mounds may have been the location of public buildings or elite residences; conical mounds may have been charnel houses. There is also evidence of a presumably defensive stockade or wall surrounding the central 80 ha (Fowler 1978:462-465). Occupational emphasis was definitely on farmable floodplain lands during the Mississippian (Milner et al. 1984:182-186).

Size differences of communities, monumental construction, status differentiation, and indications of craft specialization have led many researchers to consider the American Bottom area a ranked society at the complex chiefdom level of integration during this period, whereas others have considered a state-level society to have been present (Griffin 1984:xvii; Iseminger 1980a, 1980b; O'Brien 1972). As is the case throughout, this study takes the more conservative interpretation, that of a complex chiefdom.

The Mississippian period ended at ca. 1350 or 1400 and was followed by the poorly known Oneota period. Since the exact nature of the social organization during this final protohistoric period is not well known, the time of interest is simply considered to end at A.D. 1673 with the arrival of the first French explorers in the area, who found Cahokia abandoned (Esarey 1984:187). This yields a total of 1073 years of village farming in the American Bottom.

SUMMARY

This chapter has presented a review of basic data on the sequences without domesticated animals. Table 3 presents a tabular summary of this basic information for both the animal and the non-animal groups.

CHAPTER 3

Table 3. Summary of Archaeological Sequence Information

Sequence	Southern Britain	Carpathian Basin	South-central Bulgaria	Greece (Thessaly)	Anatolia (Konya Plain)
Approximate Duration	4000 years	6200 years	5000 years	5000 years	4600 years
Time Span[1]	4300 - ca. 300 B.C.	6300 - ca. 100 B.C.	6500 - ca. 300 B.C.	7000 - ca. 2000 B.C.	6500 - 1900 b.c.
Domestic Animals[2]	Present	Present	Present	Present	Present
Farming System[3]	Permanent Fields	Permanent Fields	Permanent Fields	Permanent Fields	Permanent Fields
Water Control	Dry Farming	Dry Farming	Dry Farming	Dry Farming	Dry Farming and Irrigation
Social Organization	State Society	State Society	State Society	State Society	State Society
References	Barker 1985 Champion 1984 Dennell 1983 Renfrew 1973 Rowley-Conwy 1981 Sherratt 1981 Smith 1974	Barker 1985 Bogucki 1983 Champion 1984 Kosse 1979 Milisauskas 1978 Sherratt 1982 Whittle 1985	Barker 1985 Champion 1984 Dennell 1978 Sherratt 1981 Whittle 1985	Barker 1985 Champion 1984 Halstead 1981 Milisauskas 1978 Renfrew 1975 Whittle 1985	French 1966 Lewy 1965 Mellaart 1965, 1967a, 1967b, 1972 Redman 1978

(continued)

Table 3. Summary of Archaeological Sequence Information (continued)

Sequence	Northern Mesopotamia	Southern Mesopotamia	Upper Egypt	Pakistan (Indus River System)	Northern China
Approximate Duration	3660 years	1900 years	2400 years	3000 years	3150 years
Time Span[1]	6000 - 2340 b.c.	5500/5300 - 3600 b.c.	5500 - 3100 B.C.	5500 - 2500 b.c.	5000 - 1850 B.C.
Domestic Animals[2]	Present	Present	Present	Present	Present
Farming System[3]	Permanent Fields	Permanent Fields/ Shifting Unirrigated Fields	Permanent Fields	Combination Shifting and Permanent Fields	Shifting Fields Give Way to Permanent Fields
Water Control	Dry Farming and Irrigation	Dry Farming and Irrigation	Irrigation	Irrigation	Dry Farming and Irrigation
Social Organization	State Society	State Society	State Society	State Society	State Society
References	Bottero 1967 Kirkbride 1972, 1973a, 1973b, 1974, 1975 Mellaart 1972 Oates 1972, 1973 Redman 1978	Adams and Nissen 1972 Edzard 1967 Falkenstein 1967 Mellaart 1975 Redman 1978	Caton-Thompson and Whittle 1975 Hassan 1985 Hoffman 1979 Redman 1978 Whittle 1975	Allchin and Allchin 1982 Jarrige 1979 Jarrige and Meadow 1980 Meadow 1979	Chang 1977 Harris 1977 Wenke 1980

(continued)

37

Table 3. Summary of Archaeological Sequence Information (continued)

Sequence	Peru (Ayacucho Basin)	Mexico (Valley of Oaxaca)	Basin of Mexico	Mexico (Tehuacan Valley)	Chaco Canyon	Cahokia
Approximate Duration	3650 years	1400 years	1400 years	1750 years	800 years	1073 years
Time Span[1]	4000 - 350 B.C.	1600 - 200 b.c.	1500 - 100 B.C.	1900 - 150 B.C.	A.D. 500 - 1300	A.D. 600 - 1673
Domestic Animals[2]	Present	Absent	Absent	Absent	Absent	Absent
Farming System[3]	Permanent Fields	Permanent Fields	Permanent Fields	Permanent Fields	Permanent Fields	Combination Shifting and Permanent Fields
Water Control	Dry Farming and Irrigation	Dry Farming and Irrigation	Dry Farming and Irrigation	Dry Farming and Irrigation	Dry Farming and Irrigation	Dry Farming
Social Organization	State Society	State Society	State Society	State Society (Chiefdom)	Ranked Society (Chiefdom)	Ranked Society
References	MacNeish et al. 1980 MacNeish et al. 1981	Flannery 1976 Flannery and Marcus 1983 Ford 1976 MacNeish et al. 1967	MacNeish et al. 1967 Sanders, Parsons and Santley 1979 Santley and Rose 1979 Whalen 1981	Johnson and MacNeish 1972 MacNeish et al. 1967 Woodbury and Neely 1974	Hayes, Brugge and Judge 1981 Lagasse, Gillespie and Eggert 1984 Schelberg 1983 Toll 1985 Vivian 1970 Windes 1987	Bareis and Porter 1984 Esarey 1984 Fortier et al. 1984 Fowler 1978 Johannessen 1984 Kelly and Cross 1984 Kelly et al. 1984 Milner et al. 1984 Smith 1978

[1] "B.C." refers to calibrated radiocarbon dates. "b.c." refers to uncalibrated radiocarbon dates. All dates are taken directly from the sources.
[2] Cattle, sheep, goats, pigs or llamas are the domesticated animals examined in this study.
[3] Permanent fields are fields that are either continuously cropped, annually cropped or under a system of short-fallow rotation as discussed by Boserup (1965:16). Shifting fields are under long-fallow rotation (Boserup 1965:16). This information is estimated as accurately as possible from the published sources.

Chapter 4

DISCUSSION OF THE PATTERN

Sixteen archaeological sequences from eight general areas were used to define the pattern of differential duration of the pre-state farming lifeway. The eight general areas reviewed in Chapters 2 and 3 are southern Britain and Europe, the Near East, Egypt, China, India and Pakistan, the Andes, Mesoamerica, and North America. Table 1 lists the specific sequences used to define the pattern of interest. Table 3 briefly summarizes information on sequence duration, time span, domestic animals, farming system, and social organization. Table 2 and Figure 2 give the duration of the pre-state farming period for each sequence, ordered from longest to shortest.

Sequences from these sixteen groups were selected because they give wide areal coverage of temperate zone groups and also have sufficient high-quality archaeological information. The sequences do vary in geographic extent, number of sites, and amount of information in general, owing to the varying amount, intensity, and quality of research in the different geographic areas.

The durations of the pre-state farming periods listed in Tables 1 and 2 show the pattern of greater length when domesticated animals are present and shorter length when they are absent. The average duration of the sequences with animals is 3978 years; the average duration of the sequences without animals is 1285 years. There is a difference of 2693 years between the means of the animal and non-animal groupings.

A one-way, or one-factor, analysis of variance and a Mann-Whitney nonparametric test were run on the two groups of sequence durations to determine if there is a statistically significant difference between the durations of the animal- and non-animal-using groups (Arkin and Colton 1970; Blalock 1960; Glass and Stanley 1970; Hays 1973). The Mann-Whitney test provides a check on the results of the analysis of variance. It can be used when the assumptions required for analysis of variance, such as a normal distribution, are not met. Since the sequence durations used in this study are not normally distributed and since the sample size is small, the Mann-Whitney test was used in addition to the analysis of variance. Results of both of the analyses indicate that the difference between the group means is greater than that ascribable to sampling fluctuations, and it can be said that the two groups are not from the same population. In other words, there is a statistically significant difference between the group means at the .01 level of significance. Computations for these tests are given in the Appendix.

These results strengthen the case for the presence of the pattern of differential duration between the pre-state farming periods of groups with domestic animals as opposed to those of groups without domestic animals.

GROUPS WITH DOMESTIC ANIMALS

Considerable variation can be seen in the range of durations of the sequences under consideration. This difference is especially apparent within the grouping of eleven sequences representing the groups that possess medium to large domestic animals. This grouping ranges in duration from the 6200-year European spans to the spans from Upper Egypt and southern Mesopotamia (2400 and 1900 years, respectively; Table 2).

The sequences from Upper Egypt and southern Mesopotamia have several factors in common that seem to lead to their being the shortest pre-state farming periods in which domesticated animals are present. In general, several of the factors considered to lead to changes in social organization, or growing social complexity, come together in these areas (Flannery 1968; Flannery and Marcus 1983; Rathje 1971; Redman 1978; Sanders 1968; Wittfogel 1957; Wright and Johnson 1975). This combination of factors may have hastened the development of organizational complexity and state-level society in Egypt and southern Mesopotamia. The following factors contributing to complexity are discussed by Redman (1978:247-251, 253-266, 281-286).

Population growth can be seen in both areas. Both internal expansion and external migration into the region can be seen in southern Mesopotamia. In combination with these growing populations, the amount of the best agricultural land, on which various forms of water control were possible, was limited in both cases. Full-time farming communities were not realistically possible in either locus without some form of water control or without the annual flooding of the Nile, which limited intensive farming to the flooded or irrigated lands. Intensification of irrigation systems and technology, which requires at least some degree of organization, was possible and in fact advanced fairly rapidly in both areas. In addition to these factors, intra- and interregional trade were important. Southern Mesopotamia lacked several critical resources — wood, stone, and metals, for example — and its occupants were forced to trade for these items from the time of the earliest occupations. Thus, the combination of population

SEQUENCES

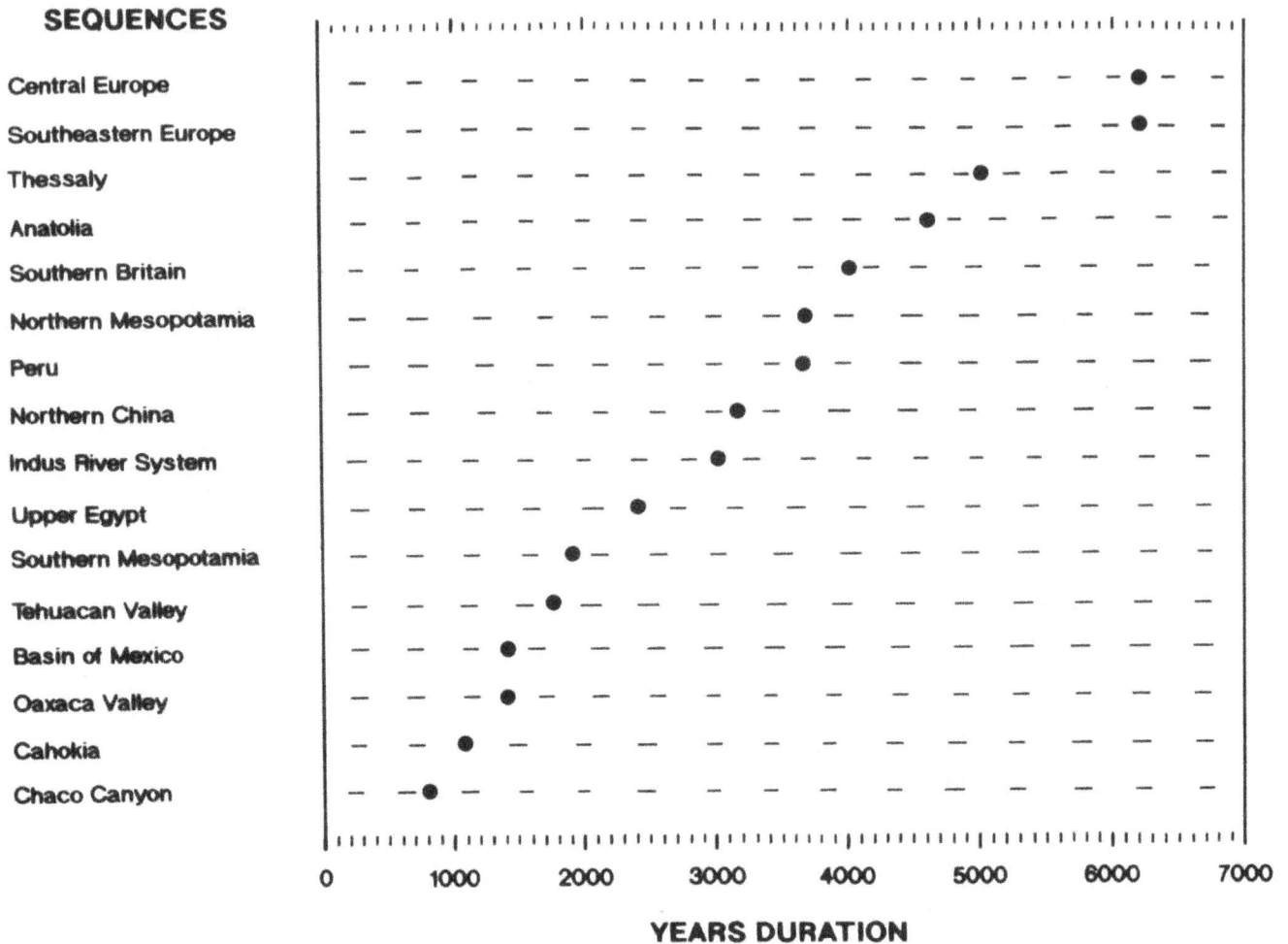

Figure 2. Durations of the pre-state farming periods from sixteen archaeological sequences

growth, limited access to good land, the necessity of some form of water control, and trade may have hastened the appearance of organizational complexity in these areas.

The long time spans of pre-state village farming, on the other hand, occur in areas of rainfall agriculture where quality land is fairly abundant (Barker 1985; Bogucki 1983; Dennell 1978; Kosse 1979; Milisauskas 1978; also see Table 3). Population growth is apparent in these areas as well, but there was sufficient land to absorb it for a longer period. Small daughter communities were able to split off and find new land until the landscape was full (Milisauskas 1978:44-50, 76-80). The land constriction seen in the areas with short sequences is not present in the regions with long sequences.

In general, the shorter Old World sequences examined for this study are those in which irrigation played a necessary or important role (Table 3): if not from the beginning, then as agricultural intensification began to develop (as in the case of northern China; Chang 1976:30). The average duration of the pre-state farming period of groups that used domestic animals and also irrigation, including Peru, is 3194 years. The average duration of the pre-state farming period among rainfall-farming groups with domestic

animals is 5350 years, a difference of 2156 years. The point of this discussion is not to promote the view that irrigation, along with its technology and organization, led to a more rapid development of complex social organization. It is simply that though a pattern of slower state development is evident among domestic-animal-using groups, there is indeed variability within that pattern. Obviously, many factors enter into the rate of development of complex social organization. This study indicates that two important factors seem to be the necessity of some form of water control and land constriction, which can be related both to differential access to irrigable lands and to population growth, among other things.

GROUPS WITHOUT DOMESTIC ANIMALS

There is a smaller range of variation, 950 years, among the sequences in which domesticated animals are absent (Table 2), probably because fewer groups are examined. The durations are all fairly short; some are simply shorter than others. The two shortest durations are the North American sequences from Chaco Canyon, 800 years, and Cahokia, 1073 years. Most researchers are of the opinion that although ranked societies did develop, state-level organization was never reached in either of these areas (Ford 1974; Fowler 1978; Griffin 1984; Schelberg 1983; also see the Chaco and Cahokia sections of Chapter 3). Thus, the time periods of interest end with the effective abandonment of the area in the case of Chaco (Windes 1987) and colonial occupation in the case of Cahokia (Esarey 1984:187). Since state-level organization did not develop in these areas, they are not precisely comparable to the previously discussed Old World sequences. Some of the same "sequence shortening" factors seem to be in operation, however, with the addition of others.

Both population growth and land constriction (Schelberg 1983) were present in the Chaco Canyon area of the San Juan Basin. Recent studies show this growth, though the population was probably never as high as the earliest estimates indicated (discussed in Lekson 1984:64, 69 and especially in Windes 1984:75-87). Schelberg (1983) discusses problems of land availability in Chaco with respect to the shortage of irrigable lands and poor soil quality in many parts of the canyon. Water control in Chaco was practiced from about A.D. 1000 on, was always fairly simple, and was designed to manage runoff in various forms (Lagasse et al. 1984:187; Vivian 1970: 75). The water sources for the canyon were never amenable to the complex forms of canal irrigation that were eventually in use in the Near East and Mesoamerica, however (Schelberg 1983).

The Chaco sequence is quite short compared with the other non-domestic animal sequences from Mesoamerica in which population growth and irrigation were also present (Flannery and Marcus 1983; MacNeish et al. 1967; Sanders et al. 1979; also see Table 3). This seems to be due to the fact that the Chaco area is very marginal for corn agriculture in terms of available moisture and frost-free days (Clary 1984:265-279; Schelberg 1983), as the following discussion drawn from Schelberg (1983) points out. Around 115-130 days is usually considered necessary for the maturation of the types of corn traditionally used in the American Southwest (Bradfield 1971; Cordell et al. 1984; Minnis 1981). According to Schelberg's calculations (1983), there was a 30% chance that the growing season would be less than or equal to only 100 days in Chaco Canyon in any given year. Thus, limitations on the frost-free period were a serious constraint on Chacoan agriculture, as was scant rainfall. A minimum of 16 inches of rainfall, with 6.4 inches falling in the summer months, is necessary to produce corn in the Hopi area (Hack 1942). The total for Chaco is barely half that amount. Thus, Chaco Canyon is definitely marginal in terms of both precipitation and growing season.

As mentioned previously, water control in Chaco depended on simple forms of irrigation from runoff and impermanent water sources (Lagasse et al. 1984:187; Schelberg 1983). Under drought conditions, these systems were not sufficient to meet the needs of growing agricultural production, and the canyon was eventually abandoned by village farmers before the state level of organization was ever reached.

The other short New World sequence under discussion is the Cahokia sequence of the American Bottom of the Mississippi River. Though the sequence was cut off by colonial exploration and expansion into the area, the major developmental climax apparently ended approximately 200-300 years earlier, around A.D. 1350-1400 (Milner et al. 1984). The first European explorers in the area found the site of Cahokia abandoned (Esarey 1984). The period between A.D. 1350-1400 and European contact is not well known, however. Uncertainty over both the amount of occupation in the area and the level of social organization of that occupation caused the time period of interest to be extended up until the entrance of the French into the area (Esarey 1984). This extension produces a duration of 1073 years.

Village farming began at A.D. 600, with social complexity apparent by A.D. 1000 or Mississippian times (Kelly et al. 1984; Milner et al. 1984). Within an approximate period of 400 years, the level of complex chiefdom was reached in the American Bottom area (Ford 1974; Fowler 1978; Milner et al. 1984). Some researchers would even define the presence of state-level society in the American Bottom during Mississippian times, from ca. A.D. 1000 to 1350-1400 (Iseminger 1980a, 1980b; O'Brien 1972). Whether this level of complexity was reached or not, the Cahokia sequence is quite abbreviated and worth examining in order to determine the factors that might have contributed to its brevity.

Population growth was apparent in the American Bottom from Late Woodland through Mississippian times, from A.D. 600 to 1350-1400 (Kelly et al. 1984:126-127; Milner et al. 1984:182-186). Trade and interaction with other areas appeared during the Emergent Mississippian, ca. A.D. 800, and grew throughout the following Mississippian period (Kelly et al. 1984:157; Milner et al. 1984: 186). Irrigation was not practiced in the American Bottom, but both periodic and annual flooding of the Mississippi River were used to renew the fertility of the floodplain farmlands, which occurred in restricted areas (Bareis and Porter 1984:83). A decrease in the availability of prime agricultural land was noted by Emergent Mississippian times, after A.D. 800 (Kelly et al. 1984: 157). Land constriction, under conditions of population growth, was apparently a major problem that was exacerbated by the absence of the plow, animal traction, and metal agricultural implements with which the heavier soils could be brought under cultivation (Barker 1985: 110). Thus, growing population and limitations on agriculturally productive lands under a primitive farming technology may have hastened the development of social complexity at Cahokia.

The remaining sequences in which domesticated animals were not present are from Mesoamerica (Table 3). Their pre-state village farming period durations have a fairly tight range of 350 years, with the Oaxacan period lasting 1400 years, the Basin of Mexico 1400 years, and the Tehuacan Valley 1750 years (Table 2). The average duration of the Mesoamerican sequences is 1517 years.

In contrast to the previously discussed short New World sequences, the Mexican sequences all ended in state formation after fairly similar amounts of time (Table 3). In all of these areas, population growth, irrigation, limited access to the best lands, and intra- and interregional trade were present to some degree. They differ from their shorter New World cousins in that considerable agricultural intensification was possible in the form of complex canal irrigation systems based on permanent water sources and double cropping based on considerably longer growing seasons (Flannery and Marcus 1983:96; MacNeish et al. 1967:3-13; Sanders et al. 1979:94-108). Thus, state-level societies of increasing complexity formed in these areas as opposed to the relatively short-lived chiefdoms followed by abandonment of one form or another seen in Chaco and Cahokia.

COMPARISONS AMONG GROUPS THAT USED IRRIGATION

For purposes of this study, it is instructive to compare the three Mexican sequences to the domesticated animal sequences in which irrigation was also used. Only sequences in which water control was present are used for this discussion in order to hold the farming systems as constant as possible. Chaco and Cahokia are not used in this comparison either, since the state level of organization was not present in these areas nor were complex irrigation systems based on permanent water sources used.

The seven sequences in which both domesticated animals and irrigation were present are from Upper Egypt, southern Mesopotamia, Pakistan (Indus River system), northern China, Peru (Ayacucho Basin), northern Mesopotamia, and Anatolia (Konya Plain; see Tables 2 and 3). The durations of pre-state farming in these areas range from 1900 years for southern Mesopotamia to 4600 years for the Konya Plain. The average duration for these sequences is 3194 years as compared to an average duration of 1517 years for the three Mesoamerican sequences, in which irrigation was present but domesticated animals were not. The difference of 1677 years between the averages of the two groupings indicates that the Mexican sequences are considerably shorter than those in which domesticated animals were present. In other words, the state developed ca. 1700 years more rapidly in the non-animal areas, though all the areas were experiencing to some degree the same constricting factors examined in this study (Chang 1977; Flannery and Marcus 1983; Hoffman 1979; Jarrige and Meadow 1980; MacNeish et al. 1967; MacNeish et al. 1980; Meadow 1979; Mellaart 1967b, 1972; Redman 1978; Sanders et al. 1979; Wenke 1980).

Identification of these constricting factors is unfortunately quite impressionistic in some cases, especially with respect to definitive statements concerning land constriction. The previously discussed factors are population growth, the presence of water-control systems that grew increasingly complex through time, various forms of limited access to or availability of prime agricultural lands, and intra- and interregional trade and interaction (Redman 1978:215-243).

To continue this series of comparisons, it is also instructive to compare the three Mesoamerican sequences with the two most abbreviated Old World sequences, those from Upper Egypt and southern Mesopotamia. As discussed previously, these two areas show the strongest presence of those conditioning factors that seem to hasten the development of organizational complexity (Redman 1978:215-243, 247-251, 253-266, 2891-286). An examination of the three Mexican sequences shows that these factors were also present in Mesoamerica but not to the extent that they appear in southern Mesopotamia and Upper Egypt, especially the necessity for water control and the resulting land constriction brought on by the severity of the water problem. The necessity for various forms of water control and the resultant restriction of the prime agricultural lands to those on which irrigation was possible were especially critical in the two Old World areas (Redman 1978:247-251, 253-266, 281-286). Though irrigation systems that grew in complexity through time were important components of the farming system and the intensification process in Mesoamerica, lands on which rainfall farming is possible were always present and in use (Flannery 1976:106; Flannery and Marcus 1983:96; Ford 1976:261; MacNeish 1967:306-309; MacNeish et al. 1967:3-13; Sanders et al. 1979:94-108; Woodbury and Neely 1972:95; The farming system in each of these areas is described in detail in Chapter 3). Thus, the water and land problem was apparently not as severe in Mesoamerica as it was in southern Mesopotamia or Upper Egypt. This situation is not reflected by the sequence durations, however. As shown in Table 2, the Mesoamerican sequences are all shorter than the sequences from the two most constricted animal-using Old World areas. The average duration of the southern Mesopotamian and Upper Egyptian village farming periods is 2150 years whereas the Mesoamerican average is 1517 years, a difference of nearly 650 years. In all probability, the difference may actually be much greater. The estimated 1900-year southern Mesopotamian sequence undoubtedly lasted considerably longer; it is believed that alluviation has buried many earlier sites in the area (as mentioned in Chapter 2).

The final comparison in this examination of the pattern of differential duration of the pre-state farming periods of domestic-animal and non-domestic-animal-using groups involves examination of the Peruvian Ayacucho Basin sequence in comparison to both Old World and Mesoamerican groups. The Peruvian sequence is particularly informative because it is the only sequence used in this study that has both the New World crop complex and medium to large domesticated animals.

The Peruvian sequence is compared to the Old World sequences in which water control was used, since water control was an important component of the Peruvian farming system (MacNeish et al. 1980:11-13). Tables 2 and 3 show that the duration of pre-state farming in the Ayacucho Basin was 3650 years, which puts the Peruvian sequence at the long end of the Old World sequences in which irrigation was present. The Peruvian duration is shorter than the Anatolian duration of 4600 years and is virtually identical to the northern Mesopotamian one of 3660 years (Table 2). It is longer than the remaining Old World irrigation sequences (Tables 2 and 3). Thus, the Peruvian sequence fits in well with those of groups that used domestic animals and practiced a combination of irrigation and rainfall agriculture (Table 3). As far as the Peruvian case is concerned, reliance on the New World complex of domesticated plants and animals produced a village farming period that equaled those of the Old World. If nothing else, this information indicates that no innate New World peculiarity produces short village farming periods.

When the length of the Ayacucho Basin sequence (3650 years) is compared to the average length of the Mesoamerican sequences (1517 years), it can be seen that the average Mesoamerican length is 2133 years shorter. In other words, the span from the beginning of the village farming lifeway to the appearance of the state was 2000 years shorter in Mesoamerica. This figure is particularly significant in light of the similarities between the two areas (Steward and Faron 1959:11-13). Though the two regions are certainly not equivalent, they are similar in several important respects.

The following discussion of these similarities is taken from Flannery (1976), Flannery and Marcus (1983), Ford (1976), MacNeish (1967), MacNeish et al. (1967), MacNeish et al. (1980), Sanders et al. (1979), and Woodbury and Neely (1972) unless otherwise cited. State-level societies developed in each of the sequences under consideration. Both rainfall farming and irrigation agriculture were practiced in these areas, and intensification of the irrigation systems was possible, with extensive systems of canal irrigation based on permanent water sources eventually being used. The primary crops in both areas were the New World staples of corn, beans, and squash supplemented by a wide variety of subsidiary cultigens. In the Peruvian area, more than 40 domesticates were grown, including corn, beans, squash, quinoa, amaranth, achira, potatoes, sweet potatoes, and avocados (Steward and Faron 1959:49-50). The Mesoamerican groups also relied on the New World triad of corn, beans, and squash as well as amaranth, chia, tomatoes, avocados, chili peppers, various chenopods, and white zapotes (Santley and Rose 1979). Thus, the major crop complex was similar in the two New World regions although variations occurred in the secondary crops.

Though figures and methods of calculation vary considerably and fluctuations occurred, growing populations are documented in both the Mexican and Peruvian areas (Santley and Rose 1979). Limitations on prime land under conditions of population growth were also present. In the Central Andean area much of the land is inhos-

pitable; it is either complete desert or the tundra and alpine zones of the high mountains (Steward and Faron 1959:53). Steward and Faron (1959:53) estimate that not more than 2% of the land in modern Peru is farmed, and they state that the portion cultivated in native times could not have been much greater. Thus, quality land is at a premium in general in the Andean area. Another example of land constriction is from the Basin of Mexico sequence and resulted from loss of land because of a natural disaster. A major pre-state center, Cuicuilco, was depleted when its farmlands were destroyed by volcanic ash and lava flows. This catastrophe was presumably a major contributing factor to the subsequent nucleation of population at the competing center of Teotihuacan.

Both intra- and interregional trade and interaction flourished in each of the regions; there is evidence that the Mesoamerican groups were interacting with each other as well as with other areas. Much of Andean development was linked to what MacNeish et al. (1980) refer to as the Andean vertical economy in which highland herding and potato-growing groups maintained close social and kinship ties with lowland groups practicing seed agriculture (see Chapter 2). Trade and interregional interaction were apparently important to these groups, though none was as dependent on trade for critical resources as groups in southern Mesopotamia, for example.

Thus, there are indeed areas of similarity between the two regions that can be held fairly constant to allow examination of other factors that might be contributing to the difference in sequence duration. One such factor, of course, is the contribution of domesticated animals to the economy. These contributions in general, as well as in the Peruvian case in particular, are the topic of Chapter 5.

SUMMARY

A pattern of significantly shorter duration of the pre-state farming period has been identified among groups that do not possess medium to large domesticated animals when compared to groups that do. A one-factor analysis of variance and a Mann-Whitney test performed on the durations of the pre-state farming periods from the two groups showed the difference to be significant at the .01 level of confidence (Appendix). Only temperate zone, noncoastal groups with primary agricultural reliance on grain crops were used in this study in order to maintain a degree of consistency among the groups studied. The archaeological sequences used to define the pattern were also examined for variation within the larger groupings of sequences with and without domestic animals. In general, it was found that areas in which water control was present and for which limited access to prime lands could be identified developed more rapidly, and had shorter pre-state farming periods, than areas in which rainfall agriculture was practiced and land was relatively abundant. In a further examination of inter- and intragroup variation, the Peruvian case was compared to both the Old World animal-using groups that practiced irrigation and the Mesoamerican groups that also practiced irrigation but had no medium to large domesticated animals. The duration of the Peruvian case was considerably longer than the non-animal Mesoamerican sequences and fit in well with the duration of the animal-using Old World groups. The possible input of the presence or absence of domesticated animals to the difference in sequence duration is explored in the next chapter.

ECONOMIC CONTRIBUTIONS
OF DOMESTICATED ANIMALS

THE ETHNOGRAPHIC CASES

The contributions of domesticated animals to subsistence-level farming economies were determined by examination of ethnographic and ethnohistoric sources that describe the uses of domesticated animals among such groups. The *Ethnographic Atlas* (Murdock 1967) was used to select groups useful for this study. To be consistent with the archaeological cases, these groups should be subsistence-level, mixed farmers as opposed to casual horticulturalists, pastoralists, or groups whose primary reliance is on cash cropping. Thus, groups were selected on the basis of the following criteria. Groups with at least a 36% dependence on agriculture and no greater than 65% dependence on domesticated animals were chosen. These criteria exclude casual horticulturalists by insuring that agricultural crops make up at least one-third of the subsistence base. They also exclude purely pastoralist groups by limiting the dependence on domesticated animals. In addition, the principal crops must be food crops, such as cereals or tubers. This excludes groups whose primary means of subsistence is cash cropping of nonfood items, such as tobacco and cotton.

Since this study is concerned with pre-state farming groups, an attempt was made to select farmers at this level of social organization. It must be noted, however, that the majority of these groups are presently incorporated within the realm of larger state-level societies. This is unavoidable for most nineteenth and twentieth century ethnographic sources. These groups do subsist primarily from their own produce, which is the main criterion. The only state-level society examined directly is that of the Inca. Ethnohistoric information on the Inca is used because they were a New World group with medium to large domesticated animals at the time of European contact. Their animal use patterns are therefore of particular interest.

Identification of societies in the *Ethnographic Atlas* (Murdock 1967) that meet these criteria initially yielded 210 cases. Of these, 188 possess the appropriate domestic animals. From this listing of 188, 15 cases or 8% were selected for in-depth examination of domestic animal uses. Fifteen is not a "magic" number. These groups were selected on the basis of locally available, quality information. The Human Relations Area Files (HRAF) and other sources were used to obtain information on these groups. These groups, their geographic locations,

and specific sources of information are shown on Figure 3 and listed in Table 4.

Since the objective of this part of the study is to explore the diversity of domestic animal uses under a wide range of environmental conditions, no geographic or climatic restrictions were placed on the ethnographic sample. The detail of coverage possible in the ethnographic studies allows the exclusion of groups that rely heavily on resources not covered by this study, such as fish or root crops. Thus, some coastal and tropical groups could be used even though these groups were excluded from the archaeological sequence sample. The fifteen societies were selected to represent worldwide coverage, different crop complexes, and different geographic conditions. This section of the study does not attempt to use a statistically valid cross-cultural sample, unlike that described by Murdock (1967:1-6). More germane criteria are employed that meet the needs of the present study, which does not require this type of sample. An in-depth examination of each selected case with respect to animal uses is desired, as opposed to a few general statements on a large number of cases. The goal of this study is to document the varied uses of domesticated animals and their importance to the farming economy. This requires only a sufficient number of cases with a wide geographical spread to insure that a particular use is not unique, unusual, or case- or region-specific.

USES OF DOMESTICATED ANIMALS

The major uses of domesticated animals determined from the ethnographic sources are as follows: *(a)* consumption of meat and animal by-products; *(b)* use of dung as fertilizer; *(c)* use of animals as a means of amassing wealth, as a back up resource in lean times, and as a form of live storage; and *(d)* use of animal traction for transport and plowing. These uses and their frequency of occurrence in the fifteen groups under examination are listed in Table 5. In general, these sources show that domesticated animals are used as both an added food source and a means of diversifying the resource base (Flannery 1969). They also spread the risk of storage loss and serve as a back-up resource since they are not subject to the same forms of loss as agricultural crops. In addition, they renew the fertility of certain types of agricultural fields and lead to further agricultural intensification with use of the plow. The most common use of domesticated animals

Figure 3. Locations of the ethnographic cases

Table 4. Ethnographic Groups, Geographic Locations, and References

Ethnographic Group*	Geographic Location	References
Balinese (1)	Bali	Covarrubias 1938; Geertz 1959
Bambara (2)	Mali	Paques 1954
Coorg (3)	Southern India	Krishna Iyer 1948; Richter 1870; Srinivas 1952
Ifugao (4)	Northern Luzon, Philippines	Barton 1922
Inca (5)	Peru	Garcilaso de la Vega 1869-1871; Rowe 1946
Rural Irish (6)	Ireland	Arensberg 1937; Evans 1942; Freeman 1958; Messenger 1969
Kikuyu (7)	Kenya Highlands	Lambert 1950; Leakey 1953; Middleton 1953
Kurds (8)	Northern Iraq	Barth 1953; Leach 1940; Masters 1953
Mapuche (9) (Araucanians)	Chile and Argentina	Cooper 1946; Faron 1961; Hilger 1957; Titiev 1951
Miao (10)	Hainan Island and northern Thailand	Graham 1937a, 1937b
Rif (11)	Northern Morocco	Coon 1931; Mikesell 1961
Serbs (12)	Yugoslavia	Halpern 1958; Lodge 1942
Shluh (13)	Northern Morocco	Berque 1955; Montagne 1930
Tallensi (14)	Ghana	Fortes 1936; Fortes and Fortes 1936; Lynn 1937
Zuni (15)	U.S. Southwest	Bohrer 1960; Cushing 1920; Leighton and Adair 1963; Roberts 1956; Stevenson 1904

* Numbers in parentheses refer to location in Figure 3.

is as a food source, and this contribution will be discussed first.

Domesticated Animals as Food Sources

All of the ethnographic groups consume the meat of their animals, though they may actually rely more heavily on use of by-products in the form of milk and milk products. Eleven of these groups consume milk and milk products; four do not (Table 5). All eleven archaeological cases with domesticated animals also show evidence of use of the animals as a meat source. In addition, seven of the groups show milk consumption with probable use of other milk products. Information on milk consumption is not available for three of the groups (Konya Plain, Indus River system, and northern China); the Peruvian group definitely did not consume milk (Chapter 2). Generally, the societies that do not use dairy products are those whose primary reliance is on pigs or llamas. The manner in which meat and milk products are used and the societies that use them will be discussed in detail shortly. First a brief review of the importance of domesticated animals as a food source for agriculturalists is provided.

Various anthropological and archaeological studies have dealt with nutrition in low-protein, high-carbohydrate diets (e.g., Ferguson 1980; Minnis 1981; Reidhead 1980;

Santley and Rose 1979; Young 1980). Though nutritional studies are subject to controversy and differences of opinion, these studies suggest that nutritional problems may occur as agriculture becomes more intensified. They also suggest that diets that are heavily reliant on cereal products provide adequate nutrition if certain processing techniques are used and if they are supplemented with some meat, vegetables, and (in the case of maize) beans (Haas and Harrison 1977; Santley and Rose 1979). Animal secondary products, such as milk, are also considered to be important dietary supplements. Milk is a source of the amino acid lysine, which can be deficient in cereal-based diets (Sherratt 1981:275). Major supplementary meat sources (fish are excluded for purposes of this examination) are either hunted game or domesticated animals. Only domesticated animals are considered as sources of edible secondary products in this study.

Information from the 210 ethnographic groups reviewed and the 15 groups selected for detailed study indicates that the use of domesticated animals as food sources becomes more important as populations increase and agriculture becomes more intensified. Intensification cuts down on hunting time and also limits the amount of fields under long fallow as well as virgin, uncultivated areas, which are favored locations of wild game (Harris 1977: 67-78). The ethnographic groups under study show a decline in the importance of hunting and in the presence

Table 5. Uses of Domestic Animals from Fifteen Ethnographic Groups

	Presence		Absence		No Info.		Total
	N	%	N	%	N	%	N
Consumption	15	100	0		0		15
By-product consumption	11	73	4	27	0		15
Use of dung as fertilizer	10	67	5	33	0		15
Indirect use of fertilizer (Animals graze fallow fields)	9	60	3	20	3	20	15
Accumulated wealth	13	87	2	13	0		15
Back-up for lean times	6	40	2	13	7	47	15
Plowing	10	67	5	33	0		15

of wild game as agriculture becomes more important. Of the initial sample of 210 groups with 36% or more dependence on agriculture, 55% are categorized as having a 0-5% dependence on hunting, 38% are listed as having a 6-15% dependence, and only 7% have a 16-25% dependence on hunted resources (Murdock 1967). Eighty-seven percent of the 15 selected societies show a maximum of 15% dependence on gathering, hunting, and fishing (Murdock 1967). Many of the agricultural systems of groups with a high dependence on nondomesticated food sources have an extensive component, which tends to preserve the advantage of greater game availability (Harris 1977:67-78) found in the less-intensive farming systems.

The following statements taken from the ethnographic sources give an especially clear picture of the declining importance of hunting to full-time agriculturalists. Game is not abundant, and hunting and fishing do not add an important supplement to the diet of the Kurds (Masters 1953). For the Mapuche, hunting was of minor importance in the early days; it is nonexistent today (Hilger 1957). Rabbit, deer, and antelope (now vanished) used to be an important part of the Zuni economy (Bunzel 1932). Information on the Serbs presents the following picture. During the nineteenth century, when the area was farmed extensively, hunting was of some importance. The woods had bear, deer, marten, and other game. Hunting is no longer important for subsistence, however. Its importance declined as the population grew and the virgin forest was put under cultivation (Halpern 1958). For the Tallensi, fish are fairly important as a lean-season resource but game is now scarce in the bush on the peripheries of their lands (Fortes and Fortes 1936). Hunting was of minor importance and was strictly regulated by the government in Inca times. Game was in preserves (Rowe 1946). This information presents a picture of growing scarcity of game and growing scheduling problems as agricultural intensity increases. The declining importance of hunted game appears to be the result of reduced availability of game and reduced time in which to hunt, as opposed to a lack of desire or a declining need to hunt.

This drop in the availability of game as agriculture becomes more important can also be observed in the archaeological record from some areas. New World areas are particularly informative, since the effect of declining game can be seen without the ameliorating effect of the presence of medium to large domesticated animals. Santley and Rose (1979) present a well-reasoned argument for nutritional stress arising from deficiencies in protein quality and availability, as well as possible iron and zinc deficiencies, during certain periods in the Basin of Mexico. They relate these nutritional problems to scarcity of animal products and other high-quality protein coupled with heavy reliance on maize. Their simulation uses reconstructed dietary information and shows a sharp, early drop-off in the percentage of the diet represented by deer, which was the main fauna. The following figures are maximum amounts that could have been consumed; in reality, less meat was probably eaten. Deer declined from 33.7% of the diet at the beginning of sedentary village life in the Basin of Mexico to 7% in the following phase, which began 350 years later. Near the end of the pre-state farming period, deer accounted for only 1.3% of the diet (Santley and Rose 1979:194).

The faunal and skeletal data from Tijeras Canyon and other pueblos in the American Southwest provide additional information on this subject (Ferguson 1980:121-148; Young 1980:88-120). In her summary of the faunal information from Tijeras, Coconito, and San Antonio pueblos, Young (1980:109) concludes that during the period of highest population concentrations in the area the groups may have been experiencing difficulties in obtaining adequate supplies of meat. She bases this view on a change in the hunting pattern from deer to the more distant antelope, on higher frequencies of small rodents showing evidence of having been consumed by humans, and on skeletal evidence of a significant incidence of possible iron-deficiency anemia in the most vulnerable age/sex groups.

Another example of possible meat acquisition problems comes from Fort Ancient times in the middle Ohio Valley

(A.D. 1000-1700) and is discussed by Reidhead (1980: 141-186). He cites a skeletal analysis conducted by Cassidy (1973), which indicates that people at the Late Fort Ancient Hardin Village site may have been experiencing some nutritional problems. These problems appear as abnormally high infant mortality between the ages of two and four. Cassidy (1973) posits protein deficiency during weaning as a possible cause of the increased infant mortality. The Hardin Village midden shows a relative paucity of deer bone (Hansen 1966, cited in Reidhead 1980), which was the primary large fauna of the area. Reidhead reviews information that indicates that meat acquisition and protein capture were not a problem in the Ohio Valley during Late Archaic hunter-gatherer times, but that agriculturalists in the valley appear to have been unable to achieve a nutritionally satisfactory diet. Reidhead suggests that this problem may have resulted from declining supplies of meat owing to overexploitation of game in the area during the later times.

Such studies as these are by no means definitive, but they do lend credence to the ethnographic information concerning the declining role of wild game with the rising importance of agriculture. They indicate the potential importance of domesticated animals to the farmers who possess them and suggest that the role of these animals gains in importance as dependence on cultivated crops increases.

Patterns of Meat and Secondary-Product Consumption

As mentioned previously, all the groups under study eat the meat of their domestic animals, and the majority of them make heavy use of the secondary products as well. Two patterns of meat consumption were identified from the ethnographic information. The first, and most common for mixed farmers, is that of heavy reliance on cereal crops with periodic inputs of animal meat. The second is that of groups with larger herds and flocks and heavier reliance on animal meat.

The Kikuyu are an excellent example of the first pattern of consumption when flocks and herds are relatively small and carefully tended. The information on the Kikuyu describes their diet as mainly vegetarian except for meals at festivals and sacrifices. Animals are never killed solely for meat but are eaten only on ceremonial occasions or after they have died a natural death. The information on sacrifices, however, is highly instructive. There are 108 occasions from birth to death that require the slaughter, sacrifice, and consumption of a sheep or goat on behalf of an individual. This averages out to 1.5 occasions per year per family member (Leakey 1953). A family of four, then, would slaughter six sheep or goats per year; a family of five, seven and a half. The Kikuyu live in extended family groups so these numbers would probably be higher. When natural animal deaths and participation in the ceremonial feasts of other community members are added to the above total, it can be seen that

the mainly vegetarian Kikuyu diet receives a small but steady input of meat throughout the year.

The Zuni illustrate the second pattern of consumption. In fairly recent times, their meat consumption pattern has been that of stockmen and craftsmen with relatively large flocks. During the 1940s (1942-1948), the sources report 6000 sheep slaughtered for home consumption per year and 2000 slaughtered during Shalako (Leighton and Adair 1963), one of the most important annual ceremonies. When the 1950 Zuni population of 2563 and the 6000 count are used, it can be estimated that roughly 2.3 sheep were consumed per person per year. A family of five would then slaughter 11.5 sheep per year for home consumption, as well as consuming all animals that die a natural death and participating in the consumption of those animals slaughtered during Shalako. Meat is also dried and stored for later consumption.

The other contribution of animals to the diet comes from the use of secondary products as dietary supplements. This consumption is greater than the use of animals as meat sources in most groups of mixed farmers. Milk, butter, ghee, yogurt, curds, and cheese are all consumed. Some groups also tap the animals' blood as a food source.

Eleven of the fifteen ethnographic groups studied consume or sell edible animal by-products to some degree. Of the four groups that do not consume secondary products, two have animals that were not used for secondary food products — the Ifugao raise primarily pigs and the Inca raised llamas. The Miao and the Balinese have cattle, which do produce edible secondary products, but they do not consume them. Many people cannot consume milk directly owing to lactose intolerance (discussed in Sherratt 1981, 1983). The ability to digest milk is very low or absent in Mongoloid, New World, Melanesian, Australoid, and Khoisan populations (Sherratt 1983). This could be why the Miao and the Balinese do not consume secondary products. Lactose intolerance does not preclude the consumption of fermented milk products, such as yogurt and cheese, however.

A small amount of by-product consumption is reported for the Zuni. They exemplify groups that follow the pattern of heavy consumption of meat with much less reliance on dairy products. In 1920, goatherds are reported to have milked their goats; later reports state that cattle are not milked, and no mention is made of milking sheep (Cushing 1920; Bunzel 1932). None of the means of storing dairy products, such as butter, cheese, or yogurt production, is reported for the Zuni.

The more common pattern of heavy reliance on dairy products is shown by the rural Irish farmers, who are an excellent example of heavy dependence on animal by-products with a much smaller consumption of animal meat. Animal meat is consumed in much the same pattern as that of the Kikuyu. Animals are slaughtered for festival occasions and when they have become old and unproductive. Animals that die natural deaths are also consumed, or their meat is salted and stored. The heaviest meat consumption is in winter, whereas heavy dependence on dairy products occurs during summer. Sheep as well as cows are milked, and milk, butter, cheese, and curds are eaten. Dairy products, in the form of butter, are stored for the lean days of spring. Ireland has one of the highest rates of butter consumption in the world. Animals are also bled and the blood is consumed in the form of blood pudding and sausage. Small amounts of meat and considerable amounts of milk products are added to a diet of potatoes, oats, rye, cabbage, and other vegetable products.

The Serbs are another example of this pattern of consumption. They are light users of meat and have a heavy reliance on dairy products and lard. They store both meat and dairy products for winter and they milk their sheep. The Kurds also follow a pattern of heavy use of milk and milk products, which form a large portion of their diet. The sources state that meat is consumed almost every day in richer households, whereas the poorer classes eat meat only once or twice each week.

Information on the remaining groups indicates patterns of use similar to or somewhere in between those of the Zuni and the rural Irish. In general, groups that are more reliant on meat are less reliant on dairy products and vice versa. Taken together, the ethnographic sources indicate a considerable dietary input of protein and calories from the use of domesticated animals as sources of meat and dairy products. These sources also demonstrate the importance of this dietary input as wild meat sources decline with the intensification of agriculture.

Domesticated Animals
as a Source of Fertilizer

Aside from their use as a food source, one of the major contributions of domesticated animals is production of fertilizer. The ethnographic information indicates that ten of the fifteen groups apply dung directly to their fields and nine of them allow animals to graze fallow fields, which is a form of indirect manuring (Table 5). Evidence from the eleven archaeological cases with domesticated animals indicates probable manuring in six of the cases; five of the cases do not present information on the subject (Chapter 2). The five ethnographic groups that do not manure include the Kikuyu, who are primarily extensive farmers and do not manure, and two paddy rice cultivators, the Balinese and the Ifugao. The Ifugao also have an extensive component to their farming system. These types of systems generally do not use manure to maintain fertility because the rice receives nutrients from irrigation water. If paddy cultivation is practiced in an extremely intensified form, as is described for Japan (Geertz 1963), manure or nightsoil may be applied. The Village Kurds, who also do not fertilize, consider dung such an important fuel source that it is not used for manure. The final group that does not report manuring is the Zuni. They are apparently deemphasizing agriculture somewhat and

moving into herding and silversmithing. Thus, they are not attempting to increase agricultural production with fertilizer.

It can be seen that manuring, though important, is not needed by all groups under all conditions. Extensive, slash-and-burn cultivation does not require animal manure to maintain fertility. When extensive farming gives way to intensive farming, however, fallow time is reduced or eventually eliminated altogether. Maintenance of soil fertility can then become a problem on certain kinds of lands (Boserup 1965:25). Manuring generally attains its greatest importance on dry-farmed lands that are annually cropped or under short-fallow rotation (Boserup 1965:25).

Other types of land may never require manuring. Lands that are flooded annually or even periodically maintain their fertility by receiving nutrients and fresh soil in solution. Land along the Nile and the American Bottom of the Mississippi are two examples (discussed in Chapters 2 and 3). For the same reason, plots near the mouths of arroyos do not require fertilizing (Bradfield 1971; Hack 1942). Land under flow irrigation is also revitalized through the addition of nutrients and soil in solution, though fertilizer may also be added to irrigated lands. These lands remain fertile as long as salinization does not become a major problem (Gibson 1974). Paddy rice cultivation also maintains soil fertility by the addition of nutrients and fresh soil in solution plus decayed organic matter from the previous year's cultivation (Geertz 1963:28-37). Paddies grow more fertile as they age. The lands that do not require fertilization are generally limited in extent. The much more abundant dry-farmed lands, which are watered by rainfall and therefore do not maintain their fertility, are those to which fertilization makes its greatest contribution. Both crop rotation, such as the use of leguminous plants to replenish nitrogen, and manuring are used on these lands.

Three main strategies of direct and indirect manuring were noted in the ethnographic information: (a) maintaining a dung heap from which manure is carried to the fields, (b) corralling animals over sequential patches of a fallow field until each area has been well manured, and (c) allowing animals to graze randomly in fallow fields. These strategies are often used in combination; the choice of strategies depends on the number of animals owned and the ways in which they are tended and fed. Certain animals may be allowed to graze a fallow field, while others are penned and a dung heap is maintained nearby. Several examples of manuring techniques from both arid and nonarid regions where rainfall agriculture is practiced are presented below to clarify the patterns of manure use and demonstrate its importance under both climatic regimes. Sources for these descriptions are listed in Table 4 unless otherwise cited.

The ethnographic information on the Shluh describes a combination of the first and third strategies listed above and also indicates the importance of animal waste as fertilizer. This importance is shown by the fact that there are litigations over who owns the manure from which animals. Manure deposited on collectively owned lands or sanctuary lands is even controlled by law and is sold at auction, with the proceeds being used to support the mosques.

The Shluh are sedentary, mixed agriculturalists who inhabit both plain and mountain areas. The Shluh who inhabit the plains are described here. Their lands are arid, receiving some 30 cm of precipitation annually in the coastal regions and an average of 20 cm annually in the interior (approximately 8 to 12 inches). They have unirrigated fields under short fallow and small, irrigated fields under continuous cropping. They allow their animals, which consist of sheep, goats, cattle, and mules, to graze the unirrigated stubble fields. Mountain groups also bring their animals down to the plain seasonally to graze these fallow fields. Their gift to the Plainsmen for this right is the manure from the grazing animals. Manure is also collected in the village and transported to the irrigated fields, which are the most abundantly manured. For these smaller irrigated fields, a compost is made from manure and vegetal materials. Ovine manure is considered the warmest, with an effect that lasts three or four years. Bovine manure lasts only one season. Thus, two layers of ovine manure are alternated with a layer of bovine and equine manure. During food shortages, these abundantly fertilized plots enable the group to survive. The remaining manure is placed in piles in the unirrigated, fallow fields. After a rain, it is spread and the field is ready for use.

The Tallensi information shows a less intensive form of this pattern. Their area is also arid with marked rainy and dry seasons and the real possibility of drought. They do not irrigate but have three different types of farmland: intensively cultivated farms located near the house compounds, short-fallow lands, and extensively cultivated bush farms.

The compound farms are manured from the dung heap. Animals graze the stubble fields of the short-fallow lands and in defined grazing grounds. The average Tallensi extended family compound has two head of cattle, one donkey, three sheep, six goats, and about twenty fowl. Because they have relatively few animals (compared to the Shluh, for example), less manure is available and only the most intensively cultivated land is manured from the dung heap. Lynn (1937) states that 12% of the total area cultivated receives an average dressing of from 2 to 5 tons of manure per acre; 10 tons per acre would be desirable. Information is given on a four-year period for manured and unmanured lands producing early millet, late millet, and guinea corn. The most striking effect is on early millet — the yield from manured lands is almost double that from other lands. The guinea corn yield from fertilized fields is one-third larger, whereas the late millet yield is virtually the same. Late millet is often planted on extensively cultivated bush farms. During the first seasons of cultivation these areas have very high fertility,

which explains the equal yields. The Tallensi consider manure to be critical for maintaining their farming system, especially for producing greater yields of early millet, which is the first crop harvested and ends the spring/early summer lean season.

The ethnographic studies of the groups under examination indicate that patterns of fertilizer use for rainfall agriculture are much the same in both arid and nonarid regions. The rural Irish farmers are an example of rainfall agriculturalists in a decidedly nonarid area. They receive an average of 30 to 50 inches of rain per year and do not irrigate. Their farmlands consist of intensively cultivated infields and outfields under short fallow. Manure from the household dung heap, from 10 to 15 tons per year, is applied to the infield. Animals are also allowed to graze the infield for short periods. They normally graze in the outfield and on pure pasture lands, however. In the outfield, they are penned in temporary enclosures over particular areas that are due for cultivation. This practice is also reported by the Tarahumara of northern Mexico, who state that this practice allows them to keep farming the same land for long periods of time without resorting to moving (Kennedy 1978). Manuring is considered vital by both of these groups.

These examples demonstrate the ways in which manure is used and its importance to intensive, rainfall agriculturalists in both arid and nonarid regions. Though these groups may possess some lands that are extensively farmed or periodically flooded and never need fertilization, these lands are limited and access to them may be cut off as regional populations grow. Thus, the importance of fertilizer and fertilizer producers tends to increase in an area as populations grow and access to extensively farmed lands becomes restricted.

Domesticated Animals as Security and Savings

The next category of animal use covers the function of animals as a means of amassing wealth, as a back-up resource in lean times, and as a form of live storage. In these roles, domesticated animals augment and diversify the resource base. They increase security by spreading the risk of resource loss both from the regular pool of resources used on a daily basis and from stored resources, because they are subject to different forms of loss than the agricultural crops (Flannery 1969; Halstead and O'Shea 1982).

The use of animals as a form of wealth and savings is extremely common in subsistence-level farming societies. Thirteen of the fifteen ethnographic societies studied use animals in this way (Table 5). When amassing more land is not realistically possible, animals are the major form of investment. The two societies whose major investment is not in animals invest in acquiring more land (the Coorg and Village Kurds). A family with no animals is poor indeed, and one of the worst disasters that can occur is the loss or illness of animals. Money from surplus crops and extra cash obtained from the sale of craft items is spent on buying more animals. The standard of exchange is often fixed in terms of animals, and they serve as bridewealth and dowry (refer to the ethnographic sources listed in Table 4). According to the ethnographic information on all of these groups, the prestige value of animals is enormous: a rich man is measured in terms of his animals.

For these subsistence-level farming groups, animals serve not only as a means of amassing extra wealth and displaying prestige but also as a form of live storage. Especially in hot or wet climates, animals have a much longer "shelf life" than stored grain or tubers. They are also subject to different forms of storage loss than stored crops. So, storage in animals and in agricultural products spreads the risk of storage loss (Flannery 1969).

An even more sophisticated form of storage involves an inedible animal by-product, such as wool, that can be converted into edible products should the need arise. The ethnographic sources (Table 4) show that nine of the groups use wool from sheep or llamas. Two of the groups do not possess or do not emphasize wool producers (the Balinese and Ifugao); no information on wool use is available for the four remaining groups that do possess sheep (the Tallensi, Rif, Coorg, and Kikuyu). Of the eleven archaeological cases with domesticated animals discussed in detail in Chapter 2, nine show evidence of wool use and information is not available for the other two (Konya Plain and Indus River system). As discussed by Sherratt (1981), the use of wool and textiles comes into full flower during the period of nation-state economic interaction, which occurs after the period of prime interest to this study. Sherratt (1981:283) describes the use of woolen goods as follows:

> items of inter-regional trade, and are usually the first manufactured goods to be traded on a large scale. Exports in developing areas shift from basic subsistence items like grain to manufactured products. This process can be observed in Mesopotamia during the course of the third millennium, and the development of such trade may have had an important role in extending the urban network.

Trade in such commodities as wool allows longer storage and a greater trading distance for the traded product, which enables a larger area to be included in the inter-action sphere. This expansion increases group security by providing a wider range of options and opportunities to obtain desired goods. This topic is discussed in greater detail in Chapter 6.

The domesticated animals maintained by a society can also serve as back-up resources in lean times. There is less information on this category of use, but ethnographies of six of the societies (Inca, rural Irish, Kikuyu, Mapuche, Tallensi, and Zuni) state that in hard times animals are either sold, traded for grain, or consumed directly. Generally, animals are sold or traded for grain,

since a considerable amount of grain can be obtained for one animal. In this manner, more mouths can be fed over a longer period than if the animal were consumed directly. As described for the Kikuyu, if the harvest is bad, the Kikuyu buy grain from the Wakemba with sheep, goats, cows, or ivory — cows are rarely consumed directly and are only slaughtered in times of famine.

Two groups do not follow the pattern of lean-times reliance on domesticated animals; seven do not have information on this subject. The two groups that do not use animals in this way are the Ifugao and the Balinese. They are primarily dependent on rice, tubers, and pigs, and they seem to have a system of borrowing rice at high interest on an individual basis. The Ifugao, who still have an extensive component to their farming system, are also able to use wild game as a back-up.

Despite some exceptions, the majority of the studied societies do rely on their animals to a greater or lesser degree to diversify and augment their resource bases and to serve as an added source of security on which to rely in hard times.

Domesticated Animals for Transport and Plowing

Two other vital uses of domesticated animals are transport and plowing. All of the ethnographic cases and all but one of the archaeological cases with domesticated animals describe use of their animals for traction and to pack goods (Table 4; also see Chapter 2). The Inca are the only group whose animals were apparently not suitable for traction, and they were used as pack animals. Use of animal power for transport and packing enables movement of more goods with less human labor over a wider geographic area.

Ten of the fifteen ethnographic societies and nine of the eleven archaeological cases with animals also use their animals for plowing (Table 5; Chapter 2). Use of the plow allows broadcast sowing and expands the area that an individual can cultivate. The two aberrant archaeological examples are the Konya Plain group, for which there is no information, and the Inca, whose animals, llamas, were unsuitable for pulling a plow (Chapter 2). The Inca are also one of the ethnographic (ethnohistoric) groups included in this study that do not use plows. The four remaining groups are the Kikuyu, Ifugao, Tallensi, and Bambara. All of these groups have an important extensive component to their agriculture that does not use the plow. The Ifugao also have small, terraced ricefields arranged in a complicated vertical manner that is not suitable for the plow. The Bambara tried to use the plow on the intensively cultivated lands but discontinued this attempt because deep plowing of the soil brings up the laterite-forming layer, rendering the soil unusable.

As with woolen commodities, the uses of domestic animals for transport and plowing make their most significant contributions to the initial stages of industrialization of nation-state economies (Sherratt 1981:261), which occurs after the period of primary focus in this study. They do also contribute to the stability of pre-state farming economies, however. As discussed by Sherratt (1981:261-262), use of the plow and cart are the first applications of animal power to the mechanization of agriculture and the transport of agricultural products. These uses of animals make important contributions to both the intensification of agricultural production and the development of trade. The plow increases production and makes possible the cultivation of a range of poorer-quality and heavier soils. This process brings more land into cultivation by allowing use of previously unculti-vated areas. Thus, greater population or greater economic elaboration can be supported. The use of wheeled vehicles and pack animals opens new possibilities for bulk transport and reduces the impact of distance. Animal-powered transport makes feasible a range of locations and settlement types, including cities, that would not be possible otherwise (Sherratt 1981:261-262). These economic contributions are explored in greater detail in Chapter 6.

SUMMARY

From the described uses of domesticated animals, it can be seen that animals make a substantial contribution to village farming economies. Their role in helping to maintain economic stability seems especially important as agricultural intensification increases, with attendant loss of fallow time and extensively cultivated fields. Animals serve as a replacement source of both meat and secondary products at a time when hunted game may be declining, and they serve as a means of replenishing the fertility of certain types of fields. They diversify the subsistence base by providing both additional resources and alterna-tive forms of storage that are not subject to the same risks as agricultural crops. Ultimately, they lead to further intensification of field agriculture with use of the plow. In addition, the use of wheeled vehicles and pack animals allows transport of both agricultural produce and other traded items over a much wider range than was previously realistic. This ability to transport in bulk increases the probability that members of the group can obtain needed goods.

ECONOMIC OPERATION OF SOCIETIES WITH AND WITHOUT DOMESTICATED ANIMALS

Both archaeological and ethnographic data have been used to examine pre-state farming groups with and without medium to large domesticated animals. This chapter presents a summary of this information in the form of descriptive models of the economic operation of the two different groupings. The economic roles of agricultural crops and farming techniques, land-use patterns, hunted resources, domesticated animals, and trade are discussed. A comparison of the economic strategies of the two systems is presented along with a discussion of the areas in which economic problems might result in the absence of domesticated animals. The ways in which increased social complexity might ameliorate these problems are also examined.

GROUPS WITH DOMESTIC ANIMALS

A brief picture of the economic pursuits of subsistence-level farmers with domesticated animals, drawn primarily from the archaeological and ethnographic information used in this study, is presented below. These groups have primary agricultural reliance on cereal crops, such as wheat, barley, millet, oats, rice, and maize. They practice irrigation and various forms of manuring under certain circumstances and often have an infield/outfield farming system. The plow is used in field cultivation. Domesticated animals are heavily relied upon as a source of food from secondary products and occasionally as a source of meat, whereas the importance of hunted resources declines through time. Domesticated animals are also used as a form of wealth and storage. Trade among these groups is active and seems to intensify as the political systems become more complex. Long-distance exchange of manufactured goods using animal transport is ultimately the major form of trade among these systems. This economic pattern is discussed in detail below.

Agricultural Crops

Agricultural crops and farming techniques are examined first. The groups selected for use in this study are primarily reliant on grain crops. This type of crop was used by the majority of the groups that went on to develop intensified forms of agriculture and complex societies, the societies of interest to this study. Wheat, barley, millet, oats, rice, and maize are the cultivated grains. Of the eleven archaeological cases discussed in Chapter 2, nine

cultivated wheat and barley as their primary food crops. The northern Chinese cultivated primarily millet, with a later introduction of wheat, barley, and rice. The one New World case with domesticated animals, the occupants of the Central Andes, cultivated the New World crops of corn, beans, and squash supplemented by a wide variety of highland Andean cultigens. The fifteen ethnographic groups discussed in Chapter 5 cultivate the full range of grain crops, including wheat, barley, oats, rye, millet, rice, and maize, as well as a variety of root crops and cash crops. In addition to their field crops, vegetable gardens are of considerable importance to all these groups.

As discussed by Haas and Harrison (1977), since the advent of agriculture most human populations have relied on cereal cultigens for their major source of energy. These crops are closely associated with the origins of complex societies, population growth, and major changes in social organization. Harris (1969, 1972b) views these systems, which place primary reliance on cereal grain staples, as unstable or as less stable than the more diversified vegecultural cropping systems of the nonseasonal tropics. Rindos (1984) argues to the contrary that systems that emphasize seasonal grain staples are not inherently unstable or ill adapted in all environmental settings, but are suited to the seasonal environments in which they have evolved and spread. In his view, they are no less stable than other cropping systems. Rindos states that the stability of agricultural systems in general must be viewed in a variety of different contexts (1984). Agricultural systems have been globally persistent (stable) but locally unstable in that they are successful and productive on the larger level but can be subject to recurrent and catastrophic episodes of local failure (Rindos 1984). Such episodes are of considerable interest to this study. Local wisdom would dictate that as one crop or set of staple crops becomes increasingly emphasized, perturbations affecting those crops would have greater economic repercussions.

Though primary crops are definitely present and are heavily relied upon, the possibility of local failures seems to be the reason why both the archaeological and the ethnographic crop lists are long and generally include several different staples (e.g., Rowe 1946; Steward and Faron 1959; also see Table 4). The importance of vegetable gardens is also stressed. It is interesting that a greater number of crops and, more significant, a greater number of staples are listed for the ethnographic cases than for the archaeological ones (Chapters 2 and 3; Table 4). This distinction is undoubtedly due in part to archaeological preservation problems; however, it also seems to indicate a willingness to cultivate many new crops as they became available to the New World from the Old World and vice versa. When cash cropping becomes an option, that is also undertaken. This willingness to cultivate a wide range of crops seems to be an attempt to spread the risk of local failure by relying on crops that are subject to different limiting factors, such as soil quality, precipitation, temperature, and insect pests. Some examples are the use of barley as opposed to wheat in areas of high soil salinity (Gibson 1974) and the planting of potatoes in wetter areas and wheat in drier locales (Messenger 1969). Another example is the planting of different varieties of maize with varying maturation rates and levels of drought and wind resistance. This strategy is a form of protection against variations in growing season length, precipitation, and wind strength (discussed by Bradfield 1971; Cordell 1984; Hack 1942).

The nutritional qualities of the major staple crops used by the societies in this research are reviewed by Haas and Harrison (1977). Wheat, which is the major staple cereal of the domestic-animal-using groups under study, seems to present fewer nutritional problems related to protein-energy malnutrition and vitamin deficiencies than diets based on either rice or maize. According to Haas and Harrison (1977), this is partly because wheat diets are more often supplemented with animal products and other foods than rice or corn diets. They do find that diets based on unrefined wheat consumed in large quantities (50-70% of energy intake), as in some parts of rural Iran, may pose a problem with mineral absorption. The phytate found in the unrefined wheat combines with calcium, iron, and zinc to produce compounds that are poorly absorbed. This poor absorption can lead to rickets, osteomalacia, hypogonadal dwarfism from zinc deficiency, and iron-deficiency anemia. The solution is better refining techniques to remove a larger percentage of the phytate from the wheat kernel.

The chief limitation of rice-based diets lies in the quantity of protein, which may be insufficient to meet the needs of a growing child. Protein quality may also be a problem. Milling and washing also remove protein and water-soluble vitamins, such as thiamine. Thus, beriberi and protein-energy malnutrition may be present in populations that subsist on milled rice. Consumption of meat, fish, and vegetable products with the rice and parboiling before milling can help to alleviate these problems.

The nutritional problems of maize-based diets have been examined by Santley and Rose (1979) as well as by Haas and Harrison (1977), among others. Pellagra can be a problem for groups that are reliant on maize, since the protein component of maize is fairly low in the amino acids lysine and tryptophan and high in leucine. Corn is also relatively low in nicotinic acid, most of which is in a form that cannot be utilized. The protein value of maize-based diets can be improved by processing the maize with lime and by consuming meat and beans, whose amino acid make-up complements that of maize. Thus, the cereal staples do provide adequate nutrition when they are properly processed and consumed in conjunction with some meat and other foods.

Farming Techniques and Land-use Systems

This portion of the economic model for village farmers with cattle, sheep, goats, pigs, or llamas examines the farming techniques and land-use systems used to produce the mix of cereal staples and other crops discussed above. Both Rindos's work (1984) and the ethnographic information used in this study (Table 4) indicate that these farmers generally maintain monocultural cereal fields. They devote separate fields to the cultivation of the different staple grains. Exceptions to this pattern include Mediterranean interculture of cereals, figs, olives, and vines; another occurs when outfields are extensively cultivated without the use of a plow or when planting is done by hand. In these cases, cereals are interplanted with other cereals, root crops, beans, or peanuts. Reported combinations are guinea corn and late millet for the Tallensi (Lynn 1937), maize and camotes for the Ifugao (Barton 1922), millet and peanuts for the Bambara (Paques 1954), and corn and beans for the Zuni (Bunzel 1932). The Zuni fields are not extensively cultivated but the cornfields are planted by hand, so they are discussed here. These interplanted cereal fields are secondary in importance to the main cereal fields, which are planted in monocultural plots. The main staples in these cases are paddy rice or wheat. According to the information gained from these examples, it appears that interplanting is inconsistent with use of the plow and broadcast sowing. Interplanting is apparently used as a means of buffering by crop diversification in the extensively cultivated, or long-fallow, fields. Its role as a means of maintaining soil fertility in extensively cultivated fields is unclear. These fields are generally quite fertile in the first seasons of cultivation, and no other means of increasing fertility is needed. The planting of corn and beans together in the Zuni fields, which are not extensive, is a measure used to replenish soil fertility. This technique is discussed in a later section on non-animal cropping systems.

The land-use systems of domestic-animal-using groups summarized below are drawn from the following sources on the studied ethnographic groups, unless otherwise cited: Barton (1922), Berque (1955), Covarrubias (1938), Evans (1942), Faron (1961), Graham (1937a, 1937b), Halpern (1958), Krishna Iyer (1948), Leakey (1953), Lynn (1937), Masters (1953), Mikesell (1961), Paques (1954), and Rowe (1946). Information from these studies is used to develop the following generalized descriptive model.

The small sample that was examined does not indicate significant differentiation in land-use systems on the basis of climate or geography. The agricultural field systems used by these groups fall into two major, related types. The first consists of small, continuously cropped dooryard gardens; intensively cultivated infields; and extensively cultivated outfields. Animals are pastured in special pasture areas but are also allowed to graze the infield and outfield areas after the harvest. The second consists of small, continuously cropped dooryard gardens; intensively cultivated infields, which may also be continuously cropped; and less extensively cultivated outfields. Among some groups the outfields have completely disappeared. Animals are still pastured in special areas in these subsistence farming systems, often in mountainous or hilly lands that are unsuitable for agriculture. The animals are also allowed to graze the stubble fields after harvest.

The most common trend seen in these systems is a gradual disappearance of the outfields and a growing intensity in cultivation of the infields. Apparently, the single most important factor conditioning the disappearance of the outfield is an absence of sufficient land, in these cases owing to growing population. The Serbian example reports infields and newly cleared, extensively cultivated outfields in the 1800s. With the founding of more villages, the outfields disappeared and the infields are now cropped continuously (Halpern 1958). The Irish examples describe continuously cropped infields and outfields under short or alternate-year fallow (Evans 1942). Both the Kurds (Masters 1953) and the Shluh (Berque 1955) report intensively cultivated infields, no outfields, and land shortages. The three African groups, the Kikuyu (Leakey 1953), Tallensi (Lynn 1937), and Bambara (Paques 1954), report infields that are fairly intensively cultivated and extensive outfields under slash-and-burn long fallow. These areas generally do not exhibit land constriction, though the Tallensi area is reported to be reaching a point of overpopulation for the type of shifting farming that is practiced (Fortes and Fortes 1936).

The size of agricultural plots, the total number of plots or amount of land owned or used by a family, and the distance of that land from the community are topics of considerable interest to this study. These factors are important to agricultural productivity and are affected by the presence or absence of domesticated animals. The quality of information on these topics is quite variable, however. Infields and outfields belonging to the same family are often reported as being scattered over a fairly wide area. This dispersion seems to be the result of division upon inheritance and piecemeal accretion of properties. Scattered plots in the American Southwest are considered to represent strategies of adaptation to patchy precipitation, temperature vagaries, and differential soil quality, and the desire to maintain the purity of different strains of corn (Bradfield 1971; Hack 1942). In areas of more uniform precipitation and temperature, scattered fields may aid in evening out plots of varying soil quality among the different families and in curtailing crop diseases. They may also be the result of taking into account the distinct soil quality requirements of different crops.

Information on distance of garden, infield, and outfield areas from the community is usually not quantified. The gardens are located within the communities or immediately adjacent to them, infields are reported as being located in close proximity to communities, whereas outfields vary in their distance from the home community. Tallensi outfields are located a mile or two from the compound (Lynn 1937); Ifugao outfields are "an hour's walk" from the village (Barton 1922). Specific distances or times are not listed for the other groups.

Of particular significance for this study is information presented by Bradfield (1971) on the effects of the introduction of draft animals (and later the pick-up truck) and the plow to the Hopi. In his opinion, the introduction of animals and the plow enabled the Hopi to abandon marginal land under worsening climatic conditions in favor of better lands located farther from the village. The draft animals and plow also enabled the Hopi to group fields on the better lands into larger, more economical holdings. Hopi fields currently may lie 8, 10, or even 20 miles from the village. Without the animals, Bradfield argues that they could not realistically have been located much more than 4 miles from the village. This figure is based on the amount of time needed to transport the entire crop back to the village before the onset of the damaging November rains. Bradfield estimates that this process would take approximately six weeks, if a man and his family brought in 20 bushels of corn a week from a 10-acre field, yielding a total production of 3 tons. He figures that approximately 10-12 acres are needed to produce sufficient corn for a family for one year. This estimate seems somewhat high, but it is used here because it is the figure suggested by Bradfield. Pedestrian harvest parties might cut the transport time down somewhat, but it would probably not be a significant reduction since all participants' crops would have to be transported. Thus, the presence of draft animals allows fields to be located over a considerably larger area than was possible without the animals. This much wider selection of land can serve as a buffer for climatic problems and for declines in soil fertility in certain fields. Of course, these more distant lands must be in areas not occupied by other groups.

The Hopi information (Bradfield 1971) indicates that amount of agricultural land may increase when draft animals are used for plowing. This information is explored in greater detail in the following sections of this chapter. Some provocative information comes to light when the ethnographic groups that possess animals but do not use the plow are examined. Plot size itself does not seem to be particularly affected by plow use as reported from this very small sample. Plot sizes range from a minimum of a quarter-acre. When plot sizes are small, farmers usually own many plots, which are often scattered. The Irish example mentions that one farmer owned 32 different plots of about 0.25 acres each for a total landholding of 8 acres (Evans 1942). A difference can be seen in the total landholding between plow-using and non-plow-using groups, however. For the plow-using groups, quantified data on total lands owned is available for the Irish (Evans 1942; Messenger 1969), Serbs (Halpern 1958), Shluh (Berque 1955), and Mapuche (Faron 1961; Titiev 1951). The Irish report an average of 15.7 acres, with farmers who own less than 4 acres considered landless. The Serbian average is 25-37.5 acres, with owners of 12.5 acres and under considered poor. The Shluh consider a family with 20 acres to be "weak." A chief would own in the neighborhood of 360 acres. The Mapuche landholdings range from 5 to 15 acres, with the lower end of the scale considered small. These variable landholding sizes among societies relate to many factors, including land quality, length of fallow and amount of land in fallow, and the social and economic requirements placed on the landholder. An average of the lowest acreages for each of the groups yields a figure of 16.4 acres, but a less conservative estimate could be considerably higher. This figure can be compared to the average suggested for two of the non-plow-using groups, the Tallensi (Lynn 1937) and the Kikuyu (Leakey 1953). These cultivators have major extensive components to their agricultural systems and an average landholding of about 3 acres. These figures lend credence to the view that plow-using farmers do cultivate more land. These numbers will be compared to field size estimates for the New World agriculturalists who did not possess draft animals in the section on subsistence farmers without animals.

Irrigation and Maintenance of Fertility

In general, the following techniques are used to farm the gardens, infields, and outfields of the mixed farmers. This information is summarized from the previously cited list of references. Dooryard gardens are the most intensively cultivated of the field types. They are manured first, irrigated by hand if necessary, and cropped continuously if climate permits. The produce from these gardens becomes very important in times of general crop failure. Infields come next in the amount of time and effort devoted to their care. Infields are located so they can be irrigated, if irrigation is practiced. They are either floodwater-farmed or under flow irrigation. Crop rotation is often, but not always, practiced on these fields. They may be continuously cropped, fallowed for six months, or under a regime of alternate-year fallowing. If manure remains after the gardens have been fertilized, it is applied to the infields. If the infields are fallowed for any amount of time, the animals are allowed to graze them. In any event, they graze the stubble fields after harvest. These practices also add manure to the fields.

Manuring is not equally important for all types of fields. It is most critical for rainfall-farmed lands under continuous cropping or alternate-year fallow, such as those worked by the Irish and the Serbians (Evans 1942; Halpern 1958). Fields that are inundated by floodwater or under flow irrigation receive nutrients and fresh soil in

solution from the waters flooding or irrigating them (Bradfield 1971; Gibson 1974; Hack 1942). Thus, manuring is not as critical for these lands, but it is reported. The Shluh (Berque 1955), Rif (Mikesell 1961), Mapuche of the north (Faron 1961), and Inca (Rowe 1946) all report manuring of lands under flow irrigation. Manuring is not reported for fields that are annually or periodically inundated by floodwater. Perhaps this type of flooding brings in a greater amount of nutrient-bearing new soil so fertilization is completely unnecessary. The main manuring strategies are discussed in detail in Chapter 5.

The outfields are either extensive fields under long or bush fallow as described by Boserup (1965), or they are simply less intensively tended fields located farther from the community. The latter is the case with the majority of the groups under study. In irrigation systems, the outfields are often located away from the water source and are dry farmed. In all the cases studied, the outfields are dry farmed and fallowed on an alternate-year or somewhat longer basis. Animals are allowed to graze these fields when they are not in production. Fields ready to be cultivated are also manured if there is sufficient manure for them. The Irish pen animals sequentially over outfield plots due for cultivation (Evans 1942).

Use of Animals for Traction and Plowing

One other aspect of the mixed farming technology will be reviewed here: use of the plow and draft animals, which were not present in the New World systems prior to European contact. Two aspects of the presence of the plow and draft animals have already been discussed under field size and distance from the community. The use of draft animals for transport to and from fields and to bring crops in from fields allows the selection of plots at a greater distance from the community. The plow also seems to facilitate the cultivation of larger landholdings. In addition, use of the metal-tipped plow enables the cultivation of heavier soils and the breaking up of heavier ground cover, such as dense prairie grasses (Barker 1985; Sherratt 1981). This technology was of importance in the expansion of European village farming groups onto heavier soils after the introduction of the plow. This type of land is not a limiting factor for agricultural expansion in all areas, but it does seem to have presented difficulties for the Middle Mississippian system in the Cahokia area, which was experiencing land constriction (Kelly et al. 1984) and was unable to expand farming onto the heavier, non-floodplain soils. Thus, when certain types of heavy, densely covered lands are present, the plow becomes a necessary adjunct to agricultural expansion.

Summary

This paragraph serves as a brief summary of the information presented above on the farming system and land-use patterns of mixed agriculturalists. These groups rely primarily on a variety of different cereal staples that are generally grown in monocultural plots. Interplanted vegetable gardens are present, and certain groups have some long-fallow, interplanted fields. Agricultural fields consist of dooryard gardens, infields, and outfields. Outfields may simply be dry-farmed fields that are more distant from the community and less intensively tended, or they may be true extensive fields under long or bush fallow. Infields are manured and irrigated, if necessary. They are under regimes of continuous cropping, six-month fallow, or alternate-year fallow. With the major exceptions of the African groups and the Inca, the mixed farmers under study use draft animals and the plow on landholdings conservatively estimated to average 16.4 acres. These fields are located at varying distances from the home villages on light or heavy soils.

The remainder of the economic model for mixed farmers is now presented. It deals with the importance of wild game to these societies, the ways in which domesticated animals are integrated into the mixed farming economy, and the many ways in which domesticated animals contribute to this type of economy. The economic role of trade and interaction with other groups is also explored.

The Role of Hunted Game

Both the archaeological (Chapter 2) and ethnographic (Table 4) sources examined for this research are used to study the importance of wild game to mixed farming economies. This study does not examine the role of fish in any great detail or groups that are heavily reliant on fish, as discussed previously. The purpose of this study is to examine the contributions of domesticated animals, one of which is as a source of protein, to these mixed farming groups. Because groups that are heavily reliant on fish have an added source of protein that could diminish the need for the contribution of domesticated animals, this difference might skew the results of a study of the role of domesticated animals. Thus, these groups were not included in this study.

The ethnographic information discusses the importance of hunting to fairly recent subsistence farming cultures, whereas the archaeological information allows study of the changing role of hunted resources through time. Both sets of information seem to present the same conclusion, however. The economic importance of hunted game declines as agriculture becomes more intensified among groups that possess domesticated animals. Two cases that vary somewhat from this pattern are discussed separately.

The ethnographic information concerning wild resources is reviewed in Chapter 5. As discussed in that chapter, the sources examined indicate that wild resources are not a major economic input for the studied groups (Table 4). Only one of the groups reports hunted game as an important economic resource. This group, the Ifugao (Barton 1922), has an extensive farming component, which tends to preserve the advantage of game availability (Harris 1977). The three African groups with extensive farming

components to their agricultural systems report minimal inputs from hunted resources (Murdock 1967), as do the other societies that do not farm extensive fields.

The archaeological information is of particular interest because it enables examination of changes through time in the role of wild game resources. This information begins with the first village farmers in an area and continues through varying levels of growing social complexity and agricultural intensification up to the appearance of the state. Thus, this body of data provides an excellent means of examining changing patterns of wild game use throughout the periods of interest.

The eleven archaeological sequences with domesticated animals fall into three categories with respect to the use of hunted game. Five of the sequences show that domesticated animals represent the primary faunal component from the time of the Early Neolithic. After the advent of mixed farming, wild game is of minor importance in these five areas: southern Britain (Legge 1981), south-central Bulgaria (Barker 1985; Dennell 1978), Thessaly (Barker 1985; Renfrew 1972), southern Mesopotamia (Redman 1978), and the Indus River system of Pakistan (Jarrige and Meadow 1980; Meadow 1979). Four of the remaining sequences show hunted game as an important resource for the earliest village farmers; however, by Middle and Late Neolithic times the role of wild game declined to one of minor importance, as it did in the other grouping. These areas are the Carpathian Basin (Barker 1985), Konya Plain (Mellaart 1967b; Perkins 1969; Redman 1978), northern Mesopotamia (Bokonyi 1973; Mellaart 1975; Oates 1973; Redman 1978), and Upper Egypt (Hoffman 1979). The third grouping consists of the Ayacucho Basin of Peru (MacNeish et al. 1980) and northern China (Chang 1977; Wenke 1980). In these two areas, hunted game retains a significant role, though a gradually declining one, throughout the time period of interest to this study. Even in these two areas, however, the domesticated animals are of primary importance.

The two larger groupings are examined first to determine if it is possible to understand why one category has an early reliance on hunting but the other does not. Since extensive, slash-and-burn farming is often associated with greater game availability and use (Harris 1977), it is tempting to assume that the areas and time periods in which hunting is important were characterized by slash-and-burn farming systems. This does not seem to be the case, however. China is the only area for which initial slash-and-burn farming is suggested, and this system gave way to permanent fields in the immediately following periods (Chang 1977). Another reason for the reliance on hunted game in the Chinese region is suggested below. According to the most current views of the several researchers, however, all of the other areas under study were initially farmed with some form of fairly permanent fields. This research, with the appropriate references, is discussed in detail under the "Farming System" section of each sequence review in Chapter 2. Thus, a slash-and-burn farming system does not seem to be contributing to the importance of wild game in some areas. It is therefore not immediately apparent why some Early Neolithic villages had important hunting components and others did not. A detailed examination of the faunal components from each of the sites in the two categories might shed light on this question, but this type of examination is well beyond the scope of the present study.

The different use patterns shown by the Chinese and Peruvian groups are probably conditioned by the fact that the domesticated animals emphasized in these zones during the periods of interest were camelids and pigs (Chang 1977; MacNeish et al. 1980). Neither of these species fulfills all the roles that the other domesticates do. Pigs are useful as a meat source only; camelids serve as a source of meat and wool and as pack animals. Neither of these domesticates are suitable for traction and plowing, and neither were used as producers of secondary food products. This latter factor is probably the most important one conditioning the difference between the Chinese/Peruvian systems and all the others. Use of animal secondary products as food and protein sources is very important to mixed farmers, in many cases outweighing the importance of use of the meat itself (Sherratt 1981, 1983). The absence of secondary food products could lead to a continued reliance on hunted game as a subsidiary food and protein source. This inference seems to be borne out by the areas that evidence an early reliance on hunted game and a decline of the importance of this resource during the later Neolithic periods (Barker 1985; Bokonyi 1973; Hoffman 1979; Mellaart 1967b, 1975; Oates 1973; Perkins 1969; Redman 1978). The middle to late Neolithic periods are precisely when Sherratt (1981, 1983) argues for the initial use of animal secondary products. These resources may have replaced or lessened the need for hunted game to some degree at a time when game may have been declining in the area, anyway.

The decline of game availability and a concomitant decline in time to hunt with the intensification of agriculture are discussed in Chapter 5. The information examined here indicates that domesticated animals and their secondary products probably replaced hunted resources as these declines came into play. Along this line, it is interesting to note that hunting finally declined to a minor role in north China during the time of state-level societies (Chang 1977). At this later time, intensified irrigation agriculture was being practiced and primary reliance was on cattle and sheep, though pigs were still important. Wild resource use among the New World groups that were not able to use domesticated animals and their secondary products as a replacement resource is discussed in a later section of this chapter.

Domestic-Animal Management and Use

This study now turns to an examination of the ways in which domesticated animals are integrated into the village farming economy and their contributions to that economy. The domesticated animals emphasized in this discussion

are cattle, sheep, goats, and pigs. Of the archaeological and ethnographic cases used in this study, only the pre-contact Andean groups used llamas exclusively, and therefore these animals are not examined here. Their use is described in detail in Chapter 2. Table 6 lists the domesticated animals used by each of the other groups. The sources for the data in this table and for the following description of animal management are listed in Table 4 and Chapter 2.

Animals in subsistence farming economies are managed in the following manner. Cattle, sheep, and goats are allowed to graze or browse the stubble fields after harvest and the fields that are in fallow. In addition, they are often taken to feed in pasture areas near the village that are never used for cultivation. In some cases, seasonal transhumance is practiced. In these cases, all or a part of the group takes the animals to more distant lands for summer or winter pasturage. Animals are often moved to more distant regions when the fields are under cultivation. In this way, they can be fed without damaging or destroying growing crops (Hilger 1957). Some animals are penned or stalled during certain parts of the year; this is the case with very valuable animals, such as plow oxen. This practice also occurs when few animals are owned, or when the climate is seasonally severe.

The feeding requirements of pigs are different from those of cattle, sheep, and goats, since they are not primarily grazers or browsers. They prefer tubers, grains, or such plants as clover (Barker 1985). They root in unculti-vated forest areas or on lands under long fallow, serve as village scavengers, or are fed grain. They are fed and maintained within or near the community.

The following paragraphs examine the use patterns of cattle, sheep, goats, and pigs among the various archaeo-logical and ethnographic cases under study. The discussion focuses on why certain domesticated animals are used by some groups but not by others. It also explores why certain animals are more important than others to the different groups and why these roles may change through time. Change through time is examined using the archaeological information. Climatic variations, differences in farming systems, and changes in the farming system through time are seen as the major conditioners of which domesticated animals are the most important in a given area at a given time.

Table 6 indicates that all of the archaeological cases show evidence of the presence of cattle, sheep, goats, and pigs. All of the ethnographic cases also record the presence of cattle, but not necessarily of sheep, goats, or pigs. The widespread presence of cattle seems to be an indicator of the importance of these animals as producers of food products and as sources of animal power for plowing and transport. Sheep and goats are also important as producers of food products and other secondary products, such as fleece, but are not useful as sources of animal power. Sheep are absent among the Ifugao and Balinese, and goats are also absent among the Balinese. In addi-

Table 6. Domesticated Animals Used by the Archaeological and Ethnographic Groups

	Cattle	Sheep	Goats	Pigs
Archaeological Groups				
Southern Britain	X	X	X	X
Central Europe	X	X	X	X
Southeastern Europe	X	X	X	X
Thessaly	X	X	X	X
Anatolia	X	X	X	X
Northern Mesopotamia	X	X	X	X
Southern Mesopotamia	X	X	X	X
Upper Egypt	X	X	X	X
Pakistan	X	X	X	X
Northern China	X	X	X	X
Ethnographic Groups				
Bambara	X	X	X	
Kikuyu	X	X	X	
Tallensi	X	X	X	
Ifugao	X		X	X
Balinese	X			X
Miao	X	X	X	X
Coorg	X	X	X	X
Rural Irish	X	X	X	X
Serbs	X	X	X	X
Kurds	X	X	X	
Shluh	X	X	X	
Rif	X	X	X	X
Mapuche	X	X		X
Zuni	X	X	X	X

tion, goats are not mentioned for the Mapuche. The absence of sheep and goats among the Balinese may relate to an absence of grazing lands on this island with its dense population and small, crowded rice paddies (Covarrubias 1938). In this case, they selected to graze cattle rather than sheep and goats. The Ifugao lands are rugged and mountainous with paddy ricefields planted in the more level areas. There are also slash-and-burn sweet potato fields under long fallow, which are more suitable for browsing goats than for sheep (Barton 1922) and apparently explains the presence of goats but absence of sheep. In the case of the Mapuche the absence of goats is less clear and may simply represent a lack of discussion of the presence of these animals. This group does use wool extensively in trade; they are also poor and presumably prefer to put their scant resources into sheep, from which they receive a greater return.

The use of pigs follows a different pattern from that of cattle, sheep, and goats, because their feeding and environmental requirements are different. Five of the ethnographic societies used in this study do not report the use of pigs: the Bambara, Kikuyu, Tallensi, Shluh, and Kurds. The Bambara, Kikuyu, and Tallensi are African groups for which the absence of pigs may be the result of historical and climatological factors. These areas have pronounced rainy and dry seasons with the real possibility of drought and water shortages during the dry season (Fortes and Fortes 1936; Lynn 1937; Paques 1954). The moisture-loving pig would not fare well in this type of rainfall regime, as discussed below.

Both the Kurds and the Shluh presently have settled village components as well as nomadic components within their cultural groupings. The more settled sections of these systems seem to be fairly recent developments, however (Berque 1955; Masters 1953). As discussed by Harris (1977), pig raising is not prevalent and the eating of pork is often prohibited in the great pastoral zones of the Old World, stretching from North Africa across the Middle East and Central Asia. Pig raising is not compatible with pastoral nomadism or with transhumance.

Pigs are also not well adapted to these arid grassland regions. Presently, pigs are raised by some groups in these areas, but they are far from the main domesticate.

Since pigs do not sweat, they are not well adapted to direct sunlight or hot, arid conditions. They need external sources of moisture to regulate their body temperature. Thus, they are well suited to moist, mild areas. Among subsistence farming groups, pigs are particularly appropriate to areas with nearby, uncultivated forest lands or fields under long, forest fallow, since they feed on roots and tubers. Pigs are important sources of meat and protein in China, Southeast Asia, Indonesia, and Melanesia (Harris 1977).

This geographic distribution is borne out by the societies used in this research. Of these groups, pigs are or were especially important domesticates to the northern Chinese groups, the Balinese, the Ifugao, the Miao, and the Coorg. All these groups except the northern Chinese are rice agriculturalists, generally exhibiting an additional extensive component to the farming system. Large areas of grazing lands are present only in China. During the time of the greatest importance of pigs in northern China, millet was the primary grain crop and shifting farming was practiced (Chang 1977), which fits well with pig raising.

Harris (1977) presents a pertinent discussion of the declining role of pigs in certain world areas. He correlates this decline with the disappearance of extensively farmed fields or virgin, uncultivated zones under conditions of agricultural intensification. This decline occurs especially rapidly in hot, arid climates. Disappearance of these lands removed the efficient, natural feeding areas for pigs. They then had to be provided with produced feed or village waste, as well as man-made, moist, cool living areas. According to Harris's argument (1977), this type of treatment is likely to be more costly than the return would justify from an animal that can only be used as a meat source. Pigs decline in importance in the more arid regions at the close of the Neolithic, when growing populations and growing agricultural intensification are evident. The rise in importance of domesticated animals as producers of secondary products and as sources of animal power for traction and plowing is correlated with the decline in the importance of the pig. Harris (1977) discusses the decline and virtual disappearance of the pig as a resource in Egypt, southern Mesopotamia, and the Indus. This decline is borne out by the archaeological information on these sequences, discussed in Chapter 2. Pigs remain important in cool, moist areas or in areas with very limited grazing lands, such as the areas of intensive, paddy rice cultivation.

The archaeological sequences also shed light on the changing roles of cattle, sheep, and goats. Again, archaeological information is particularly valuable because it enables examination of changes in the use patterns of these animals through time. The following information is taken from eight of the archaeological sequences with

Table 7. The Importance of Cattle, Sheep, and Goats in the Archaeological Sequences

Sheep and Goats Most Important Throughout the Time of Interest

> Southeastern Europe
> Northern Mesopotamia

Cattle Most Important Throughout the Time of Interest

> Southern Britain
> Anatolia
> Southern Mesopotamia
> Pakistan

Changing Importance from Sheep/Goats to Cattle and Finally to Sheep Throughout the Time of Interest

> Central Europe
> Thessaly

domesticated animals listed in Table 2 and discussed in Chapter 2. Peru is not included in this examination because cattle, sheep, and goats were not used by the pre-contact Andean groups. Upper Egypt and northern China are also excluded because the information used in this study does not include figures on the differences in importance among these animals for these two areas.

Cattle, sheep, and goats are present in all eight areas, but their primacy varies both geographically and temporally. The reasons discussed here for these variations are tentative and somewhat subjective. They have been suggested by the major researchers of each of the sequences reviewed in Chapter 2. Variations in environment and farming system are suggested as the primary conditioners of shifting emphasis on these different domesticated animals. The questions of which animals are native to a region and may have been domesticated locally or first are not really emphasized by these researchers.

Three major use patterns can be discerned from the groups that were examined (Table 7). Sheep and goats remain the most important animal domesticates throughout the pre-state farming period in the Bulgarian sequence of southeastern Europe and in northern Mesopotamia. Cattle were also very important, but they were outnumbered, especially by sheep. Sheep were always the prime animals in southeastern Europe and increased significantly in proportion to goats through time in northern Mesopotamia (Barker 1985; Dennell 1978; Oates 1973; Redman 1978). Researchers in these areas suggest that these regions evidenced fairly early clearance of many permanent fields, resulting in more cleared, open grazing lands. Animals grazed stubble fields and fields under short fallow. These conditions are more favorable for sheep than for goats, which prefer the browse of uncultivated areas and long-fallow fields (Barker 1985; Dennell 1978; Oates 1973; Redman 1978). The importance of wool as a secondary product may also have been a factor contributing to the importance of the flocks (Sherratt 1981, 1983).

Another use pattern, one in which cattle are the major domesticate throughout village farming times, is present in southern Britain, Anatolia, southern Mesopotamia, and Pakistan. Various reasons are suggested for the primacy of cattle in these areas. The ability of these animals to adapt to a hot, dry climate is suggested as a reason for their ascendancy in southern Mesopotamia (Redman 1978). Of course, this is not the case in mild, moist southern Britain. The main suggestions for the importance of cattle in all areas are use of their secondary products and use of their traction potential for plowing and transport (Barker 1985; Cohen 1970; Meadow 1979; Mellaart 1967b; Redman 1978). As Sherratt argues (1981, 1983), however, the use of animals for secondary products and as sources of power is not well documented until the Middle and Late Neolithic. Though some Early Neolithic use of secondary products and the plow may have occurred (Meadow 1979; Sherratt 1983), they were probably not common occurrences. Among the small sample used here, all the areas of early primacy of cattle, except southern Mesopotamia, are areas in which cattle are native and were domesticated locally (Barker 1985; Cohen 1970; Meadow 1979; Mellaart 1967b). This fact may help to explain their majority in the Early Neolithic somewhat better than heavy reliance on secondary products or use of the animals as power sources. Their early importance in southern Mesopotamia does seem to relate to their ability to adapt to the hot climate (Redman 1978).

The third use pattern consists of the early importance of sheep and goats with a switch to cattle during the Middle and later Neolithic periods and a return to sheep during the Final Neolithic and Bronze Age. This pattern occurs in central Europe and Thessaly (Halstead 1981; Sherratt 1982). Halstead (1981) and Sherratt (1982) are of the opinion that animals were grazing stubble fields under short fallow and small uncultivated patches during the earlier period. With the rise of the importance of cattle, they feel that cultivation may have expanded into some long-fallow fields, which provided more browse for additional cattle. The growing importance of sheep during the later periods is seen as a response to an increase in cleared lands in short or alternate-year fallow (Halstead 1981; Sherratt 1982). This type of cropping system provides excellent grazing lands for sheep in fairly close proximity to the community. The rising importance of sheep is also attributed to an increased demand for wool textiles for local use and for trade (Sherratt 1981, 1983).

The rising importance of sheep in the Late Neolithic and Bronze Age periods is not limited to Thessaly and central Europe. It is a common pattern that occurs in seven of the eight cases examined here. The exception is the Indus River area of Pakistan, for which no information is

available. In all the other areas, sheep rise in importance during the later pre-state and early state periods even though they may not be the most prevalent domesticated animal (Barker 1985; Cohen 1970; Dennell 1978; Mellaart 1967b; Oates 1973; Redman 1978). The rising importance of sheep is related to the increased importance of secondary products, such as wool. It is also related to the more open landscape created by increased clearance of farmland and more intensive cultivation of that land. This type of cropping system deemphasizes the secondary browse preferred by goats and cattle while emphasizing the short graze used by sheep. Ultimately, the growing importance of this domesticate is related to increasing population, agricultural intensification, and intensification of trade in such products as woolen goods (Sherratt 1981, 1983).

Economic Contributions of Domesticated Animals

The economic contributions of all of these domesticated animals and their secondary products are discussed in detail in Chapter 5. They are briefly reviewed here. Four use categories were determined for the animals from the ethnographic information discussed in Chapter 5: (a) consumption of meat and animal by-products, (b) use of dung as fertilizer, (c) use of animal traction for transport and plowing, and (d) use of animals as a means of amassing wealth, as a back-up resource in lean times, and as a form of live storage. These uses indicate the central value of domesticated animals as economic system buffers or spreaders of the risk of agricultural failure. As discussed by Flannery (1969), by Halstead and O'Shea (1982), and in Chapter 5, animals serve as added resources, as a means of diversifying the resource base in order to spread the risk of crop failure, and as means of spreading the risk of storage loss. When they are amassed as wealth, they are available in times of emergency for conversion into food either directly or indirectly through trade. Use of their manure adds fertility to certain lands that might otherwise be marginal or sufficiently unproductive that they would have to be abandoned. Use of animal power in traction and plowing aids in risk reduction by facilitating the cultivation of greater amounts of land and by allowing a wider range of field selection since more distant fields can be used. These buffering mechanisms function along with other previously mentioned buffers, such as crop diversification and diversification of field locations. Other suggested buffering techniques, such as rising social complexity (Halstead and O'Shea 1982), are discussed with the section on societies that do not have domesticated animals to use as risk-reduction mechanisms.

Intercommunity Trade and Interaction

The final phase of this economic description of systems with medium to large domesticated animals concerns intercommunity trade and interaction, which also serve as economic buffering mechanisms. Trade and social interaction among groups in zones characterized by different climates, topography, and biotic communities can have various functions. This trade can serve as a means of providing desired luxury goods in times of abundance, as well as keeping channels open to obtain more basic necessities in times of economic stress (discussed by Halstead and O'Shea 1982). The importance of domesticated animals in trade and transport is emphasized in this discussion. Three aspects of the contributions of domesticated animals are examined here: the actual trade of the animals and their edible and nonedible by-products, trade of such goods as textiles manufactured from animal products, and use of animal power to transport goods to be traded.

The actual exchange of domesticated animals and their secondary products is extremely important to subsistence-level farming groups, as indicated by both the ethnographic and the archaeological information used here. An example of this importance comes from research conducted by Sherratt (1982). An examination of archaeological data led him to suggest that cattle trading was a very important economic component of the early agricultural communities of the Konya Plain, Thessaly, and the Carpathian Basin. In the Carpathian Basin, exchange occurred over a 100-150 km arc and was facilitated by the ability of the livestock to walk considerable distances. Cattle fairs may also have been held; this suggestion is based on ethnographic analogy between enclosure structures found in the archaeological remains and the occurrence of these structures at historical fairs. Desired goods, such as obsidian and fine pottery from the highlands, were exchanged for cattle from the lowlands (Sherratt 1982). Other subsistence products may have formed a part of this exchange, and it probably also served as a means of maintaining open social ties between upland and lowland areas of differential productivity that could be tapped in times of economic stress (Halstead and O'Shea 1982; Sherratt 1982).

This suggested early importance of livestock trading is not at all surprising in light of the ethnographic information concerning the importance of domesticated animals as items of exchange. All of the 15 groups studied trade or sell domesticated animals and consider them one of their most important products (sources listed in Table 4). The following information on the trade and sale of animals is drawn from Fortes and Fortes (1936), Graham (1937a, 1937b), Halpern (1958), Middleton (1953), Mikesell (1961), and Paques (1954). In all the areas that use secondary animal products, products ranging from dairy products to raw wool are also traded or sold along with the animals. Domesticated animals are so highly valued as commodities that the rates of exchange are often set in terms of animals, as are dowry, bride price, fines, and loans. Spare money is invested in animals, and they are traded or sold in times of need. In the present day, they are one of the primary means of obtaining cash and are often the only form of wealth.

Animals are either taken to markets to be traded or taken directly to a specific group that traditionally purchases them. The latter is the case with the Kikuyu, who trade seasonally with the Masai and Wakemba to even out agricultural shortages. In times of bad harvests, they buy grain from the Wakemba using sheep, goats, cows, or ivory (Leakey 1953; Middleton 1953).

Domesticated animals fulfill social and kinship obligations, such as gift-giving, bride price, and dowry. When they are taken to market they are usually traded for money or, in times of emergency, for cereal staples. They are especially desirable because they serve not only as a prestige item but also as an edible resource.

Goods manufactured from animal products are also traded and sold. Woolen products are chief among these goods for many reasons. Their production and sale bring in extra resources while the animal remains intact. As discussed by Halstead and O'Shea (1982), the manufacture of woolen textiles allows maximum use of the flexibility of the sheep in its ability to provide either food in times of scarcity or the raw materials for crafts and manufactured goods in times of plenty. These manufactured items can then be used as prestige goods, which can be traded for basic subsistence goods should the need arise. Woolen textile production also does not take up fields that might otherwise be devoted to cereal staples, unlike the intensive production of flax or cotton. These factors may account for some of the growing popularity of woolen textiles as an item of exchange and social obligation under conditions of growing population and growing agricultural intensification.

Though use of woolen goods as manufactured items of trade reaches its greatest importance in the nation-state periods, it seems to be present and important in pre-state farming economies from at least the time of the Bronze Age (Sherratt 1982, 1983). The archaeological and ethnographic information examined here gives an indication of the enduring importance of wool. Of the eleven archaeological cases, ten report the use and eventual trade of woolen goods (Sherratt 1981; Chapter 2). No information is listed on this subject for the Indus system of Pakistan. The village farming level ethnographic cases also report the spinning and weaving of wool for local use and as craft production for the market. Of course, those groups that emphasize sheep are most active in this pursuit, including the Serbs, rural Irish, the Miao who live in sheep-producing areas, the Kurds, Shluh, Zuni, Mapuche, and Inca (Arensberg 1937; Berque 1955; Cushing 1920; Graham 1937a, 1937b; Halpern 1958; Hilger 1957; Leighton and Adair 1963; Masters 1953; Messenger 1969; Rowe 1946). For these groups as well as for more complexly organized preindustrial economies, woolen textiles serve as another means of amassing wealth and spreading the risk of storage loss and economic failure. Textiles are not subject to the same forms of loss as either grain crops or livestock. Thus, adding textiles to the repertoire of storable goods results in yet another measure of security by creating one more hedge against failure.

Another extremely important function of animals in trade and exchange is their use as a power source, serving as either draft or pack animals. In both cases, they enable the efficient transport of more goods over a wider area. This ability to widen the sphere of interaction and exchange in good times leads to a wider range of options for relief in bad times. More viable options for relief of stress in bad times lead to greater system security and stability. This impact is discussed by Santley and Alexander (1992) with reference to various forms of state-level territorial integration, but the point is still valid for less complexly organized systems. The amount of stress that can be buffered by a system depends in part on the scale or size of the system. Larger systems can bring more resources into the system center, leading to the creation of more work and a greater diversification of the local economic base, which in turn enhances the ability of the system center, or core, to deal with stress. One of the crucial factors determining system size is the major mode of transportation. As discussed by Santley and Alexander (1992), systems based on foot transport, such as that of the Aztecs, are generally small in geographic extent and have comparatively small capitals. They can import bulky subsistence commodities from a range of up to about 150 km; only exotics and luxury goods are imported from greater distances (Bedoian 1973, cited in Santley and Alexander 1992). Systems whose members use pack animals and carts can grow much larger and transport goods over a much wider distance. The Babylonian empire, which had a population of nearly 400,000 and stretched from Palestine to Iran, is used as an example of this type of system (Oates 1986, cited in Santley and Alexander 1992). If conditions are held equal, this type of system can buffer stress more effectively or buffer greater amounts of stress than a system of smaller dimension.

In summary, domesticated animals and their secondary products serve as highly valuable commodities in trade and exchange. Use of wool in textiles provides an easily storable cash-equivalent that can be redeemed for subsistence goods should the need arise. Finally, traction power allows the trade of more, bulkier goods over longer distances.

GROUPS WITHOUT DOMESTIC ANIMALS

The above section has examined various economic facets of subsistence-level farming groups with medium to large domesticated animals. These facets included the economic roles of agricultural crops and farming techniques, as well as patterns of land use, hunted resource use, and domesticated animal use. Trade and exchange have also been briefly reviewed. The following portions of this chapter examine these same categories for subsistence farmers without domesticated animals. Areas in which the absence of animals may have contributed to situations

of economic instability are discussed as each of the categories is reviewed. The role of increased social complexity in relieving episodes of economic stress is also suggested.

Agricultural Crops

Agricultural crops, farming techniques, and land-use patterns are examined first. The village farming societies without medium to large domesticated animals consist primarily of pre-contact New World groups that subsisted on the New World triad of corn, beans, and squash supplemented by a wide variety of other cultigens. As discussed in the earlier portions of this chapter, a maize-based diet can fulfill basic nutritional requirements if certain conditions are met: processing the maize with alkali (lye, lime, or wood ashes) before grinding, and consuming beans in conjunction with the maize. Consumption of additional vegetables and meat is also helpful. Lime processing of the maize has a beneficial effect on the availability of niacin and on the essential amino acid composition of the grain, and the amino acid composition of beans complements that of maize (discussed by Haas and Harrison 1977).

The New World agricultural groups placed their primary reliance on maize but buffered the possibility of cereal crop failure by planting different varieties of maize, as well as a long list of other cultigens. The crop lists for the highland Andean cultures document about 40 domesticates in use (Rowe 1946; Steward and Faron 1959). MacNeish (1967) lists 31 domesticates found in the Tehuacan sequence, including eight varieties of maize. Old World crop lists from northern Europe and the Mediterranean before the introduction of New World plants compare favorably with the New World lists in terms of the range of domesticates and the number of varieties of cereal grains that were grown. For example, northern European and Mediterranean groups were cultivating between 25 and 30 domesticates, including five forms of wheat and two of barley (Barker 1985). These lists do not include fruit trees other than olives and figs, which were only grown in the Mediterranean. Thus, agriculturalists in both the Old and New Worlds used crop diversity as a buffering mechanism. The absence of domesticated animals as an additional buffering agent does not seem to have caused the New World groups to buffer more intensively with domesticated plant foods than did their Old World counterparts. New World use of wild plant foods in this capacity will be examined in a later portion of this chapter.

Maintenance of Fertility

The agricultural systems without domesticated animals did not use animal traction plows or broadcast sowing. Information derived from ethnographic and ethnohistoric sources indicates that fields were planted by hand and were often interplanted (Bradfield 1971; Bunzel 1932;

Cordell 1984; Leighton and Adair 1963; Sanders et al. 1979; Stevenson 1904). Interplanting of corn, beans, and squash is discussed as a means of maintaining soil fertility when animal fertilizer is not available. The beans replace the soil's nitrogen, which has been removed by the grain crop. In addition, in the American Southwest seeds are planted by hand in small hills located to avoid the places where seeds were planted the previous season. Thus, a method of fallowing a field while that field is still in use is practiced (Cordell 1984; Cushing 1920; Hack 1942; Minnis 1981). The advantages of this type of interplanting system are maintenance of soil fertility without manuring and a probable reduction in the type of pest infestation that can afflict monoculturally planted fields (Rindos 1984). The disadvantage, especially under conditions of growing population and agricultural intensification, is lowered field productivity (Rindos 1984).

The highly intensive agricultural systems of Mesoamerica and the Andes undoubtedly also used monoculturally planted fields in some areas. These fields were in areas where fertility was renewed by manuring, as in the case of the Andean groups that used camelid and human manure as well as bird guano (Rowe 1946; Steward and Faron 1959). They could also occur in areas under flow irrigation, which also renews fertility by the addition of fresh soil and nutrients in solution (Gibson 1974; Sanders et al. 1979). Flow-irrigation systems in the New World ranged from the simple to the increasingly large and complex and were located in the Andean and Mesoamerican regions (Flannery and Marcus 1983; MacNeish et al. 1967; Rowe 1946; Sanders et al. 1979; Steward and Faron 1959). Only the more simple water-control techniques were combined with floodwater and arroyo-mouth farming in most of the Southwest. These farming systems also renew fertility as well as provide needed water (Bradfield 1971; Hack 1942; Lagasse et al. 1984). Other methods of maintaining fertility, such as fallowing and crop rotation, were also in use in the New World (Steward and Faron 1959).

The problems with these methods of maintaining fertility are that they inhibit productivity, rely on lands that are limited in extent, or both. The wide spacing of plants that is practiced in some Southwestern contexts as a means of increasing fertility is one such practice that lowers productivity. Lands that can be brought under flow irrigation or farmed using arroyo-mouth or floodwater farming techniques are not uniformly distributed across the landscape. Agriculturalists who can select only these lands for regular, intensive use will be more limited than those who can choose from the full range of available dry-farmed lands and boost productivity with fertilizer. Adding fertilizer to lands under flow irrigation also seems to provide a beneficial input and is commonly practiced (Berque 1955; Faron 1961; Mikesell 1961; Rowe 1946). This added fertility can be seen in a comparison of Peruvian lands under heavy fertilization with Mesoamerican lands that were not receiving inputs of animal manure. Steward and Faron (1959) estimate that the Inca could support a family on half an acre whereas at least

one acre was needed in Mesoamerica. These figures are for irrigated fields producing maize.

Soil fertility may also have been maintained on certain lands by the use of extensive farming techniques during the early periods of the establishment of farming villages in some areas of the New World (Sanders et al. 1979). Access to this type of land tends to decrease as populations grow, however (Boserup 1965). The decline in extensively farmed outfields was discussed earlier in this chapter using information from the ethnographic sources (Table 4). It is when the option of extensive farming disappears that manuring is needed to maintain fertility on the remaining dry-farmed lands that are undergoing shorter and shorter fallow periods. Thus, as growing populations demand more from the productive system, access to the special lands needed to meet those demands may decline. Shortages of high-quality land and food crops could occur under these conditions, unless other means of agricultural intensification were developed (Sanders et al. 1979). These conditions could indeed lead to economic stress and instability. Additional factors that might lead to economic stress and instability are discussed in the following section.

Agricultural Techniques and Land-use Systems

Ethnographic, ethnohistoric, and archaeological information has been used by New World researchers to explore patterns of pre-contact land use. Categories that roughly approximate those used to classify Old World systems include gardens, irrigated fields, and dry-farmed fields. In the Southwest, including Chaco, and in earlier times in the Tehuacan area, considerable emphasis was placed on floodwater and arroyo-mouth plots with no means of water control or irrigation in use (Judge et al. 1981; MacNeish 1967). During later times in the Chaco region, some canyon bottom fields were farmed using simple water-control techniques, such as manipulation of runoff (Judge et al. 1981). Dry-farmed plots were located in dune fields and on mesa tops (Hayes et al. 1981). As farming became more intensified, the Mesoamerican systems focused on irrigated fields located in the humid alluvium of the river floodplains, with dry-farmed fields occurring in the upper and middle piedmont zones (Flannery 1976; MacNeish 1967; Sanders et al. 1979). The latter may have been farmed extensively. Intensive drainage agriculture, as discussed by Sanders et al. (1979) for the Basin of Mexico, came into full use in the later periods of state-level integration and will be mentioned in a subsequent section.

The amount of land cultivated by farmers and the distance of that land from the community are more restricted for farmers without animals than for farmers with animals. Both sets of farmers report scattered plots owned by the same families or groups, but these plots are located closer to the villages and the total aggregate land is smaller in non-animal systems (Bradfield 1971; Hack 1942; Sanders et al. 1979). These differences are directly related to the absence of animal power in traction and plowing. As previously mentioned, Bradfield's (1971) discussion of Hopi farming before and after the introduction of animals indicates the input that traction animals have had in the ability to select more distant fields, owing to reduced transit time to and from fields and reduced transport time to bring the crop in. His paper also deals with the role plowing plays in the ability to cultivate more land in general (Bradfield 1971). This role of the plow is also mentioned by Sanders et al. (1979). The Hopi material also suggests that absence of the plow may have contributed to the buildup of soil salinity and to soil puddling, which led to the abandonment of fields in some areas. This problem can occur when slightly saline floodwater is used as a water source and turning of the soil with a plow is not possible (Stewart 1940, cited in Bradfield 1971).

The actual amount of land cultivated by the New World subsistence farmers without animals is generally estimated from ethnographic, ethnohistoric, and archaeological information. These estimates are based on amount of land cultivated, amount of maize produced per acre, amount of grain needed to support a household for a year, and amount of land that can be profitably worked without a plow (Bradfield 1971; Flannery 1976; Kirkby 1973; Sanders et al. 1979). In some cases, maize productivity figures have been calculated to account for the use of less productive varieties with smaller cobs earlier in the sequences (Kirkby 1973). Figures used here are from the Hopi Mesas (Bradfield 1971), the Basin of Mexico (Sanders et al. 1979), and the Valley of Oaxaca (Flannery 1976; Kirkby 1973) and are for dry-farmed fields. The Oaxaca figures are estimated for corn productivity at 1000 B.C. on the basis of cob sizes from archaeological contexts (Flannery 1976; Kirkby 1973); the other productivity estimates are based on modern maize. Sanders et al. (1979) argue that the pre-modern maize productivity figures from Oaxaca are too low and thus indicate a higher land requirement than necessary to support a household for a year. The Oaxaca figures are used here, but it should be borne in mind that these land requirements may be somewhat high for the humid alluvium of Oaxaca. The land requirements for the Hopi area are even higher than those for Oaxaca, but that may be due to the very marginal nature of the area for agriculture (Palkovich 1984). The Hopi information indicates that 10-12 acres are necessary to produce sufficient grain for a family of five to six for a year (Bradfield 1971). The Oaxaca estimates are 8.25 acres per household per year; those from the Basin of Mexico suggest that between 3.5 and 7 acres were needed to support an extended family of seven for a year (Flannery 1976; Kirkby 1973; Sanders et al. 1979). These figures yield an average of 7.25-9.1 acres for dry-farmed fields. Information from the Basin of Mexico for irrigated fields indicates that 1.75-3.5 acres could support a family for a year. These figures all show smaller acreages under cultivation for the non-plow-using

farmers than for the plow-using groups. The plow-using groups showed a low of 16.4 acres and a high of 22 acres for households (other than those of chiefs) using both irrigated and unirrigated lands. These groups can effectively cultivate somewhat more than twice as much land as the non-plow-using groups.

This review of farming systems without domesticated animals identifies several areas of potential agricultural risk. Especially under conditions of growing population or climatic perturbation, these areas of potential risk might indeed result in economic stress from limited or lowered productivity, which in turn could lead to economic and system instability. Possible problem areas identified by this research include the absence of animal manure to renew the fertility of nonextensive, dry-farmed fields. This disadvantage is compounded by the lack of traction and plow animals. The absence of draft and pack animals affects field selection by limiting the distance fields can be located from the home community. Fieldhouses extend the radius to some degree, but the crop must eventually be transported back to the security of (and to permit access by) the main community (Bradfield 1971). Absence of the plow reduces the amount of land that can be cultivated by about one-half in subsistence farming systems. Sanders et al. (1979) discuss the amount of land that can profitably be cultivated with hand tools and conclude that 5 hectares (12.5 acres) would be unprofitable to cultivate in terms of energy expended for return. Somewhere in the neighborhood of 2.5 hectares (6.25 acres) is considered more reasonable by contemporary hand cultivators (Sanders et al. 1979). The Hopi acreages are right at the upper limit of the amount it would be profitable to cultivate according to these calculations. The other groups are also near either the upper limit or the preferred one on their dry-farmed lands.

Thus, the absence of domesticated animals can limit the choice of land and the amount of land that can be cultivated. These limitations put crop productivity at greater risk from declining fertility and such microclimatic problems as patchy rainfall and hail damage. If less land is under cultivation, problems with any of the crops on that land are going to be felt more severely than if more land were under cultivation to serve as a buffer. As stated above, the estimates for cultivated land for these New World systems are all close to the maximum or preferred limit. More land cannot realistically be put under cultivation to enable greater productivity. The only way to buffer against crop failure by developing greater productivity is to intensify the agricultural system through various hydraulic techniques that also increase fertility and output. Some of these techniques were used in Mesoamerica during pre-state times. Others, such as intensive drainage agriculture, needed the administrative system of a state-level society to reach full development (Sanders et al. 1979). The ways in which complexly organized societies can help to buffer agricultural system and general economic risk are discussed in the concluding section.

The Role of Hunted and Gathered Resources

The use of wild resources among the New World groups without animals is examined in this section, followed by an examination of the role of trade and exchange in these societies. A cursory review of the archaeological and ethnographic information indicates that wild plant resources seem to play a slightly greater role in the New World than in the Old (Barker 1985; MacNeish 1967; Rowe 1946; Sanders et al. 1979). These groups may be using plant resources as an added food item to contribute to a "gap" left by the absence of the secondary products and the meat from domesticated animals. This certainly seems to be the case in regions with low population densities, such as the American Southwest, where these resources always played a subsistence role, especially as emergency and famine foods (Beaglehole 1937; Palmer 1871; Sebastian 1983). Ricegrass has always been particularly important in this respect (Palmer 1871). As population density rises, however, these foods fall to roles as minor contributors and supplements (Flannery and Marcus 1983; MacNeish 1967; Sanders et al. 1979).

An exception to this generalization is the suggested role of *Spirulina*, a proteinaceous algae collected from the lake and used as an important protein supplement during the Late Horizon in the Basin of Mexico (Santley and Rose 1979). Santley and Rose (1979) argue that *Spirulina* made a significant and necessary protein contribution to the Late Horizon diet in the basin. They feel that the addition of *Spirulina* to the diet brought it up to a level of adequate nutrition as measured by a resurgence of population growth, which had declined in the preceding periods. In a sense, *Spirulina* served as a replacement protein source for the animal protein that had been provided by wild game, which was no longer available in sufficient quantity.

This discussion of gathered food leads to a discussion of the major wild resource examined by this study, hunted game. As discussed in Chapter 5 and in an earlier section of this chapter, the role of hunted game declines with growing agricultural intensification (Murdock 1967). This fact seems to be related to the declining availability of game and the declining amount of time available for hunting as populations grow and agriculture becomes more time consuming. Intensification of agriculture also cuts down on the amount of land under long fallow and on uncultivated forest areas, which are favored locations of wild game (Harris 1977). Without the input of meat and edible secondary products from domesticates to replace declining wild game, nutritional problems can occur in some locales as agriculture is intensified.

The strongest cases for economic stress and instability related to declining animal protein come from the zones of highest population density, such as Mesoamerica. Santley and Rose (1979) present a detailed simulation and discussion of declining wild game availability and rising nutritional stress in the Basin of Mexico. The protein quality and availability problems are related to heavy reliance on maize and lessening availability of animal meat owing to the overexploitation of deer, which were the primary fauna. These problems continued until well after the period of state development and led to population stability as measured by lack of population growth. During the Late Horizon, changes in lake levels made the gathering and use of proteinaceous algae as a dietary supplement practical. During that time period, population growth began again. Santley and Rose (1979) attribute the renewed population growth to a return to an adequate diet owing to the use of *Spirulina*, which corrected the protein quality and abundance problems. Thus, during the periods prior to the use of *Spirulina*, the population was indeed suffering nutritional problems severe enough to disrupt population growth resulting from difficulties with protein quality and abundance.

Evidence for dietary stress related to maize-based diets and deficiencies in protein is not as clear cut in less populous areas, such as North America. The appearance of bone pathologies attributed to apparent dietary stress seems to occur in locations where several stressors come together. These stress factors include growing population, land constriction, mobility restriction, and climatic problems related to precipitation and length of growing season. The American Southwest is a prime example. Palkovich (1984) examines evidence for dietary disturbances among the Anasazi in the Southwest, which she considers a marginal environment for both agriculture and hunting and gathering. The following information is taken from her summary of dietary difficulties in the Southwest. Small hunter-gatherer groups buffered resource unpredictability by remaining highly mobile. The shift to agriculture involved population growth accompanied by decreased mobility and led to increasing problems in obtaining necessary resources. Even altered subsistence strategies involving the use of less desirable foods and the adoption of irrigation agriculture to buffer the diet met with only limited success (Wetterstrom 1976, cited in Palkovich 1984). "Apparently, continued population increase and a shift to a primary dependence on produced food served only to heighten the effects of environmental instability and to reduce resource predictability" (Palkovich 1984:427).

Palkovich (1984) focuses on information indicating nutritional stress in populations from Chaco Canyon and Arroyo Hondo, New Mexico. Both areas exhibit evidence for dietary stress in the form of protein-calorie malnutrition. She uses Wetterstrom's (1976) information from Arroyo Hondo to demonstrate that fluctuations in precipitation led to unpredictable agricultural yields and eventual abandonment of the pueblo. An important point from the skeletal study, however, is the information that dietary problems were apparent at Arroyo Hondo throughout the occupation — not just in drought years. They were simply heightened in drought years. "What were marginal protein-calorie diets in average years were virtually starvation diets in drought years" (Palkovich 1984:436). Information from the current research suggests that an insufficient input of animal protein could have exacerbated the problems of fluctuating agricultural productivity to produce marginal to inadequate levels of nutrition throughout the occupation of the pueblo.

Skeletal and faunal studies from other Southwestern sites corroborate this picture of dietary difficulties. The previously mentioned studies by Ferguson (1980) and Young (1980) indicate that obtaining adequate supplies of animal meat became more difficult under conditions of population growth and agricultural intensification in the Tijeras, Coconito, and San Antonio area of New Mexico. Evidence for this problem includes skeletal indications of possible iron-deficiency anemia and a change in hunting and animal-consumption patterns. The main fauna at these sites shifted from deer to the more distant antelope, and the combined frequency of small rodents showing evidence of consumption increased. These indicators show a tendency toward disrupted availability of wild game. These problems with resource acquisition led to the ultimate form of instability in some areas of the American Southwest — site and areal abandonments.

The more eastern North American areas are better watered and more productive for both wild and cultivated plants. In these areas, problems of resource inadequacy are more strongly related to population increases and land constriction than to drought and climatic perturbations. These areas are less marginal than the Southwest; some of them show evidence of resource acquisition problems whereas others do not. Generally, the areas with apparent resource acquisition problems are the zones of highest population and greatest constriction of prime, floodplain farmland. One such area is the American Bottom of the Middle Mississippi Valley, where agriculture is associated with population nucleation and the major center of Cahokia. In addition, natural food resources and agricultural soils are not as abundant in the American Bottom as in some of the other areas of the Mississippi River system, such as the Lower Mississippi Valley (Rose et al. 1984). Thus, stresses should be felt in this locale before they are felt in other locales. Milner's (1984) study of skeletal remains from sites in the American Bottom in proximity to Cahokia indicates the presence of stress, probably both from population aggregation and resultant exposure to density-dependent infectious diseases and from dietary deficiencies. Results of this study are summarized below. Milner's (1984) research discusses evidence of high infant mortality. One of the skeletal series, the Kane Mounds Group, also shows high mortality of young females from ages 15 to 30. This group was probably already stressed from child bearing and lactation. Several adolescent and adult crania show evidence of cribra orbitalia and porotic hyperostosis, which is taken to indicate iron-deficiency anemia (Steinbock 1976, cited in Milner 1984). These pathologies are healed, which indicates that they occurred at an early age. Milner (1984) suggests that perhaps chronic nutritional deficiencies in childhood resulted from poor diets during and immediately after the weaning period. He also

suggests that some of the bone pathologies may have been caused by infectious diseases resulting from population growth and aggregation, which culminated in the Cahokia center itself (Milner 1983).

Cook (1984) has studied settlements in the Lower Illinois Valley, which are considered to be satellites that interacted with Cahokia. She has identified bone pathologies in the skeletal remains from these sites that indicate the presence of yaws and tuberculosis. She is of the opinion that these afflictions may have been a significant disease burden for the population, and that they were probably caused by infection resulting from population nucleation rather than by poor nutrition (Cook 1984). Nevertheless, although increases in infectious diseases may reflect population aggregation and growth, they are also often aggravated by poor diet and nutritional problems (Roosevelt 1984).

Paleopathological data from several other areas in the midwestern and eastern United States show possible nutritional problems during the periods with the greatest dependence on agriculture. Information from Dickson Mounds in the Central Illinois Valley demonstrates that eight of ten indicators of stress (decreased ability to adapt biologically) increase through time in severity or frequency, becoming most severe in Mississippian times (Goodman et al. 1984). These eight indicators are (a) decreased age-specific long bone length and circumference, (b) increased frequency of enamel hypoplasias, (c) increased frequency of Wilson bands, (d) increased frequency of porotic hyperostosis, (e) increased frequency of infectious lesions, (f) increased frequency of degenerative lesions, (g) increased frequency of traumatic lesions, and (h) increased cumulative mortality (Goodman et al. 1984:297). The authors feel that these stress indicators represent nutritional deficiencies resulting from decreased quality of the diet and also increased infection rates resulting from increased population and sedentism. They also suggest that the Dickson Mounds people may have been participating in a larger interaction system centered on Cahokia and its satellites, which was exacting tribute from the local Dickson Mounds groups (Goodman et al. 1984). They suggest this relationship because the Central Illinois Valley is a very rich area that seems to be undergoing more severe health problems than should be occurring if all the potential local resources were being used by local groups (Goodman et al. 1984). It is not the purpose of this research to assess this view of resource loss to a more powerful system, but it should be borne in mind as a possibility.

Paleopathological studies from the Central Ohio River Valley, southwestern Ohio, and coastal Georgia also indicate declining health with the intensification of agriculture (Cassidy 1984; Larsen 1984; Perzigian et al. 1984). Evidence for protein-calorie malnutrition, often in the most vulnerable groups of weanlings and pregnant and lactating women, appears in these areas. The suggested causes are inadequate diet and infectious diseases.

The previously discussed decline in hunted resources under conditions of growing agricultural intensification could be an important contributing factor to the nutritional deficiencies seen in these areas. Cassidy's (1984) description of wild game acquisition in the Central Ohio River Valley shows a declining importance of wild game resources through time. Hunting was practiced throughout all time periods in the area, with deer being the favored animal. The dietary importance of animals declined as the early pattern of broad-spectrum seasonal exploitation was transformed to a pattern more narrowly focused on the local ecozones. By late prehistoric times, deer and other animals were merely supplementary to a cultivated diet of grain and legumes (Cassidy 1984:319). This pattern is also reflected in the Mississippian period information from the American Bottom. Deer were the largest animal present, but fish apparently provided the majority of the meat for daily consumption. Birds also increased considerably in importance during Mississippian times, especially waterfowl and wading birds. Several of the sites in the American Bottom study contained very scant faunal remains, although this dearth of material may be the result of poor preservation (Kelly and Cross 1984). The sites show a pattern of localized subsistence with an emphasis on aquatic habitats, which indicates that the dietary role of larger fauna, such as deer, may have been replaced by fish and waterfowl. Perhaps these smaller-size protein sources were not sufficient to meet the needs of all segments of the population. Dietary improvements for certain segments of the society under complexly organized systems are the focus of the concluding section of this chapter.

Intercommunity Trade and Interaction

This final section discussing the economic system of the New World pre-state farmers without domesticated animals examines the role of trade and interaction among these groups. A review of the contributions of domesticated animals to exchange, presented in the first portion of this chapter, shows just how important animals and their products are to trading systems. Their use as a means of transporting goods for exchange is equal in importance to their use as actual exchange items. Their absence removes a prime resource. They are truly the ultimate prestige good: not only are they highly valuable, but they can also be consumed. When times become difficult, animals do not have to be converted to food. They can be consumed directly. When they are used to keep an interaction network open in both times of plenty and times of stress, they never have to be devalued or removed from circulation as exotic offerings or burial goods to make room for new tokens to keep the system functioning. Animals can simply be consumed. In addition, animal transport extends the radius over which goods can be traded and enlarges the amount that can be traded. The trading of more goods over a wider area can buffer system stresses more effectively (Santley and Alexander 1992).

Post-contact New World groups were quick to see the advantages of domesticated animals and incorporate them into their trading systems. Information on widening trade and interaction networks as a result of the presence of domesticated animals comes from the Zuni ethnographic record (Leighton and Adair 1963). This information discusses broadening of the Zuni economic base with animals introduced by the Spaniards. After the introduction of the horse and ox-drawn *carreta* (cart), Zuni trade with the Eastern Pueblos and Hopi intensified. Carts enabled more produce to be transported and trading episodes to occur with greater frequency since transport time was reduced. Handwoven woolen textiles were also introduced as an important item of trade.

Even the very large and complexly organized New World, non-animal trading systems were at a disadvantage when compared to animal-based systems. They were not only limited in the extent over which trading could occur but also in the kind and amount of goods that could be traded. Even at the state level of integration, the Basin of Mexico trade and tribute system could only move bulky, subsistence goods over a radius of about 150 km using state-organized traders and bearers. This level of trading organization probably required state-level integration (discussed in Santley and Alexander 1992). It is instructive to compare this trading radius to that suggested for the Middle Neolithic cattle trade in the Carpathian Basin of central Europe, which was also 100-150 km (Sherratt 1982) but presumably entailed considerably less government organization. Undoubtedly, the Mexican trade was bringing in a much higher volume of goods, but distance is the only consideration being examined here. As stated, the ability to bring in resources and maintain ties over a wider area leads to greater system security and stability (Santley and Alexander 1992). This buffering can apparently occur in systems with much lower levels of societal organization when animals are present to widen the area of exchange and interaction.

As stated above, the kind and amount of traded goods also differ between animal and non-animal exchange systems. Owing to transport requirements, the lighter exotics are emphasized over bulky food items in foot transport systems (Santley and Alexander 1992). This is especially the case in smaller, less complexly organized systems, such as those that were operating in pre-contact North America. Trade in these items undoubtedly accompanied exchange of some subsistence goods and served to keep open lines of communication and interaction for mutual assistance in times of stress (Halstead and O'Shea 1982). Groups such as those found in the Chaco area or the Middle Mississippi Valley were not organized to support their systems with large amounts of imported foodstuffs or inputs of large quantities of bulky famine relief. These systems were structured to maintain open relationships so people could be moved from areas of temporary underproductivity to less affected areas with greater resource availability (discussed in Cordell 1984; Schelberg 1983 for Chaco Canyon) — hence the statement from ethnographic information that famine occasionally forced the Zuni to go live with other groups, whereas other groups came to them for help in different years (Stevenson 1904). This type of buffering mechanism seems to function fairly well in small systems with equally distributed bad and good times.

The exotics that are used to keep interactions and communications open can be anything from Mimbres pottery to turquoise, copper bells, or Knife River flint. These goods serve as prestige items that can be used as tokens or rewards both within and between groups and can ultimately be "cashed in" for subsistence goods should the need arise (Halstead and O'Shea 1982). The act of "cashing in" tokens can lead to growing dependency and the potential for developing organizational complexity if relationships become unbalanced for whatever reason and one segment of a society, or group within a region, must consistently go to another for help (Halstead and O'Shea 1982). One of the values of using animals and their edible products as prestige items lies in the fact that they do not have to be "cashed in," though they often are (usually for grain). They can be consumed directly, thus postponing the day when dependency accounts must be reckoned.

New World trade in manufactured goods can be exemplified by the Mesoamerican trade in obsidian (Sanders et al. 1979; Santley 1984). This trade was monopolized by those in control of the source and thus was limited to the groups in proximity to the source or those that could take control of the source and maintain it. Old World trade in precious metals followed the same principle (Sherratt 1982, 1983). Salt, another New and Old World item of major trade importance, was also restricted in occurrence in major deposits and controllable by those in proximity or in power (Santley and Alexander 1992). In all these cases, the benefiting groups were those in control of the sources. Thus, not all developing societies with growing populations and the need and ability to use manufactured goods as means of economic expansion and large-scale buffering were in a position to take advantage of a prime source of potential manufactured items. It has been suggested that the proximity of Teotihuacan to the central Mexican obsidian sources aided the development and expansion of that state to a considerable degree and at the expense of competitors (Sanders et al. 1979; Santley 1984). Although the unequal distribution of prime candidates for manufactured goods in Mesoamerica probably had an effect on the structure and development of the later states in the basin, discussion of this problem is well beyond the scope of this research.

In sum, New World exchange systems were more constrained than their Old World counterparts. They lacked a major resource and a major means of transport, and they may have lacked a major source of fairly widely available manufactured goods. The systems were smaller and oriented more toward the exchange of prestige items than major subsistence commodities. Owing to limitations on the size and nature of the traded items, these systems probably functioned less well as risk buffers than did their Old World counterparts.

THE ROLE OF SOCIAL COMPLEXITY AS A RISK BUFFER

This chapter has reviewed the economic systems of pre-state farming groups with and without domesticated animals. It suggests that animal domesticates serve as added resources and as added buffers against economic system failure in several different areas. Their contributions as food sources, as additions to the agricultural system, and as additions to the system of trade, interaction, and exchange were examined. Several areas of economic risk were identified among groups that did not possess domesticated animals. The overall direction of this study suggests that growing social complexity might be used to buffer these risk areas in the absence of the animals (Halstead and O'Shea 1982; Santley 1984; Schelberg 1983). This view leads to the main finding of the current research: that growing societal complexity, in this case the state level of organization, is reached more rapidly in regions without domesticated animals than in regions with domesticated animals. The concluding section of this chapter briefly reviews some of the ways in which complex social organization could serve to ameliorate the specific, identified economic system problems examined in this research.

The first component of non-animal economic systems in which potential problem areas can be identified is the agricultural system. Declines in agricultural productivity or limitations on agricultural productivity may be due to many important factors. These declines become more critical under conditions of population growth and agricultural intensification. The first problem examined here is the absence of animal fertilizer. The absence of fertilizer limits the productivity of certain lands that may be needed to increase the system output. It also limits the choice of lands that can be profitably cultivated. A second limiting factor results from the absence of draft and pack animals to transport workers, goods, and crops to and from the fields. As discussed earlier, systems without draft and pack animals are forced to select lands closer to home than systems with transport animals. Thus, some marginal lands may remain in cultivation simply because they are closer to home, while more productive lands cannot be cultivated because they are too distant. Finally, less land can be farmed by hand cultivators than by cultivators using the plow.

State-level systems cope with problems of agricultural productivity and intensification in a variety of ways. The following examples are drawn primarily from the research of Sanders et al. (1979) in the Basin of Mexico. These coping mechanisms are probably most appropriate for, but are not necessarily limited to, societies at the state level of political integration. Hence, they demonstrate the ways in which the state could ameliorate agricultural risk areas to increase and sustain productivity. Sanders et al.

(1979) suggest that the development of intensive drainage agriculture, in the form of *chinampas* or raised fields, required state-level organization and administration to function effectively and productively. Outputs from these fields quadrupled normal production levels and were used to support the Aztec period population increases in the Basin of Mexico. In addition, during the periods of state-level integration in the basin, farmers were relocated and made to farm appropriate areas and may have been provisioned by the state. Such relocation can also be seen quite clearly in the Inca system, in which massive relocation programs were a function of the integration of conquered lands into the system (Rowe 1946). These actions demonstrate the ability of the state to redistribute people as well as goods. Under these conditions, the distance of fields from specific communities becomes meaningless. State-level societies also broaden their economic bases and increase productivity through wars of conquest for both tribute and land (Flannery and Marcus 1983; Rowe 1946; Santley 1984). Payment of tribute, which included agricultural produce, was the most prevalent result of conquest in the basin. Thus, state-level societies can invest in heavily intensified hydraulic systems to raise productivity, can relocate both people and resources to areas deemed appropriate, and can bring in resources from outside the system in the form of tribute and taxes to buffer agricultural productivity problems.

Another potential problem area identified by this research consists of nutritional stress in the face of agricultural intensification and growing reliance on cereal cultigens as dietary staples. This problem appears as protein-calorie malnutrition in some groups and relates to problems with dietary adequacy and quality (Santley and Rose 1979). Periodic agricultural shortfalls (Rindos 1984), especially without the added storage mechanism provided by domesticated animals, can contribute to difficulties in both dietary adequacy and quality. It has also been suggested that an insufficient input of protein, owing in part to declining availability of wild game, may be contributing to nutritional difficulties and dietary inadequacies (Santley and Rose 1979).

Both simple and complex societies buffer dietary stress by organizing means to monitor and respond to information concerning areas undergoing stress (Schelberg 1983; Wright and Johnson 1975). State-level organization is not necessary to monitor and direct information flow concerning areas of stress; however, state systems deal with problems on a grander scale and leave behind more evidence of their efforts. Since they generally have a wider area to draw on and a more developed information-processing apparatus, they may be more effective at buffering stress, at least for some segments of the system (Schelberg 1983; Wright and Johnson 1975). Complexly organized groups deal with stressed areas within the system by implementing measures to increase productivity, as discussed in the preceding paragraph. They also assume functions of crop storage and distribution, bring in needed items as tribute, and stratify or adjust the system

so the dietary needs of at least some of the population can be met (often at the expense of others). Storage and distribution systems can range from the elaborate facilities and networks of the Inca (Rowe 1946) to the much less elaborate facilities and networks that are suggested as having redistributive functions in less complexly organized societies (Martin and Plog 1973; Peebles and Kus 1977; Schelberg 1983). The role of tribute as a provider of scarce commodities is discussed by Santley and Rose (1979) with respect to animal meat being brought into the system center as tribute, thus depleting outlying areas during certain time periods. The possibility of resource depletion through tribute requirements going into Cahokia is also discussed for the Dickson Mounds area (Goodman et al. 1984). Santley and Rose (1979) discuss the manner in which tributary meat brought to the system center in the Basin of Mexico was apportioned to favor maintenance of dietary essentials for the elites at the expense of nonelites, with the least favored segments being the nonelites of outlying areas. Thus, meat was brought in as tribute to replace declining local supplies, but it was selectively consumed. The state was able to deplete the resources of outlying areas to reduce dietary stress for certain segments of the population at the system center.

The final economic disadvantage of groups without domesticated animals examined by this study focuses on the absence of animals for use in trade and transport. This absence significantly circumscribes the area over which tribute and traded goods can be transported (Santley and Alexander 1992). The *pochteca*, a class of professional traders organized and maintained by the state, were used to transport goods on foot both inside and outside the Aztec Empire as a response to this circumscription (discussed by Santley and Alexander 1992). This type of commitment to maintaining the channels of trade, exchange, and interaction is really only possible at the state level of organization. Other systems would lack the resources to fund this type of specialization. Thus, a state-level response to constricted trade is to use humans in the role of pack animals and burden bearers.

This chapter has examined the operation of pre-state farming systems with and without domesticated animals. The roles, contributions, and methods of management of domesticated animals were reviewed from an examination of the groups that possess these animals. Problems that might arise in the absence of domesticated animals were suggested from a review of the non-animal-using groups. Ways in which subsistence farmers might replace domesticated animals by emphasizing other resources were also mentioned. Finally, the contributions of complex sociopolitical organizations to ameliorating problems caused by the absence of animal domesticates were briefly reviewed. This review lends credence to the notion that societal complexity can indeed serve as a risk buffer for economic difficulties arising from the absence of medium to large domesticated animals, especially for the elite segments of the system.

Chapter 7

CONCLUSION

The concluding chapter of this volume is divided into three sections. The first summarizes the major points of this research and briefly reviews the manner in which it was conducted. The second section examines the theoretical and methodological contributions of this type of study to archaeological research in general. The third presents topics for future research that were suggested or reemphasized by information gathered during the course of this study.

RESEARCH REVIEW AND SUMMARY

The research problem focused on an identified difference in duration of the pre-state farming period between groups that possessed medium to large domesticated animals and groups that did not. This difference constituted a pattern of interest in which considerably shorter pre-state farming periods occurred among the groups without the domesticated animals. Sixteen archaeological sequences from a wide variety of temperate-zone Old and New World regions were used to define this pattern. A one-way, or one-factor, analysis of variance and a Mann-Whitney nonparametric test were run on these data. These analyses indicated that the differences between the durations of the two groupings are statistically significant at the .01 level of significance (Appendix). These findings support the argument that a pattern is present.

This study suggested that subsistence-level farming economies with domesticated animals were more stable, measured in terms of duration, than those without animals. For purposes of this research, stability was defined as persistence through time without major modifications or changes (discussed by Hardesty 1977). Thus, a stable economy was defined as one that persisted through time without major modifications in means of production, organization of production, and resources produced and consumed. A wide range of resources and strategies that diversify the acquisition of energy aid in the reduction of subsistence risk and economic perturbations that might lead to instability (Hardesty 1977; Santley 1984). The research described in this volume demonstrated that medium to large domesticated animals served as one such alternative, as suggested by Flannery (1969). Further, it assumed that problems in the subsistence/economic component of the system can lead to instability in the system as a whole. Attempts to reduce risk and maintain stability can lead to growing organizational and technological

complexity (Halstead and O'Shea 1982; Schelberg 1984). Thus, systems with a less stable subsistence component may development organizational complexity more rapidly. This research argued that the shorter pre-state farming periods and more rapid onset of state development in the New World (excluding Peru) resulted from such economic instability. This study suggested that one cause of this greater instability was the lack of an important alternative subsistence resource, domesticated animals, which are present in the Old World and Peru but absent in the remainder of the pre-contact New World.

This volume then examined the suggested role of domesticated animals as contributors to economic stability. Fifteen ethnographic groups were used to explore the economic inputs of domesticated animals in detail. Four major uses were defined from this examination: *(a)* use of animal meat and by-products as a food source; *(b)* use of dung as fertilizer; *(c)* use of animals as a means of amassing wealth, as a back-up resource in lean times, and as a form of live storage; and *(d)* use of animal traction for transport and plowing. Descriptive models of the economic operation of systems with and without domesticated animals were developed from the archaeological and ethnographic information. Potential problems or sources of instability related to the absence of the animal domesticates were identified in systems without these animals. Finally, the ways in which growing social complexity might serve to ameliorate these problems were examined.

CONTRIBUTIONS TO
METHOD AND THEORY

The theoretical framework of this study is grounded in cultural ecology and the ecological approach (Steward 1955). The results of this research serve as additional support for the view that subsistence activities and economic arrangements are of prime importance in structuring other aspects of the cultural system. Growth in sociocultural complexity is one of these aspects.

The main contribution of this work, however, is methodological. This type of study, which focuses on pattern recognition and explanation, serves as a means of developing appropriate methods for building and augmenting useful theories of human and systemic behavior. This type of pattern-recognition study conducted at a global scale allows research to move beyond single-case, historical explanation to the examination of general cultural processes. Such examinations can lead to the development of productive theories of general anthropological relevance.

This volume focused on the specific research methods of global-scale pattern recognition and the use of nonarchaeological information to develop a warranted explanation of the observed pattern. The value of recognizing patterns of human and cultural behavior at a large scale is demonstrated by the following discussion drawn from information used in this study.

The historical events learned from the archaeological sequence of one locale cannot form a pattern and are minimally explicable unless viewed in terms of the events occurring in other areas. For example, the isolated information that the period of village farming lasted approximately 800 years in Chaco Canyon has no explanatory potential. This information does not indicate whether the adaptation was long-lived or short-lived. It was long in terms of 100 years, short in terms of 6000 years. The duration of village agriculture in Chaco Canyon has no meaning until it is compared to the durations of the agricultural periods from other areas. This examination should begin as regional pattern recognition in the American Southwest but should not stop there. Regional analysis is simply a beginning point in this type of study. Each expanded level of study increases the amount of information available and may actually alter the pattern under study and its possible explanations.

At the regional level, the information from other sequences in the American Southwest identifies village farming periods of comparable length. Persistent episodes of political decline or geographic abandonment, periodic severe drought, and a generally marginal climate for agriculture, especially with respect to precipitation and length of growing season, occur throughout the region (Cordell 1984; Palkovich 1984; Schelberg 1983, 1984). These conditions have led many investigators to the conclusion that climatic perturbations, especially periods of drought, were the causal factors behind political declines and geographic abandonments in the Southwest (discussed by Cordell 1984; Palkovich 1984).

Though general agricultural marginality was probably the major factor conditioning the specific southwestern U.S. pattern of abandonments and declines, additional interesting information can be obtained by expanding the scale of the study to include other North American regions in which village agriculture was practiced. The example used in this study is the Cahokia sequence, which had a village farming period duration of 1073 years. This area also shows evidence of decline and abandonment, as well as a length similar to that of Chaco Canyon for the period of interest. Availability of water was not a problem in this area, however. Growing population and land constriction are suggested as contributing to economic difficulties in the American Bottom (Kelly et al. 1984:156-157).

Thus, short sequences and abandonments can also occur in regions that are not considered to be climatically or environmentally marginal. Land constriction and growing population can also contribute to the appearance of the observed pattern.

When the scope of the study is widened to include the Mesoamerican zone of the New World, it can be seen that the North American periods of village farming are shorter than the Mesoamerican ones. The North American average (based on two examples) is about 900 years, whereas the Mesoamerican average (based on three examples) is about 1500 years. Thus, in New World archaeological studies the Mesoamerican sequences are considered to be long whereas the North American ones are considered to be short (Schelberg 1983). Again, environmental variables, such as climate, precipitation, and land quality, seem to be causing the differences in durations. The Mesoamerican regions of Oaxaca, Puebla, and the Basin of Mexico are more favorable for agricultural pursuits than the North American areas under study (Schelberg 1983). Growing season, precipitation, and available land are all more amenable to agricultural production and intensification in Middle America (Flannery and Marcus 1983; MacNeish et al. 1967; Sanders et al. 1979). At the New World level, then, the best explanation of the observed pattern still seems to be one that stresses the causal role of environmental variables.

It is not until pattern recognition is expanded to a global scale, with the addition of village farming sequences from the Old World and Peru, that some new and different possibilities appear. The "long" Mesoamerican sequences from climatically favorable agricultural zones no longer seem as long when they are compared to Old World village farming durations from climatically favorable regions. The Mesoamerican average duration of ca. 1500 years pales when compared to the 4000-, 5000-, and 6000-year durations of some of the Old World pre-state farming periods. From this angle, *all* the New World sequences seem short, whereas the Old World ones appear long. This expanded information gives rise to a new pattern, short New World sequences versus long Old World sequences. Since both hemispheres contain climatically favorable and unfavorable areas, this new pattern offers the possibility of adding another important dimension to the explanation that has developed from the recognition of climatic and environmental factors as conditioners of the differences in sequence duration. The new dimension examined in this research is the presence or absence of an additional, important economic resource in the form of domesticated animals. Other explanations might also be possible. If more sequences were examined, other variations on the pattern might also appear. The point of this discussion lies in the fact that the pattern and its potential explanation can change at each level of examination: local, regional, hemispheric, and worldwide. The scale of examination affects the pattern, its potential explanations, and the amount of information that is derived from the archaeological record. The full potential of pattern recognition is not reached until a world-scale examination is conducted, though smaller scale studies can also be valuable.

Development of a well-warranted explanation for the observed archaeological pattern is the other major methodological contribution of this study. The archaeological record is a present-day phenomenon in which patterns can be observed. Simple recognition of an archaeological pattern does not explain what produced that pattern, however (Binford 1983a, 1983b). As discussed by Binford (1983a, 1983b) and by Gilman (1983), a properly warranted explanation must be developed for the pattern using information independent of the archaeological problem under consideration. This study demonstrates the value of using ethnographic information, complemented by ancillary information from nutritional studies and soil science, as a means of developing a set of economic contributions of domesticated animals to pre-industrial farming economies. Ethnographic sources are especially valuable in this regard because they offer dynamic information to help with the interpretation of the static remains of the past. These sources are some of the best places for obtaining direct information on the actual operation of subsistence-level farming societies. This type of information can only be inferred from archaeological remains. The economic contributions of domesticated animals derived from the ethnographic sources, and from the ancillary information from nutrition and soil science, are used to warrant the explanation that domesticated animals made a significant economic impact on the village farming economy and led to greater economic stability and greater duration of the adaptation.

RESEARCH IMPLICATIONS

The final portion of this chapter reviews several research implications derived from information examined during the course of this research. Four topics are presented. All were initially mentioned in Chapters 4 or 6, and all have considerable potential to inform on the economic operation of subsistence-level farming economies with and without domesticated animals.

The first topic concerns the changing economic roles of hunted game and domesticated animals in early village farming groups. The eleven archaeological sequences used in this study showed three different patterns of wild game versus domesticated animal use. The two major patterns are discussed first: *(a)* domesticated animals as the primary faunal component from the earliest Neolithic, with hunted game occupying only a minor role; and *(b)* domesticated animals and hunted game as important faunal components in the Early Neolithic, with hunted game declining to a minor role by the Middle Neolithic. Geographic factors do not seem to be at the root of this observed difference. The groups that emphasized only domesticates early in the sequence and those that emphasized both domesticated and wild resources are seemingly

located at random across the Old World areas that were studied. The different types of groups do not cluster in any particular type of geographic location. In Chapter 6, the possibility was mentioned that differences in the farming system (permanent field or slash-and-burn systems) might have caused the difference in resource exploitation patterns. This possibility seemed likely because slash-and-burn farming is often associated with greater game availability (Harris 1977). This suggestion was not confirmed by the data, however, since virtually all of the groups were apparently using various forms of permanent field systems even in the earliest agricultural times. Thus, no potential explanation for the difference in resource use was suggested. This difference in resource use merits further research, perhaps beginning with a detailed examination of the faunal components from each of the sites in the two categories. This type of examination could serve as a beginning point in the development of an explanation for the difference in importance of hunted game among early village farming groups.

The third use pattern appeared in only two sequences, those from Peru and northern China. This pattern consisted of a continued, though declining, importance of hunted game throughout the periods of subsistence-level farming. The major animals used in these areas were pigs and llamas, neither of which was used to produce edible secondary products. The importance of edible secondary products to subsistence farmers is discussed by Sherratt (1981, 1983). The research presented in this volume suggested that the absence of edible secondary products as a food and protein source might have been a contributing factor to the continued reliance on hunted game. Since this idea was suggested on the basis of information from only two sequences, further research should be conducted on groups that use domesticated animals, but not edible secondary products, to determine if hunting remained an important economic pursuit among these groups. In this way, the presence of a genuine resource exploitation pattern could be confirmed. This kind of study also leads the way to a more detailed examination of the role and importance of edible secondary products among these groups.

A second implication of this research concerns patterns of changing importance through time of the various animal domesticates and the factors that seem to be causing these alterations. Different patterns of presence/absence and abundance of cattle, sheep, goats, and pigs were discussed in detail in Chapter 6. A few important points from this discussion are briefly reiterated here. Pigs are well-suited to mild, moist areas and to the long-fallow fields and uncultivated areas of Early Neolithic farming villages in some regions (Harris 1977). They are the first animal to decline and disappear under conditions of agricultural intensification in the more arid areas (Harris 1977). They become too costly when their naturally shaded rooting areas are removed to make way for permanent fields. Sheep, on the other hand, increase in importance as cultivation becomes more intensified, especially in the later pre-state and early state periods (Barker 1985; Cohen

1970; Dennell 1978; Mellaart 1967b; Oates 1973; Redman 1978). The rising importance of sheep is related to the rising importance of secondary products (such as wool) and to the more open landscape created by increased clearance of farmland and intensive cultivation of that land. This kind of farming system produces the short graze favored by sheep.

At this preliminary level of analysis, climatic variations, differences in farming system, and changes through time in farming systems seem to be the major factors conditioning which domesticated animals are the most important in a given area at a given time. Additional study is needed to add more detail to these animal use patterns and their causes. Ultimately, certain aspects of the economic and farming systems might be predicted on the basis of the percentage of particular species of domestiecated animals in use during a given time period.

Another implication of this investigation concerns the means by which state-level sociopolitical integration is used to buffer economic risk, especially in groups without domesticated animals. This topic was presented in detail in the final portion of Chapter 6. Several state-level economic functions were examined briefly in Chapter 6, and all of these functions could profit from more in-depth study.

State-level political integration can help to ameliorate economic problems in the following ways. The state can aid in increasing agricultural productivity by providing a bureaucracy to administer complex water-control systems and to relocate and provision farmers and other personnel (Rowe 1946; Sanders et al. 1979). States also increase productivity by waging wars of conquest for both land and tribute. They cope with agricultural and resource shortfalls by maintaining elaborate information systems to identify areas suffering from agricultural problems and by maintaining storage facilities to provision those areas (Rowe 1946; Schelberg 1983; Wright and Johnson 1975). States can also stratify the population so the dietary needs of some (usually elites) can be met, usually at the expense of others (Santley and Rose 1979). Finally, state-controlled systems of trade can bring in more goods from a wider range than non-state-controlled trade and exchange systems (Santley and Alexander 1992). Other risk-reducing functions of the state could undoubtedly also be identified. A more detailed study of the function of the state as a supplier of risk-reduction strategies would lend additional support to the arguments set forth by this research — namely, that state-level sociopolitical organization developed more rapidly in areas of greater economic risk as a means of buffering those risks.

The final implication of this study focuses on New World systems and the developmental differences between the North American and Mesoamerican systems discussed in this volume. The specific developmental differences concern the growing social complexity and state development that occurred in Mexico compared to the growing social complexity that led to decline or abandonment in

some of the North American areas. The Mesoamerican sequences come from the Basin of Mexico, the Tehuacan Valley, and the Valley of Oaxaca. The North American sequences come from Chaco Canyon and the Four Corners area, and from Cahokia. The implication of this research centers on why population growth and agricultural intensification led to state development in some areas and effective abandonment in others.

As discussed earlier in this chapter, the pattern found in this study indicates that environmental and climatological factors are the crucial variables leading to developmental differences among these New World areas. Others have noted this pattern as well, especially in comparisons between Mesoamerica and the Southwest (Schelberg 1983). Evidently, a certain base productive capacity is necessary before state-level society can develop. The information presented in this volume indicates that neither the American Bottom nor the Four Corners area could provide this productive potential. This statement is not new (Cordell 1984; Schelberg 1983), but the information provided by this study lends additional confirmation to this view.

Land constriction (Kelly et al. 1984) seems to be the primary problem in the Cahokia area. The land in the American Bottom of the Mississippi River is probably as fertile as any land in the world. The easily cultivated, river-bottom lands are limited in extent, however. Without metal agricultural implements and the draft animals to pull them, Mississippian cultivation could not expand onto the heavy, grass-covered prairie lands. Thus, agricultural expansion was limited. A more in-depth study of the precise nature of these limitations would add greatly to the knowledge base concerning the Mississippian adaptation.

Climatic marginality in general served to limit the productivity of the areas under study in the American Southwest (Cordell 1984; Palkovich 1984). This marginality centered on length of growing season and on precipitation (Clary 1984; Cordell 1984; Minnis 1981; Palkovich 1984; Schelberg 1984). In good years, both precipitation and growing season were adequate. In bad years of late frosts, early frosts, or drought, crop failures or very small yields could occur. Repeated episodes of stress seem to have preceded specific site and areal abandonments (Palkovich 1984; Schelberg 1983). These agricultural difficulties were compounded by other environmental and geographic problems that inhibited or lowered productivity, including limited amounts of quality land and inability to develop large-scale irrigation systems in certain areas. Dry farming was practiced widely in the Southwest, but the prime lands were those that could receive extra water from various fairly simple water-control techniques, such as diversion and runoff manipulation (Bradfield 1971). These lands were limited in extent, however. Large-scale canal irrigation systems that could bring a considerably greater amount of land under cultivation, or bring added security to the cultivated lands, were not possible in the Four Corners area owing to the entrenched or ephemeral nature of the water sources (Schelberg 1983). All these factors combined to lower the productive potential of the Four Corners region.

On the other hand, the Mexican climate and environment were much more favorable for agriculture and agricultural intensification. The length of the growing season permitted double cropping, there was adequate precipitation for rainfall farming in many areas, and large-scale irrigation systems based on permanent water sources were possible. In this region, growing population was met with growing agricultural intensification and increasing societal complexity rather than the short-term increases in agricultural intensification and societal complexity followed by effective abandonment found to the north. This study follows others in suggesting that the ability or inability to produce sufficient agricultural produce over the long term was the key factor in this developmental difference.

CONCLUSION

The contribution of this research is both methodological and informational. This study has demonstrated the value and importance of global-scale pattern recognition and explanation. It has also defined and examined an archaeological problem of considerable relevance. A significant difference in duration between the pre-state farming periods of groups with and without domesticated animals was identified. The economic effects of the presence or absence of these animals was examined using ethnographic information. It was demonstrated that the economic functions of domesticated animals contributed to greater economic stability among the subsistence farming groups that possessed them. Evidence for this greater stability appears as village farming sequences of significantly greater duration.

REFERENCES CITED

Adams, Robert McC. (1972). Patterns of Urbanization in Early Southern Mesopotamia. In *Man, Settlement and Urbanism*, eds. Peter J. Ucko, Ruth Tringham, and G. W. Dimbleby, pp. 735-749. London: Duckworth.

Adams, Robert McC. and Nissen, Hans J. (1972). *The Uruk Countryside*. Chicago: University of Chicago Press.

Allchin, Bridget and Allchin, Raymond (1982). *The Rise of Civilization in India and Pakistan*. Cambridge: Cambridge University Press.

Anderson, Dana and Oakes, Yvonne (1980). A World View of Agriculture. In *Tijeras Canyon: Analyses of the Past*, ed. Linda Cordell, pp. 12-40. Albuquerque: University of New Mexico Press.

Arensberg, Conrad Maynadier (1937). *The Irish Countryman: An Anthropological Study*. London: Macmillan.

Arkell, A. J. and Ucko, Peter J. (1965). Review of Pre-Dynastic Development in the Nile Valley. *Current Anthropology* 6:145-166.

Arkin, Herbert and Colton, Raymond R. (1970). *Statistical Methods* (fifth ed.). New York: Barnes and Noble.

Bareis, Charles J. and Porter, James W. (1984). Research Design. In *American Bottom Archaeology*, eds. Charles J. Bareis and James W. Porter, pp. 1-14. Urbana and Chicago: University of Illinois Press.

Barker, Graeme (1985). *Prehistoric Farming in Europe*. Cambridge: Cambridge University Press.

Barker, Graeme and Webley, P. D. (1978). Causewayed Camps and Early Neolithic Economies in Central Southern England. *Proceedings of the Prehistoric Society* 44:161-186.

Barnard, Noel (1975). *The First Radiocarbon Dates from China* (rev. edition). Monographs on Far Eastern History 8. Canberra: Australia National University.

Barnard, Noel (1979). *Radiocarbon Dates and Their Significance in the Chinese Archaeological Scene: A List of 280 Entries Compiled from Chinese Sources Published up to Close of 1978*. Canberra: Australia National University.

Barnard, Noel (1980). *Radiocarbon Dates and Their Significance in the Chinese Archaeological Scene: A List of 420 Entries Compiled from Chinese Sources Published up to Close of 1979*. Canberra: Australia National University.

Barth, Fredrik (1953). *Principles of Social Organization in Southern Kurdistan*. Oslo: Brodrene Jorgensen.

Barton, Roy Franklin (1922). *Ifugao Economics*. Berkeley: University of California Press.

Beaglehole, Ernest (1937). *Notes on Hopi Economic Life*. Yale University Publications in Anthropology 15. New Haven.

Bedoian, William (1973). *Oro y Maiz: The Economic Structure of the Mexica Empire and Its Effects on Social Stratification and Political Power*. Unpublished M.A. thesis, Department of Anthropology, Pennsylvania State University, University Park.

Berque, Jacques (1955). *Social Structures of the High Atlas*. Paris: Presses Universitaires de France.

Binford, Lewis R. (1983a). *In Pursuit of the Past: Decoding the Archaeological Record*. London and New York: Thames and Hudson.

Binford, Lewis R. (1983b). *Working at Archaeology*. New York: Academic Press.

Blalock, Hubert M. (1960). *Social Statistics*. New York: McGraw-Hill.

Bogucki, Peter I. (1983). The Social Archaeology of the Danubian Farmers. Paper presented at the Annual Meeting of the American Anthropological Association, December 1983, Chicago.

Bohrer, Vorsila L., Kaplan, Lawrence, and Whitaker, Thomas W. (1960). Zuni Agriculture. *El Palacio* 67:181-202.

Bökönyi, Shandor (1964). The Vertebrate Fauna of the Neolithic Settlement at Maroslele Pana. *Archaeologia Ertesítö* 91:87-93.

Bökönyi, Shandor (1973a). The Fauna of Umm Dabaghiyah: A Preliminary Report. *Iraq* 35:9-12.

Bökönyi, Shandor (1973b). Stock Breeding. In *Neolithic Greece*, ed. D. R. Theocharis, pp. 165-178. Athens: National Bank of Greece.

Bökönyi, Shandor (1974). *History of Domestic Animals in Central and Eastern Europe*. Budapest: Akadémiai Kiadó.

Boserup, Ester (1965). *The Conditions of Agricultural Growth*. Chicago: Aldine.

Bottéro, Jean (1967). The First Semitic Empire. In *The Near East: The Early Civilizations*, ed. Jean Bottéro, Elena Cassin, and Jean Vercoutter, pp. 91-132. New York: Delacorte.

Bradfield, Maitland (1971). *The Changing Pattern of Hopi Agriculture*. Royal Anthropological Institute of Great Britain and Ireland, Occasional Paper 30. London.

Brand, Donald D., Hawley, Florence M., and Hibben, Frank C. (1937). *Tseh So, a Small House Ruin, Chaco Canyon, New Mexico*. University of New Mexico Anthropological Series 2(2). Albuquerque.

Brumfiel, Elizabeth (1976). Regional Growth in the Eastern Valley of Mexico: A Test of the "Population Pressure" Hypothesis. In *The Early Mesoamerican Village*, ed. Kent V. Flannery, pp. 234-249. New York: Academic Press.

Bunzel, Ruth L. (1932). *Introduction to Zuñi Ceremonialism*. U.S. Bureau of American Ethnology, Annual Report 47. Washington, D. C.: Smithsonian Institution.

Cassidy, Claire Monod (1973). Nutrition and Health in Hunter-Gatherers and Agriculturalists, an Archaeological Case Study. Paper presented at the 38th Annual Meeting of the Society for American Archaeology, San Francisco.

Cassidy, Claire Monod (1984). Skeletal Evidence for Prehistoric Subsistence Adaptation in the Central Ohio River Valley. In *Paleoanthropology at the Origins of Agriculture*, ed. Mark N. Cohen and George J. Armelagos, pp. 307-345. New York: Academic Press.

Caton-Thompson, G. and Whittle, E. (1975). Thermoluminescence Dating of the Badarian. *Antiquity* 49:89-97.

Champion, Timothy, Gamble, Clive, Shennan, Stephen, and Whittle, Alasdair (1984). *Prehistoric Europe*. London: Academic Press.

Chang, Kwang-Chih (1976). *Early Chinese Civilization: Anthropological Perspectives*. Cambridge, Massachusetts: Harvard University Press.

Chang, Kwang-Chih (1977). *The Archaeology of Ancient China* (third rev. ed.). New Haven: Yale University Press.

Chang, Te-Tzu (1983). The Origins and Early Cultures of the Cereal Grains and Food Legumes. In *The Origins of Chinese Civilization*, ed. David N. Keightley, pp. 65-94. Berkeley: University of California Press.

Clary, Karen H. (1984). Anasazi Diet and Subsistence as Revealed by Coprolites from Chaco Canyon. In *Recent Research on Chaco Prehistory*, eds. W. James Judge and John D. Schelberg, pp. 265-279. Reports of the Chaco Center 8. Albuquerque: Division of Cultural Research, National Park Service.

Clutton-Brock, Juliet (1981). Discussion. In *Farming Practice in British Prehistory*, edited by Roger Mercer, pp. 218-220. Edinburgh: Edinburgh University Press.

Cohen, Harold R. (1970). The Palaeoecology of South Central Anatolia at the End of the Pleistocene and the Beginning of the Holocene. *Anatolian Studies* 20:119-137.

Collis, John (1971). Markets and Money. In *The Iron Age and Its Hillforts*, eds. D. Hill and M. Jesson, pp. 97-104. University Monograph Series. University of Southampton, England.

Collis, John (1982). Gradual Growth and Sudden Change — Urbanisation in Temperate Europe. In *Ranking, Resource and Exchange: Aspects of the Archaeology of Early European Society*, eds. Colin Renfrew and Stephen Shennan, pp. 73-78. Cambridge: Cambridge University Press.

Cook, Della Collins (1984). Subsistence and Health in the Lower Illinois Valley: Osteological Evidence. In *Paleopathology at the Origins of Agriculture*, eds. Mark N. Cohen and George J. Armelagos, pp. 235-269. New York: Academic Press.

Coon, Carleton Stevens (1931). *Tribes of the Rif*. Cambridge, Massachusetts: Peabody Museum of American Archaeology and Ethnology.

Cooper, John Montgomery (1946). The Araucanians. In *Handbook of South American Indians*, Vol. 2, ed. Julian H. Steward, pp. 687-760. Bureau of American Ethnology Bulletin 143. Washington, D. C.: U.S. Government Printing Office.

Cordell, Linda S. (1984). *Prehistory of the Southwest*. Orlando: Academic Press.

Cordell, Linda S., Earls, Amy C., and Binford, Martha R. (1984). Subsistence Systems in the Mountainous Settings of the Rio Grande Valley. In *Prehistoric Agricultural Strategies in the Southwest*, eds. Suzanne K. Fish and Paul R. Fish, pp. 233-241. Arizona State University Anthropological Research Papers No. 33. Tempe.

Covarrubias, Miguel (1938). *Island of Bali*. New York: Knopf.

Cunliffe, B. W. (1974). *Iron Age Communities in Britain*. London: Routledge and Kegan Paul.

Cushing, Frank Hamilton (1920). *Zuñi Breadstuff*. New York: Museum of the American Indian, Heye Foundation.

Dennell, Robin W. (1978). *Early Farming in South Bulgaria from the VI to the III Millennia b.c.* British Archaeological Reports, Internatl. Series 45. Oxford.

Dennell, Robin W. (1983). *European Economic Prehistory*. New York: Academic Press.

Dennell, Robin W., and Webley, D. (1975). Prehistoric Settlement and Land Use in Southern Bulgaria. In *Palaeoeconomy*, edited by E. S. Higgs, pp. 97-109. Cambridge: Cambridge University Press.

Drennan, Robert D. (1976). Religion and Social Evolution in Formative Mesoamerica. In *The Early Mesoamerican Village*, ed. Kent V. Flannery, pp. 345-364. New York: Academic Press.

Earle, Timothy K. (1976). A Nearest Neighbor Analysis of Two Formative Settlement Systems. In *The Early Mesoamerican Village*, ed. Kent V. Flannery, pp. 196-223. New York: Academic Press.

Edzard, Dietz Otto (1967). Early Dynastic Period. In *The Near East: The Early Civilizations*, eds. Jean Bottéro, Elena Cassin, and Jean Vercoutter, pp. 52-90. New York: Delacorte.

Esarey, Mark E. (1984). Historic Period. In *American Bottom Archaeology*, eds. Charles J. Bareis and James W. Porter, pp. 187-196. Urbana and Chicago: University of Illinois Press.

Evans, Emyr Estyn (1942). *Irish Heritage: The Landscape, the People and Their Work*. Dundalgan Press, Dundalk, Ireland.

Falkenstein, Adam (1967). The Prehistory and Protohistory of Western Asia. In *The Near East: The Early Civilizations*, eds. Jean Bottéro, Elena Cassin, and Jean Vercoutter, pp. 1-51. New York: Delacorte.

Faron, Louis C. (1961). *Mapuche Social Structure: Institutional Reintegration in a Patrilineal Society of Central Chile*. Urbana: University of Illinois Press.

Feinman, Gary, and Neitzel, Jill (1984). Too Many Types: An Overview of Sedentary Prestate Societies in the Americas. In *Advances in Archaeological Method and Theory*, Vol. 7, ed. Michael B. Schiffer, pp. 39-102. New York: Academic Press.

Fenton, Alexander J. (1981). Early Manuring Techniques. In *Farming Practice in British Prehistory*, ed. Roger Mercer, pp. 210-217. Edinburgh: Edinburgh University Press.

Ferguson, Cheryl (1980). Analysis of Skeletal Remains. In *Tijeras Canyon: Analyses of the Past*, edited by Linda Cordell, pp. 121-148. Albuquerque: University of New Mexico Press.

Flannery, Kent V. (1968). The Olmec and the Valley of Oaxaca: A Model for Inter-Regional Interaction in Formative Times. In *Dumbarton Oaks Conference on the Olmec*, ed. Elizabeth P. Benson, pp. 119-130. Washington, D. C.: National Park Service.

Flannery, Kent V. (1969). Origins and Ecological Effects of Early Near Eastern Domestication. In *The Domestication and Exploitation of Plants and Animals*, eds. P. J. Ucko and G. W. Dimbleby, pp. 73-100. London: Duckworth.

Flannery, Kent V. (1972a). The Cultural Evolution of Civilizations. *Annual Review of Ecology and Systematics* 3:399-426.

Flannery, Kent V. (1972b). The Origins of the Village as a Settlement Type in Mesoamerica and the Near East: A Comparative Study. In *Man, Settlement and Urbanism*, eds. Peter J. Ucko, Ruth Tringham, and G. W. Dimbleby, pp. 23-53. London: Duckworth.

Flannery, Kent V. (1976). Empirical Determination of Site Catchments in Oaxaca and Tehuacán. In *The Early Mesoamerican Village*, ed. Kent V. Flannery, pp. 103-117. New York: Academic Press.

Flannery, Kent V. (1983). *The Cloud People: Divergent Evolution of the Zapotec and Mixtec Civilizations*. New York: Academic Press.

Ford, Richard I. (1974). Northeastern Archaeology: Past and Future. *Annual Review of Anthropology* 3:385-413.

Ford, Richard I. (1976). Carbonized Plant Remains. In *Fabrica San Jose and Middle Formative Society in the Valley of Oaxaca*, by Robert D. Drennan, pp. 261-268. Memoirs of the Museum of Anthropology, University of Michigan No. 8. Ann Arbor.

Fortes, Meyer (1936). Ritual Festivals and Social Cohesion in the Hinterland of the Gold Coast. *American Anthropologist* 38:590-604.

Fortes, Meyer, and Fortes, Sonia L. (1936). Food in the Domestic Economy of the Tallensi. *Africa* 9:237-276.

Fortier, Andrew C., Emerson, Thomas E., and Finney, Fred A. (1984). Early Woodland and Middle Woodland Periods. In *American Bottom Archaeology*, eds. Charles J. Bareis and James W. Porter, pp. 59-103. Urbana and Chicago: University of Illinois Press.

Fowler, Melvin L. (1978). Cahokia and the American Bottom: Settlement Archeology. In *Mississippian Settlement Patterns*, ed. Bruce D. Smith. pp. 455-478. New York: Academic Press.

Freeman, T. W. (1958). Inishbofin: An Atlantic Island. *Economic Geography* 34:202-209.

French, David H. (1966). Excavations at Can Hasan: Fifth Preliminary Report. *Anatolian Studies* 16:113-124.

French, David H. (1972). Settlement Distribution in the Konya Plain, South Central Turkey. In *Man, Settlement and Urbanism*, eds. Peter J. Ucko, Ruth Tringham, and G. W. Dimbleby, pp. 231-238. London: Duckworth.

Fried, Morton (1960). On the Evolution of Social Stratification and the State. In *Culture and History*, ed. S. Diamond, pp. 713-731. New York: Columbia University Press.

Fried, Morton (1983). Tribe to State or State to Tribe in Ancient China? In *The Origins of Chinese Civilization*, ed. David N. Keightley, pp. 467-493. Berkeley: University of California Press.

Garcilaso de la Vega, el Inca (1869-1871). *First Part of the Royal Commentaries of the Yncas*. London: Hakluyt Society.

Geertz, Clifford (1959). Form and Variation in Balinese Village Structure. *American Anthropologist* 61:991-1012.

Geertz, Clifford (1963). *Agricultural Involution: The Processes of Ecological Change in Indonesia*. Berkeley: University of California Press.

Gibson, McGuire (1974). Violation of Fallow and Engineered Disaster in Mesopotamian Civilization. In *Irrigation's Impact on Society*, eds. Theodore E. Downing and McGuire Gibson, pp. 7-18. Anthropological Papers of the University of Arizona 26. Tucson: University of Arizona Press.

Gilman, Patricia (1983). *Changing Architectural Forms in the Prehistoric Southwest*. Unpublished Ph.D. dissertation, Department of Anthropology, University of New Mexico, Albuquerque.

Glass, Gene V., and Stanley, Julian C. (1970). *Statistical Methods in Education and Psychology*. Prentice-Hall, Englewood Cliffs, New Jersey.

Goodman, Alan H., Lallo, John, Armelagos, George J., and Rose, Jerome C. (1984). Health Changes at Dickson Mounds, Illinois (A.D. 950-1300). In *Paleopathology at the Origins of Agriculture*, eds. Mark N. Cohen and George J. Armelagos, pp. 271-305. New York: Academic Press.

Graham, David Crockett (1937a). The Customs of the Ch'uan Miao. *West China Border Research Society Journal* 9:13-70.

Graham, David Crockett (1937b). The Ceremonies of the Ch'uan Miao. *West China Border Research Society Journal* 9:71-119.

Griffin, James B. (1984). A Historical Perspective. In *American Bottom Archaeology*, eds. Charles J. Bareis and James W. Porter, pp. xv-xviii. Urbana and Chicago: University of Illinois Press.

Haas, Jere, and Harrison, Gail (1977). Nutritional Anthropology and Biological Adaptation. *Annual Review of Anthropology* 6:69-101.

Hack, John T. (1942)*The Changing Physical Environment of the Hopi Indians of Arizona*. Papers of the Peabody Museum of American Archaeology and Ethnology 35(1). Cambridge, Massachusetts.

Halpern, Joel Martin (1958). *A Serbian Village*. New York: Columbia University Press.

Halstead, Paul (1981). Counting Sheep in Neolithic and Bronze Age Greece. In *Pattern of the Past: Studies in Honour of David Clarke,* eds. Ian Hodder, Glynn Isaac, and Norman Hammond, pp. 307-339. Cambridge: Cambridge University Press.

Halstead, Paul, and O'Shea, John (1982). A Friend in Need Is a Friend Indeed: Social Storage and the Origins of Social Ranking. In *Ranking, Resource and Exchange: Aspects of the Archaeology of Early European Society,* eds. Colin Renfrew and Stephen Shennan, pp. 92-99. Cambridge: Cambridge University Press.

Hansen, L. (1966). *The Hardin Village Site.* University of Kentucky Studies in Anthropology 4. Louisville.

Hard, Robert J. (1986). *Ecological Relationships Affecting the Rise of Farming Economics: A Test from the American Southwest.* Unpublished Ph.D. dissertation, Department of Anthropology, University of New Mexico, Albuquerque.

Hardesty, Donald (1977). *Ecological Anthropology.* New York: John Wiley and Sons.

Harris, David R. (1969). Agricultural Systems, Ecosystems and the Origins of Agriculture. In *The Domestication and Exploitation of Plants and Animals,* eds. P. J. Ucko and G. W. Dimbleby, pp. 3-14. London: Duckworth.

Harris, David R. (1972a). Swidden Systems and Settlement. In *Man, Settlement and Urbanism,* eds. Peter J. Ucko, Ruth Tringham, and G. W. Dimbleby, pp. 245-262. London: Duckworth.

Harris, David R. (1972b). The Origin of Agriculture in the Tropics. *American Scientist* 60(2):180-193.

Harris, Marvin (1977). *Cannibals and Kings: The Origins of Cultures.* New York: Random House.

Haselgrove, C. C. (1976). External Trade as a Stimulus to Urbanisation. In *Oppida: The Beginnings of Urbanisation in Barbarian Europe,* eds. B. W. Cunliffe and T. Rowley. British Archaeological Reports, International Series 11. Oxford.

Hassan, Fekri A. (1985). Radiocarbon Chronology of Neolithic and Predynastic Sites in Upper Egypt and the Delta. *The African Archaeological Review* 3:95-116.

Hayes, Alden C., Brugge, David M., and Judge, W. James (1981). *Archeological Surveys of Chaco Canyon, New Mexico.* Publications in Archeology 18A, Chaco Canyon Studies. Washington, D. C.: National Park Service.

Hays, William L. (1973). *Statistics for the Social Sciences.* New York: Holt, Rinehart and Winston.

Helbaek, H. (1952). Early Crops in Southern England. *Proceedings of the Prehistoric Society* 18:194-233.

Helbaek, H. (1964a). First Impressions of the Catal Hüyük Plant Husbandry. *Anatolian Studies* 14:121-124.

Helbaek, H. (1964b). Early Hassunan Vegetable Food at es-Sawwan near Samarra. *Sumer* 20:45-48.

Helbaek, H. (1970). The Plant Husbandry of Hacilar. In *Excavations at Hacilar,* Vol. 1, ed. James Mellaart. Edinburgh: Edinburgh University Press.

Helbaek, H. (1972a). Traces of Plants in the Early Ceramic Site of Umm Dabaghiyah. *Iraq* 34:17-19.

Helbaek, H. (1972b). Samarran Irrigation Agriculture at Choga Mami in Iraq. *Iraq* 34:35-48.

Hilger, M. Inez (1957). *Araucanian Child Life and Its Cultural Background.* Washington, D. C.: U.S. Government Printing Office.

Hoffman, Michael (1979). *Egypt Before the Pharaohs: The Prehistoric Foundations of Egyptian Civilization.* New York: Knopf.

Hole, Frank (1977). *The Excavation of Chagha Sefid: Studies in the Archaeological History of the Deh Luran Plain.* Memoirs of the Museum of Anthropology No. 9. University of Michigan, Ann Arbor.

Huber, Louisa G. Fitzgerald (1983). The Relationship of the Painted Pottery and Lungshan Cultures. In *The Origins of Chinese Civilization,* ed. David N. Keightley, pp. 177-216. Berkeley: University of California Press.

Iseminger, William R. (1980a). Cahokia: A Mississippian Metropolis. *Historic Illinois* 2(6):1-4. Springfield: Illinois Department of Conservation.

Iseminger, William R. (1980b). Yes, a True Metropolis. *Cahokian* (July):6-8. Collinsville, Illinois: Cahokia Mounds Museum Society.

Jarrige, Jean-François (1979). Economy and Society in the Early Chalcolithic/Bronze Age of Baluchistan: New Perspectives from Recent Excavations at Mehrgarh. In *South Asian Archaeology,* ed. Herbert Hartel, pp. 93-114. Berlin: Dietrich Reimer Verlag.

Jarrige, Jean-François, and Meadow, Richard H. (1980). The Antecedents of Civilization in the Indus Valley. *Scientific American* 243(2):122-133.

Johannessen, Sissel (1984). Paleoethnobotany. In *American Bottom Archaeology,* edited by Charles J. Bareis and James W. Porter, pp. 197-214. Urbana and Chicago: University of Illinois Press.

Johnson, Frederick, and MacNeish, Richard S. (1972). Chronometric Dating. In *Chronology and Irrigation,* ed. Frederick Johnson, pp. 3-55. The Prehistory of the Tehuacan Valley, Vol. IV. Austin: University of Texas Press.

Jope, M. (1965). Frequencies and Age of Species (Faunal Remains). In *Windmill Hill and Avebury,* ed. I. F. Smith. Oxford: Oxford University Press.

Judge, W. James, Toll, H. Wolcott, Gillespie, William B., and Lekson, Stephen H. (1981). Tenth Century Developments in Chaco Canyon. In *Collected Papers in Honor of Erik Kellerman Reed,* ed. A. H. Schroeder, pp. 65-98. Papers of the Archaeological Society of New Mexico 6. Albuquerque.

Kelly, John E., Finney, Fred A., McElrath, Dale L., and Ozuk, Steven J. (1984). Late Woodland Period. In *American Bottom Archaeology,* eds. Charles J. Bareis and James W. Porter, pp. 104-127. Urbana and Chicago: University of Illinois Press.

Kelly, Lucretia S., and Cross, Paula G. (1984). Zooarchaeology. In *American Bottom Archaeology,* eds. Charles J. Bareis and James W. Porter, pp. 215-232. Urbana and Chicago: University of Illinois Press.

Kemp, Barry J. (1977). The Early Development of Towns in Egypt. *Antiquity* 51:185-200.

Kennedy, John G. (1978). *Tarahumara of the Sierra Madre: Beer, Ecology and Social Organization.* Arlington Heights, Illinois: AHM.

Kirkbride, Diana (1972). Umm Dabaghiyah 1971: A Preliminary Report. An Early Ceramic Farming Settlement in North Central Jazira, Iraq. *Iraq* 34:3-15.

Kirkbride, Diana (1973a). Umm Dabaghiyah 1972: A Second Preliminary Report. *Iraq* 35:1-7.

Kirkbride, Diana (1973b). Umm Dabaghiyah 1972: A Third Preliminary Report. *Iraq* 35:205-209.

Kirkbride, Diana (1974). Umm Dabaghiyah: A Trading Outpost. *Iraq* 36:85-92.

Kirkbride, Diana (1975). Umm Dabaghiyah 1973: A Fourth Preliminary Report. *Iraq* 37:3-10.

Kirkby, Anne V. T. (1973). *The Use of Land and Water Resources in the Past and Present Valley of Oaxaca.* Memoirs of the Museum of Anthropology, University of Michigan No. 5. Ann Arbor.

Klebs, L. (1915). *Die Reliefs des Alten Reiches.* Heidelberg: Abhandlungen der Heidelberger Akademie der Wissenschaften.

Klein, Jeffrey, Lerman, J. C., Damon, P. E., and Ralph, E. K. (1982). Calibration of Radiocarbon Dates: Tables Based on the Consensus Data of the Workshop on Calibrating the Radiocarbon Time Scale. *Radiocarbon* 24(2):103-150.

Kosse, K. (1979). *Settlement Ecology of the Koros and Linear Pottery Cultures in Hungary.* British Archaeological Reports, International Series 64. Oxford.

Kretchmer, N. (1972). Lactose and Lactase. *Scientific American* 227:70-79.

Krishna Iyer, L. A. (1948). *The Coorg Tribes and Castes.* Gordon Press, Madras.

Lagasse, Peter F., Gillespie, William B., and Eggert, Kenneth G. (1984). Hydraulic Engineering Analysis of Prehistoric Water-Control Systems at Chaco Canyon. In *Recent Research on Chaco Prehistory,* eds. W. James Judge and John D. Schelberg, pp. 187-208. Reports of the Chaco Center 8. Albuquerque: Division of Cultural Research, National Park Service.

Lamberg-Karlovsky, C. C., and Sabloff, Jeremy A. (1979). *Ancient Civilizations: The Near East and Mesoamerica.* Menlo Park, California: Benjamin Cummings.

Lambert, H. E. (1950). *The Systems of Land Tenure in the Kikuyu Land Unit, Part 1: History of the Tribal Occupation of the Land.* Cape Town: University of Cape Town.

Larsen, Clark Spencer (1984). Health and Disease in Prehistoric Georgia: The Transition to Agriculture. In *Paleopathology at the Origins of Agriculture,* edited by Mark N. Cohen and George J. Armelagos, pp. 367-392. New York: Academic Press.

Leach, Edmund Ronald (1940). *Social and Economic Organization of the Rowanduz Kurds.* London: P. Lund, Humphries.

Leakey, L. S. B. (1953). *Mau Mau and the Kikuyu.* London: Methuen.

Lees, Susan H., and Bates, Daniel G. (1974). The Origins of Specialized Nomadic Pastoralism: A Systemic Model. *American Antiquity* 39:187-193.

Legge, A. J. (1981). Aspects of Cattle Husbandry. In *Farming Practice in British Prehistory,* ed. Roger Mercer, pp. 169-181. Edinburgh: Edinburgh University Press.

Leighton, Dorothea C., and Adair, John (1963). People of the Middle Place: A Study of the Zuni Indians. Ms. New Haven: Human Relations Area Files.

Lekson, Stephen H. (1984). Standing Architecture at Chaco Canyon and the Interpretation of Local and Regional Organization. In *Recent Research on Chaco Prehistory,* eds. W. James Judge and John D. Schelberg, pp. 55-73. Reports of the Chaco Center 8. Albuquerque: Division of Cultural Research, National Park Service.

Lewy, Hildegard (1965). Anatolia in the Old Assyrian Period. In *The Cambridge Ancient History,* Vol. 1 (rev. ed.). Cambridge: Cambridge University Press.

Li, Hui-Lin (1983). The Domestication of Plants in China: Ecogeographical Considerations. In *The Origins of Chinese Civilization,* ed. David N. Keightley, pp. 3-63. Berkeley: University of California Press.

Lightfoot, Kent (1985). *The Dynamics of Social Change.* Carbondale: Southern Illinois University Press.

Lloyd, Seton, and Safar, Fuad (1945). Tell Hassuna. *Journal of Near Eastern Studies* 4(4):255-289.

Lodge, Olive (1942). *Peasant Life in Jugoslavia.* London: Seeley, Service.

Lynch, Thomas F. (1982). Current Research: Andean South America. *American Antiquity* 47:209-214.

Lynch, Thomas F. (1983). Current Research: Andean South America. *American Antiquity* 48:169-173.

Lynch, Thomas F. (1984). Current Research: Andean South America. *American Antiquity* 49:416-420.

Lynn, Charles William (1937). *Agriculture in North Mamprusi.* Accra, Ghana: Director of Agriculture.

MacNeish, Richard S. (1967). A Summary of the Subsistence. In *Environment and Subsistence,* ed. Douglas S. Byers, pp. 290-309. The Prehistory of the Tehuacan Valley, Vol. I. Austin: University of Texas Press.

MacNeish, Richard S., Nelken-Turner, Antoinette, and Johnson, Irmgard W. (1967). *Nonceramic Artifacts.* The Prehistory of the Tehuacan Valley, Vol. II. Austin: University of Texas Press.

MacNeish, Richard S., Cook, Angel García, Lumbreras, Luis J., Vierra, Robert K., and Nelken-Turner, Antoinette (1981). *Excavations and Chronology.* Prehistory of the Ayacucho Basin, Peru, Vol. II. Ann Arbor: University of Michigan Press.

MacNeish, Richard S., Nelken-Turner, Antoinette, Vierra, Robert K., and Phagan, Carl J. (1980). *Nonceramic Artifacts.* Prehistory of the Ayacucho Basin, Peru, Vol. III. Ann Arbor: University of Michigan Press.

Martin, Paul S., and Plog, Fred (1973). *The Archaeology of Arizona.* Garden City, New York: Doubleday/Natural History Press.

Masters, William Murray (1953). *Rowanduz: A Kurdish Administrative and Mercantile Center.* Unpublished

Ph.D. dissertation, Department of Anthropology, University of Michigan, Ann Arbor.

Meadow, Richard H. (1979). Early Animal Domestication in South Asia: A First Report on the Faunal Remains from Mehrgarh, Pakistan. In *South Asian Archaeology*, ed. Herbert Härtel, pp. 143-179. Berlin: Dietrich Reimer Verlag.

Mellaart, James (1965). Anatolia c. 4000-2300 B.C. In *The Cambridge Ancient History*, Vol. 1 (rev. ed.). Cambridge: Cambridge University Press.

Mellaart, James (1966). Excavations at Catal Hüyük, 1965, Fourth Preliminary Report. *Anatolian Studies* 16:165-191.

Mellaart, James (1967a). *Catal Hüyük: A Neolithic Town in Anatolia*. New York: McGraw-Hill.

Mellaart, James (1967b). Anatolia before c. 4000 B.C. and c. 2300-1750 B.C. In *The Cambridge Ancient History*, Vol. 1 (rev. ed.). Cambridge: Cambridge University Press.

Mellaart, James (1972). Anatolian Neolithic Settlement Patterns. In *Man, Settlement and Urbanism*, eds. Peter J. Ucko, Ruth Tringham, and G. W. Dimbleby, pp. 279-284. London: Duckworth.

Mellaart, James (1975). *The Neolithic of the Near East*. London: Thames and Hudson.

Messenger, John C. (1969). *Inis Beag, Isle of Ireland*. New York: Holt, Rinehart and Winston.

Middleton, John (1953). *The Central Tribes of the Northeastern Bantu: The Kikuyu, Including Embu, Meru, Mbere, Chuka, Mwimbi, Tharaka, and the Kamba of Kenya*. London: International African Institute.

Mikesell, Marvin Wray (1961). *Northern Morocco: A Cultural Geography*. Berkeley and Los Angeles: University of California Press.

Milisauskas, Sarunas (1978). *European Prehistory*. New York: Academic Press.

Milner, George R. (1983). The Cultural Determinants of Mississippian Community Health: An Examination of Populations from Two Areas of Western Illinois. *American Journal of Physical Anthropology* 60:227-228.

Milner, George R. (1984). Bioanthropology. In *American Bottom Archaeology*, eds. Charles J. Bareis and James W. Porter, pp. 233-240. Urbana and Chicago: University of Illinois Press.

Milner, George R., Emerson, Thomas E., Mehrer, Mark W., Williams, Joyce A., and Esarey, Duane (1984). Mississippian and Oneota Period. In *American Bottom Archaeology*, eds. Charles J. Bareis and James W. Porter, pp. 158-186. Urbana and Chicago: University of Illinois Press.

Minnis, Paul (1981). *Economic and Organizational Responses to Food Stress by Non-Stratified Societies: An Example from Prehistoric New Mexico*. Unpublished Ph.D. dissertation, Department of Anthropology, University of Michigan, Ann Arbor.

Montagne, Robert (1930). *The Berbers and the Makhzen in the South of Morocco; Essay on the Political Transformation of the Sedentary Berbers (the Chleuh Group)*. Paris: Librairie Felix Alcan.

Mughal, M. Rafique (1974). New Evidence of the Early Harappan Culture from Jalilpur, Pakistan. *Archaeology* 27(2):106-113.

Murdock, George (1967). *Ethnographic Atlas*. Pittsburgh: University of Pittsburgh Press.

Oates, Joan (1972). Prehistoric Settlement Patterns in Mesopotamia. In *Man, Settlement and Urbanism*, eds. Peter J. Ucko, Ruth Tringham, and G. W. Dimbleby, pp. 299-310. London: Duckworth.

Oates, Joan (1973). The Background and Development of Early Farming Communities in Mesopotamia and the Zagros. *Proceedings of the Prehistoric Society* 39:147-181.

O'Brien, Patricia J. (1972). Urbanism, Cahokia, and Middle Mississippian. *Archaeology* 25(3):189-197.

Palkovich, Ann M. (1984). Agriculture, Marginal Environments, and Nutritional Stress in the Prehistoric Southwest. In *Paleopathology at the Origins of Agriculture*, eds. Mark N. Cohen and George J. Armelagos, pp. 425-438. New York: Academic Press.

Palmer, E. (1871). *Food Products of the North American Indians*. U.S. Commissioner of Agriculture Report for 1870. Washington, D. C.

Paques, Viviana (1954). *The Bambara*. Paris: Presses Universitaires de France.

Peebles, Christopher S., and Kus, Susan M. (1977). Some Archaeological Correlates of a Ranked Society. *American Antiquity* 42:421-448.

Perkins, Dexter, Jr. (1969). Fauna of Catal Hüyük: Evidence for Early Cattle Domestication in Anatolia. *Science* 164:177-179.

Perzigian, Anthony J., Tench, Patricia A., and Braun, Donna J. (1984). Prehistoric Health in the Ohio River Valley. In *Paleopathology at the Origins of Agriculture*, eds. Mark N. Cohen and George J. Armelagos, pp. 347-366. New York: Academic Press.

Rathje, William L. (1971). The Origin and Development of Lowland Classic Maya Civilization. *American Antiquity* 36:275-285.

Rathje, William L. (1979). Modern Material Culture Studies. In *Advances in Archaeological Method and Theory*, Vol. 2, ed. Michael B. Schiffer, pp. 1-37. New York: Academic Press.

Redman, Charles (1978). *The Rise of Civilization*. San Francisco: W. H. Freeman.

Reidhead, Van (1980). The Economics of Subsistence Change. In *Modeling Change in Prehistoric Subsistence Economies*, eds. Timothy Earle and Andrew Christenson, pp. 141-186. New York: Academic Press.

Renfrew, Colin (1972). *The Emergence of Civilization: The Cyclades and the Aegean in the Third Millennium B.C.* London: Methuen.

Renfrew, Colin (1973). Monuments, Mobilisation and Social Organisation in Neolithic Wessex. In *The Explanation of Culture Change*, ed. Colin Renfrew, pp. 539-558. London: Duckworth.

Renfrew, Colin (1982). Introduction to Chapter One. In *Ranking, Resource and Exchange: Aspects of the Archaeology of Early European Society*, eds.

Colin Renfrew and Stephen Shennan, pp. 1-8. Cambridge: Cambridge University Press.

Renfrew, J. M. (1969). The Archaeological Evidence for the Domestication of Plants: Methods and Problems. In *The Domestication and Exploitation of Plants and Animals*, eds. P. J. Ucko and G. W. Dimbleby, pp. 149-172. London: Duckworth.

Renfrew, J. M. (1973). *Palaeoethnobotany*. London: Methuen.

Richter, J. (1870). *Manual of Coorg: A Gazetteer of the Natural Features of the Country and the Social and Political Conditions of Its Inhabitants*. Bangalore, India: C. Stolz, Basel Mission Book Depository.

Rindos, David (1984). *The Origins of Agriculture: An Evolutionary Perspective*. New York: Academic Press.

Roberts, John Milton (1956). Zuni Daily Life. Ms. Department of Anthropology, University of Nebraska, Lincoln.

Roosevelt, Anna Curtenius (1984). Population, Health, and the Evolution of Subsistence: Conclusions from the Conference. In *Paleopathology at the Origins of Agriculture*, eds. Mark N. Cohen and George J. Armelagos, pp. 559-583. New York: Academic Press.

Rose, Jerome C., Burnett, Barbara A., Blaever, Mark W., and Nassaney, Michael S. (1984). Paleopathology and the Origins of Maize Agriculture in the Lower Mississippi Valley and Caddoan Culture Areas. In *Paleopathology at the Origins of Agriculture*, eds. Mark N. Cohen and George J. Armelagos, pp. 393-424. New York: Academic Press.

Rowe, John Howland (1946). Inca Culture at the Time of the Spanish Conquest. In *Handbook of the South American Indians*, Vol. 2, ed. Julian H. Steward, pp. 183-330. Bureau of American Ethnology Bulletin 143. Washington, D. C.: U.S. Government Printing Office.

Rowley-Conwy, P. (1981). Slash and Burn in the Temperate European Neolithic. In *Farming Practice in British Prehistory*, ed. Roger Mercer, pp. 85-96. Edinburgh: Edinburgh University Press.

Sahlins, Marshall (1972). *Stone Age Economics*. New York: Aldine.

Sanders, William T. (1968). Hydraulic Agriculture, Economic Symbiosis and the Evolution of States in Central Mexico. In *Anthropological Archaeology in the Americas*, edited by Betty J. Meggars, pp. 88-107. Washington, D. C.: Anthropological Society of Washington.

Sanders, William T., Parsons, Jeffrey R., and Santley, Robert S. (1979). *The Basin of Mexico*. New York: Academic Press.

Santley, Robert S. (1984). Obsidian Exchange, Economic Stratification, and the Evolution of a Complex Society in the Basin of Mexico. In *Trade and Exchange in Early Mesoamerica*, ed. Kenneth G. Hirth, pp. 43-86. Albuquerque: University of New Mexico Press.

Santley, Robert S. (1986). Prehispanic Roadways, Transport Network Geometry, and Aztec Politico-Economic Organization in the Basin of Mexico. In *Research in Economic Anthropology*, Supplement 2, ed. B. L.

Isaac, pp. 223-244. Greenwich, Connecticut: JAI Press.

Santley, Robert S., and Alexander, Rani T. (1992). The Political Economy of Core-Periphery Systems. In *Resource, Power, and Interregional Interaction*, eds. Edward M. Schortman and Patricia A. Urban, pp. 17-43. New York: Plenum.

Santley, Robert S., and Rose, Eric K. (1979). Diet, Nutrition and Population Dynamics in the Basin of Mexico. *World Archaeology* 2(2):185-207.

Schelberg, John D. (1983). The Chacoan Anasazi: A Stratified Society in the San Juan Basin. Paper presented at the Second Anasazi Symposium, February 1983, San Juan County Archaeological Research Center and Library, Bloomfield, New Mexico.

Schelberg, John D. (1984). Analogy, Complexity and Regionally Based Perspectives. In *Recent Research on Chaco Prehistory*, eds. W. James Judge and John D. Schelberg, pp. 5-21. Reports of the Chaco Center 8. Albuquerque: Division of Cultural Research, National Park Service.

Sebastian, Lynne (1983). Anasazi Site Typology and Chronology. In *Economy and Interaction along the Lower Chaco River: The Navajo Mine Archeology Program*, eds. Patrick Hogan and Joseph C. Winter, pp. 403-419. Albuquerque: Office of Contract Archeology, University of New Mexico.

Service, Elman (1962). *Primitive Social Organization: An Evolutionary Perspective*. New York: Random House.

Sherratt, Andrew (1981). Plough and Pastoralism: Aspects of the Secondary Products Revolution. In *Pattern of the Past: Studies in Honour of David Clarke*, eds. Ian Hodder, Glynn Isaac, and Norman Hammond, pp. 261-305. Cambridge: Cambridge University Press.

Sherratt, Andrew (1982). Mobile Resources: Settlement and Exchange in Early Agricultural Europe. In *Ranking, Resource and Exchange: Aspects of the Archaeology of Early European Society*, eds. Colin Renfrew and Stephen Shennan, pp. 13-26. Cambridge: Cambridge University Press.

Sherratt, Andrew (1983). The Secondary Exploitation of Animals in the Old World. *World Archaeology* 15(1): 90-104.

Simoons, F. J. (1969). Primary Adult Lactose Intolerance and the Milking Habit: A Problem in Biological and Cultural Interrelations (I). *American Journal of Digestive Diseases* 14:819-836.

Simoons, F. J. (1971). The Antiquity of Dairying in Asia and Africa. *Geographical Review* 61:431-439.

Smith, Bruce D. (1978). Variation in Mississippian Settlement Patterns. In *Mississippian Settlement Patterns*, ed. Bruce D. Smith. pp. 479-503. New York: Academic Press.

Smith, I. F. (1974). The Neolithic. In *British Prehistory: A New Outline*, ed. Colin Renfrew, pp. 100-136. London: Duckworth.

Srinivas, M. N. (1952). *Religion and Society among the Coorgs of South India*. Oxford: Clarendon Press.

Steinbock, R. Ted (1976). *Paleopathological Diagnosis*

and Interpretation: Bone Diseases in Ancient Human Populations. Springfield: Thomas.

Stevenson, Matilda Coxe (1904). The Zuñi Indians; Their Mythology, Esoteric Fraternities, and Ceremonies. U.S. Bureau of American Ethnology, Annual Report 23. Washington, D. C.: Smithsonian Institution.

Steward, Julian H. (1955). Theory of Culture Change: The Methodology of Multilinear Evolution. Urbana: University of Illinois Press.

Steward, Julian H., and Faron, Louis C. (1959). Native Peoples of South America. New York: McGraw-Hill.

Stewart, G. R. (1940). Conservation in Pueblo Agriculture. Science Monthly 51:201-220, 329-340.

Titiev, Mischa (1951). Araucanian Culture in Transition. Ann Arbor: University of Michigan Press.

Toll, Mollie S. (1985). An Overview of Chaco Canyon Macrobotanical Materials and Analyses to Date. In Environment and Subsistence of Chaco Canyon, ed. Frances Joan Mathien, pp. 247-277. Publications in Archeology 18E, Chaco Canyon Studies. Albuquerque: National Park Service.

Truell, Marcia L. (1986). A Summary of Small Site Architecture in Chaco Canyon, New Mexico. In Small Site Architecture of Chaco Canyon, by Peter J. McKenna and Marcia L. Truell, pp. 115-508. Publications in Archeology 18D, Chaco Canyon Studies. Santa Fe: National Park Service.

Vivian, R. Gwinn (1970). An Inquiry into Prehistoric Social Organization in Chaco Canyon, New Mexico. In Reconstructing Prehistoric Pueblo Societies, ed. William Longacre, pp. 59-83. Albuquerque: University of New Mexico Press.

Watson, William (1974). Ancient China. Greenwich, Connecticut: New York Graphic Society.

Wenke, Robert J. (1980). Patterns in Prehistory. New York: Oxford University Press.

Wetterstrom, Wilma (1976). The Effects of Nutrition on Population Size at Pueblo Arroyo Hondo, New Mexico. Unpublished Ph.D. dissertation, Department of Anthropology, University of Michigan, Ann Arbor.

Whalen, Michael E. (1981). Excavations at Santo Domingo Tomaltepec: Evolution of a Formative Community in the Valley of Oaxaca, Mexico. Memoirs of the Museum of Anthropology, University of Michigan No. 12. Ann Arbor.

Wheeler, Jane C. (1984). Review of Prehistoric Hunters of the High Andes. American Antiquity 49(1):196-198.

White, William P., Johannessen, Sissel, Cross, Paula G., and Kelly, Lucretia S. (1984). Environmental Setting. In American Bottom Archaeology, eds. Charles J. Bareis and James W. Porter, pp. 15-33. Urbana and Chicago: University of Illinois Press.

Whittle, Alasdair (1985). Neolithic Europe: A Survey. Cambridge: Cambridge University Press.

Whittle, E. (1975). Thermoluminescent Dating of Egyptian Pottery from Hemamieh and Qurna Tarif. Archaeometry 17:119-122.

Windes, Thomas C. (1984). A New Look at Population in Chaco Canyon. In Recent Research on Chaco Prehistory, eds. W. James Judge and John D. Schelberg, pp. 75-87. Reports of the Chaco Center 8. Albuquerque: Division of Cultural Research, National Park Service.

Windes, Thomas C. (1987). The Pueblo Community and Results of Tests and Excavations. Investigations at the Pueblo Alto Complex, Chaco Canyon, New Mexico: 1975-1979, Vol. I. Publications in Archeology 18, Chaco Canyon Studies. Santa Fe: National Park Service.

Wing, Elizabeth S. (1978). Animal Domestication in the Andes. In Advances in Andean Archaeology, ed. David L. Browman, pp. 167-196. The Hague: Mouton.

Wittfogel, Karl A. (1957). Oriental Despotism: A Comparative Study of Total Power. New Haven: Yale University Press.

Woodbury, Richard B., and Neely, James A. (1972). Water Control Systems of the Tehuacan Valley. In Chronology and Irrigation, ed. Frederick Johnson, pp. 81-153. The Prehistory of the Tehuacan Valley, Vol. IV. Austin: University of Texas Press.

Wright, Henry T., and Johnson, Gregory A. (1975). Population, Exchange, and Early State Formation in Southwestern Iran. American Anthropologist 77:267-289.

Young, Gwen (1980). Analysis of Faunal Remains. In Tijeras Canyon: Analyses of the Past, ed. Linda Cordell, pp. 88-120. Albuquerque: University of New Mexico Press.

Appendix

COMPUTATIONS

I. Analysis of Variance on Sequence Durations from Domestic Animal and Non-domestic Animal Groups

Total Sum of Squares: $SS_{Total} = \Sigma(X^2) - (T^2 \div n)$

Among Sum of Squares: $SS_{Among} = \Sigma(T_i^2 \div n_i) - (T^2 \div n)$

Within Sum of Squares: $SS_{Within} = \Sigma(X^2) - (T_i^2 \div n_i)$

where

X = each observation (each sequence duration)
T = total value of observations
T_i = total value of observations in each group (domestic animal, non-domestic animal)
n = number of observations in all groups
n_i = number of observations in each group

GROUP	X (YEARS)
Central Europe	6200
Southeastern Europe	6200
Greece	5000
Anatolia	4600
Great Britain	4000
Northern Mesopotamia	3660
Peru	3650
Northern China	3150
Pakistan	3000
Upper Egypt	2400
Southern Mesopotamia	1900
Tehuacan	1750
Basin of Mexico	1400
Oaxaca	1400
Cahokia	1073
Chaco	800

$T = 50{,}183$
T_i (domestic) $= 43{,}760$
T_i (non-domestic) $= 6{,}423$
$n = 16$
n_i (domestic) $= 11$
n_i (non-domestic) $= 5$
$\Sigma(X^2) = 202{,}824{,}429$

$$SS_{Total} = 202,824,429 - (2,518,333,489 \div 16)$$
$$= 202,824,429 - 157,395,843$$
$$= 45,428,586$$

$$SS_{Among} = [(43,760)^2 \div 11] + [(6,423)^2 \div 5] - 157,395,843$$
$$= 174,085,236 + 8,250,986 - 157,395,843$$
$$= 24,940,379$$

$$SS_{Within} = 202,824,429 - [(43,760)^2 \div 11] + [(6,423)^2 \div 5]$$
$$= 202,824,429 - 174,085,236 + 8,250,986$$
$$= 20,488,207$$

Degrees of Freedom (df):	Total	$= n - 1$
		$= 16 - 1$
		$= 15$

Among $= C - 1$ (where C is the number of groups)
$= 2 - 1$
$= 1$

Within $= \Sigma (n - 1)$
$= (11 - 1) + (5 - 1)$
$= 10 + 4$
$= 14$

Mean Square: Among $= SS_{Among} \div df_{Among} = 24,940,379 \div 1 = 24,940,379$
Within $= SS_{Within} \div df_{Within} = 20,488,207 \div 14 = 1,463,443$

SOURCE OF VARIATION	SS	df	Mean Square
Among groups	24,940,379	1	24,940,379
Within groups	20,488,207	14	1,463,443

$$F = 24,940,379 \div 1,463,443 = 17.0$$
$$.99\ F_{1,14} = 8.86 \text{ or } F.01 = 8.86$$

The null hypothesis of no significant difference between the means of the groups is rejected at the .01 level of significance (formulas from Arkin and Colton 1970:163-169; Glass and Stanley 1970:338-380).

II. Mann-Whitney Test, Nonparametric Alternative to Analysis of Variance, Computed on Sequence Durations from Domestic and Non-domestic Animal Groups

The Mann-Whitney test is used when the assumptions required for analysis of variance, such as a normal distribution, are not met. It can be used only for two groups. Two computation methods are presented here: Blalock (1960) and Hays (1973). Tables for critical value of U are from Blalock (1960). Computations are based on the ranked scores listed below.

GROUP (N_2)	X (YEARS)	RANK
Central Europe	6200	1.5
Southeastern Europe	6200	1.5
Greece	5000	3
Anatolia	4600	4
Great Britain	4000	5
Northern Mesopotamia	3660	6
Peru	3650	7
Northern China	3150	8
Pakistan	3000	9
Upper Egypt	2400	10
Southern Mesopotamia	1900	11

GROUP (N_1)	X (YEARS)	RANK
Tehuacan	1750	12
Basin of Mexico	1400	13.5
Oaxaca	1400	13.5
Cahokia	1073	15
Chaco	800	16

The critical value of U can be calculated in two ways for small samples.

A. For each rank score from N_1 add together the scores higher than that rank score listed in N_2. In the data presented above, N_2 contains no higher rank scores than those listed in N_1 (small samples).

$$U = 0 + 0 + 0 + 0 + 0$$
$$= 0$$

B. (Larger samples)

$$U = N_1 N_2 + N_1(N_1 + 1) - T_1$$
$$= 5(11) + [5(6) \div 2] - 70$$
$$= 55 + 15 - 70$$
$$= 70 - 70$$
$$= 0$$

A critical U value of 7 or smaller is needed to reject the null hypothesis that samples have been drawn from the same population at the .01 level of significance.

The null hypothesis is rejected at the .01 level of significance.

www.ingramcontent.com/pod-product-compliance
Lightning Source LLC
Chambersburg PA
CBHW061301270326
41932CB00029B/3427